41
43

FEARLESS COOKING FOR CROWDS

FEARLESS
COOKING FOR
CROWDS

◇ ═══════════════════ ◇

*Beautiful Food for Groups
of Eight Through Fifty*

◇

MICHELE EVANS

Times
BOOKS

Library of Congress Cataloging-in-Publication Data
Evans, Michele.
Fearless cooking for crowds.
Includes index.
1. Quantity cookery. 1. Title.
TX820.E83 1986   642'.4   85-40738
ISBN 0-8129-1209-8
BVA
Manufactured in the United States of America

9 8 7 6 5 4 3 2

First Edition

Coordinating Editor: Rosalyn Badalamenti

Designed by Ann Gold

FOR NANCY DUSSAULT

ACKNOWLEDGMENTS

I am indebted to the following family members, friends, and acquaintances for sharing their recipes, imagination, knowledge, and enthusiasm with me on the subject of cooking for crowds: Ellie Ashworth, Margot Bachman, Diana Backus, Ernesto Ballarin, Frances Bangel, Sir Charles Batchelder, Joelle and William E. Burrows, Midge and Bobby Connors, Barbara Cossman, Nadia Cossman, Raymond Etchenis, Mary Eustis, Ima Evans, Doris Farrington, Edwina Farrington, the late Sam Gallu, Gray, Steven Gregor, Bobbe Hart, Penelope Jago, John Larson, James Levi, Julie and Bruce McClennan, the late Emily McCormack and Edward McCormack, Chris Pappas, Shirley Petrofsky, Sylvia Putziger, Angel Noño Ramirez, Robbie Robinson, Daniel Rospond, Fulvia Sesane, the late Sylvia Shapiro, Martha Rose Shulman, Bruce Thomas, Katharine and Kevin White, Judy Witty, Jack Yogman, and Diane Young.

Eternal thanks again, to Tully Plesser and Esther Newberg for always being there, along with my editors, Rosalyn Badalamenti, Ruth Fecych, and Kathleen Moloney.

Contents

◇ ══ ◇

Introduction

◇ ══════════════════════ ◇

The wealthy Palm Beach dowager who once said that all you needed for a great party was a bowl of salted peanuts and lots of whiskey may have been right in her time. But things have changed since the days when a cocktail party meant cheese and crackers and dinner for more than six invariably called for a ham, roast beef, or turkey.

Travel, venturesomeness, education, interest, and availability where food is concerned have broadened American awareness and taste for a wider variety of foods than was ever imagined twenty years ago. From the elite restaurant to the modest motel-chain dining room, we are now routinely exposed to multidish salad bars with a tempting variety of dressings, ethnic food, fresh seafood, choice meat cuts, and fresh poultry, legions of pasta dishes, freshly steamed baby vegetables, elaborate pastries, and exotic fruits flown in from other continents.

The nation's catering establishments have also contributed substantially to the *finishing* of American appreciation for large-scale entertaining—teaching us at weddings, cocktail parties, corporate conventions, religious functions, charity receptions, testimonial dinners, political inaugurations, celebrity roasts, alumni homecomings, award dinners, cruise ship buffets, special holiday celebrations, boutique openings, and birthday parties right at home just how exciting, original, and delicious cooking for crowds can be.

In theory, cooking for a crowd should be a celebration, an event to be anticipated with excitement and pleasure. Unfortunately, cooking for eight or more guests often has an intimidating effect on many otherwise confident cooks. The same person who approaches a dinner for four as

1

a routine exercise can find serving eight, twelve, sixteen, twenty-four, or more to be a frightening challenge. The mere thought of cooking for a large group seems to conjure up images of overflowing shopping carts, huge cauldrons bubbling over onto the stove, crowds of people lined up at buffet tables where the main course has just run out, the family dog gobbling up the pâté, a no-show bartender, and mountains of dirty dishes after the last guests have departed at 2 A.M.

We are at once bewildered and overwhelmed as we consider the components involved in cooking for crowds: guest lists, budget, menus, shopping, serving methods, weather, tableware, serving dishes, pots and pans, flower arrangements, lighting, help, and service, storage space in the refrigerator and freezer, the bar, timetables for the meal, cleanup, and even where the cars will park. And above all, we want our celebration to be a stunning success.

Things are bound to go wrong. How can these things be anticipated, and what *early warning* systems can we rely on to avoid disaster?

In real estate we are told that the three most important elements for success are location, location, location. In cooking for crowds, the magic ingredient is organization, organization, organization.

Through the chapters that follow on organization, strategic planning, and the recipes themselves, I hope to turn the quite normal feelings of anxiety and panic over the thought of cooking for crowds into confident, fearless entertaining.

How many constitute a crowd? As many as three can, as the adage goes. For most people, though, cooking for a crowd is cooking for double or more than is usual in our day-to-day lives. In this book, the first group to constitute a crowd is eight. This number was selected because of the large and ever-growing number of households made up of single individuals, couples, and families with one or two children. For these households cooking for eight represents a substantial increase in servings.

Most of the recipes here that are for eight can be doubled to serve sixteen, so those adept and comfortable at cooking for eight should consider the recipes in this category, too.

The other recipes are listed in the various food categories for twelve, sixteen, twenty-four, thirty-six, and fifty, often with instructions for doubling or cutting the recipes in half.

Because of the limited space in our apartments and homes, kitchen logistics, equipment, and cost, twelve, sixteen, and twenty-four are the numbers most of us can realistically consider manageable crowds in our homes. But for those unusual occasions, I've included a substantial number of recipes listed for thirty-six and fifty as well.

Cooking for a large number will take extra time, careful systematic organization, and scheduling, and things will go wrong. Being flexible and having a positive attitude, common sense, a sense of humor, and imagination can solve almost any problem.

To cite an example: Last year a friend was remodeling his home, and he had planned to have the work completed in time to serve his annual Thanksgiving sit-down dinner with several tables on his expanded new terrace around his new pool. He had invited thirty people. Just a week before the event, the new kitchen, terrace, and pool were all far behind schedule. Not only could he not have the tables around the pool, he couldn't even cook the food in the unfinished kitchen. Pandemonium and dust were everywhere, yet he was determined—and resourceful. He called up all the guests and asked them to bring their own dinner plates, flatware, glasses, and napkins. He set up unmatching tables in one long row in the driveway, and covered them with the same colored tablecloths with a flower arrangement on each. The food was cooked at a friend's home, and served buffet style from two card tables under trees at one side of the driveway. Guests arrived carrying their own tableware, which ranged from paper plates, plastic knives, forks and spoons, styrofoam cups, and sheets of paper towels to elegant china, silverware, Baccarat crystal, and monogrammed linen napkins. This colorful improvised dinner turned out to be such delightful fun that many guests are sorry that it won't be the same next year. The imagination, sense of humor, common sense, and positive attitude paid off.

Cooking for a crowd is not something we generally do weekly or even monthly, but when the time comes to entertain and celebrate with a group of friends or relatives, feelings of love, hospitality, and giving are foremost in our minds. There is something uniquely special about cooking and serving a meal in our own home that is, perhaps, the ultimate expression of friendship: a combined social custom and culinary joy.

Preparing a meal for fifty is *not* ten times more difficult than preparing a meal for five; it's just that there's more food to work with. Stuffing twelve chicken breasts instead of six takes only a few minutes longer and the same amount of cooking time. Cooking in large quantities often gives the cook greater latitude and margin for error than that faced with in more precise dishes for a few. And shortcuts and quick recipes are very acceptable; in fact, today they are mandatory, because of our busy lives.

Part of our new sophistication about food is that we demand quality while at the same time we welcome simplicity. These recipes are tested crowd-pleasers that are easy to prepare, utilizing a broad spectrum of ingredients, cuisines, and cooking techniques.

Another crucial element that should also be kept in mind when you entertain crowds has to do with the mood you create—warm hospitality and a relaxed atmosphere. The guests play a large part in the event. If they feel welcome, if they sense that you are relaxed, and that they are being graciously served a thoughtfully prepared, delicious meal, guests will take care of themselves and enjoy one another's company. Happy crowds need little looking after.

New York
January 1986

Strategic Planning

◇━━━━━━━━━━━━━━━━━━━━━◇

The social function of the meal you are planning, the number of guests, the season, time of day, where and how the meal will be served, and the menu—all these determine a particular strategy. Each of the following headings should serve as a master guide for the lists that you will need to make. Remember, lists are an essential ingredient for organization, organization, organization.

The Event, Date, Time, and Place

The event, date, time, and place are the first four decisions that must be made.

The event, whether a relaxed family get-together, specific celebration or holiday, or outing for a group of friends, will determine the setting, serving style, and menu.

The date, time, and place must suit the requirements of the event, your own schedule, as well as that of your guests, and your home.

Number of Guests and Invitations

The number of guests depends on the specific occasion and your own needs and capabilities.

Invitations can be written and mailed, or you can call and invite your guests. Today we are informal. However, it is important to remember

5

how lovely it is to receive an invitation, and that the physical invitation helps remind the forgetful of the event, and to R.S.V.P. as requested.

For spur-of-the-moment or spontaneous events, of course, telephone calls must be made.

Whether written with an R.S.V.P. or made by phone, an invitation should be made a month to three weeks in advance, giving everyone plenty of time to respond and to save the date. Most important, it gives you the required planning time.

Regrets only written on invitations can be tricky, because there is always the possibility that some guests just might forget to call or might not have received the invitation.

Themes and Entertainment

Having a theme, or entertainment at a party, although not necessary, usually adds to the conviviality and relaxes a party. For friends as hooked as we were on *The Jewel in the Crown* television series, we decided to have an Indian dinner party and to watch a Sunday night episode. We dressed in 1940s English raj outfits, and the guests all appeared in saris or simulated Indian attire. We served vodka nimboo sodas (lime, soda, and vodka cocktails) and Pimm's Cups and then an Indian dinner, followed by the show. It was a delightful evening.

I once attended a formal dinner party given by an extremely serious cook. All of the guests felt some advance tension, because we knew that our host would be upset if every one of his masterpieces didn't turn out perfectly. A clever fellow, he anticipated our and his concerns, and hired a classical guitarist, who played quietly in a corner of the living room all evening. It relaxed us all.

The event itself will often determine a theme or entertainment, such as for international meals, specific holidays, boating trips, summer picnics, and football tailgates, but a little imagination and initiative go a long way in making a party fun.

Some hosts have fortune-tellers, caricaturists, or have everyone dress in costume, such as a character in a favorite Impressionist painting, or wear a certain color. A successful hostess I know has all the men at her dinner parties change seats for dessert. She also gives out amusing door prizes selected for the occasion. It's all a matter of your own imagination, taste, and the social function. A good mixture of friends and conversation is what most people are looking for in terms of entertainment.

If you do have music, anything from classical to *reggae*, keep the volume low, so that conversation can flow.

Sit-down Dinners, Buffets, and Serving Styles

Clearly the most comfortable way to serve any meal is a sit-down table arrangement. Seating guests at one table is normally limited from eight to twelve. Two tables, a series of tables in one room, throughout the apartment or home, and/or outdoors on a deck, terrace, porch, patio, or in the backyard are all possibilities. (If an outdoor meal is planned, consider an alternative in case of bad weather.) You must determine the capabilities of your apartment or home and the space available.

Tables can be made of anything that's sturdy, such as card tables, patio tables, plywood tabletops on boxes or saw horses, borrowed or rented tables. The large makeshift variety can be used for diners, as the bar, or for the buffet. Cover the tables with attractive sheets or large pieces of fabric.

If you don't own enough chairs, borrow or rent them for the day.

The easiest way to serve a sit-down dinner to a crowd is a buffet. Guests can select the foods and amounts that they want. The buffet can be set up on any table large enough to hold the food, and a centerpiece, comfortably. Of course, some buffet tables must also have room to hold the dinner plates, flatware, napkins, wineglasses, and wine. Having more than one buffet table is a good idea for a large group of people, which keeps everyone moving. Whichever setup you select, make sure the area allows the traffic to flow; corners are not good.

Lap-style buffet dinners for crowds will sometimes be necessary, due to limited space. Unless the event is very crowded, there should be a seat for everyone.

For lap-style dinners, serve fork food; dishes with small pieces of meat or dishes made with ingredients that are easily cut with a fork. Chicken Cutlets Pojarsky is an excellent "fork" entrée, as well as shellfish or fish dishes or pastas, salads, stews, ragouts, or casseroles.

It is extremely helpful to guests who are dining lap-style if the required flatware is rolled up inside individual napkins. Wielding utensils and a dinner plate while serving oneself can be awkward. Sometimes the wineglasses and wine will be situated at the end of the table. If this can be avoided, all the better. Wineglasses and wine should be passed separately, just after people are seated and are ready to eat.

The last serving style is what I like to call "restaurant serving." The host or help arranges individual dinner plates in the kitchen, which are served to diners at the table. I do this often when entertaining up to twelve. For second helpings, serving dishes can be put out buffet style, or the dishes can be individually passed around the table to each guest. The latter takes a little time and is, perhaps, more formal, but it allows guests the comfort of remaining seated and carrying on conversation.

The Menu

In selecting a menu, consider the season first. Compose a dinner utilizing the best vegetables and fruit, seafood, and any other seasonal food.

Balance the menu with complementing textures, colors, flavors, and various cooking methods.

Plan to serve as many dishes as possible that can be partially or totally made or cooked ahead of time.

Prepare some cold hors d'oeuvres and desserts which can be frozen, along with casseroles, ragouts, stews, or other entrées and speciality breads. This will leave only a hot hor d'oeuvre, the starch, salad, and vegetables, which can be washed and cut hours before dinner, and perhaps an entrée that requires last-minute cooking. Salad dressings can usually be made at least the morning of the event and, in many cases, several days ahead.

If your menu requires a lot of last-minute cooking, involve your guests in carving the roast, tossing the salad, slicing the bread, or opening the wine. Guests will generally be delighted to be in the kitchen where the action is, especially if it's a casual affair. In fact, I find that I have trouble keeping guests out of the kitchen.

Today it just isn't necessary to serve an eight-course meal. You should include hors d'oeuvres, an entrée, a vegetable or two—or an interesting combination—a rice, potato, or noodle dish, if desired, a salad, and dessert selection. For dessert, never discount ripe fresh fruit with a variety of cheeses, or a composed fresh fruit salad, a sorbet, and cookies, or brownies for any meal.

Be sure to serve a few simple dishes, such as fresh cooked asparagus and a plain green salad with a freshly made vinaigrette sauce. Balance these two honest dishes with a spectacular entrée, such as Moroccan Lamb Tagine, and for dessert, Fresh Lemon Tarts.

You will find several menu suggestions at the end of the book.

The Bar

The bar is probably the easiest element to assemble in entertaining crowds. A guideline for a standard bar for twenty-four follows; it can be halved, doubled, or tripled.

Because of individual drinking habits and diets, it is wise to have plenty of soda water, wine, diet soda, fruit juice, and even some beer.

For some functions, serving special drinks can be extremely successful: Margaritas, Bloody Marys, Pimm's Cups, Piña Coladas, White or Red Sangria, Mint Juleps, or Gluevine can really hit the spot, given the right weather, atmosphere, and group of people. But always have plenty of regular liquor, wine, and setups on hand.

Situate the bar or bars in free-flowing areas . . . a corner is not a good bar area.

Friends who regularly entertain large groups gave me an ice formula, which has never failed. Figure on 1 pound of ice per person, plus 10 extra pounds for every 25 guests. If space permits in the freezer, the ice can be made in advance and stored in plastic bags. Making the ice is much less of a problem than storing it, though. For very large crowds, buy the ice at the last minute and store it in coolers or tubs.

Where the bar is concerned, it is always better to have too much liquor, wine, and setups than too little. Since liquor, wine, soda, beer, etc., can be kept indefinitely, there is never any waste. Even the water from melted ice can be conserved and used to water plants, as is necessary in St. Thomas where water is precious, and in New York, where there is often a shortage.

The Well-stocked Bar for Twenty-four

The items listed below cover most reasonable requests. A bottle of bourbon may not even be opened. If you know your guests' drinking habits, some of the liquor amounts below can be adjusted.

Different seasons will call for more or less of certain liquors and setups. More gin and vodka and tonic will be called for in the summer. In the winter, more Scotch and whiskey and soda will be needed.

2 liters Scotch (3 in winter)   1 liter gin (3 in summer)
2 liters vodka (3 in summer)   1 liter light rum (2 in summer)

1 liter bourbon
1 liter Canadian whiskey
 (optional)
1 liter dry vermouth
1 bottle dry sherry
8 bottles dry white wine

4 bottles dry red wine
 (For dinner, provide at least a
 bottle of red or white wine
 for every three people.)
12 bottles or cans of beer

Have on hand after-dinner brandy or Cognac and liqueurs.

1 bottle brandy or Cognac
2 bottles of liqueurs—Grand
 Marnier and a cream liqueur,
 such as Bailey's Irish Cream
 or Frangelico

6 quarts tonic water (10 in
 summer)
6 quarts club soda (8 in winter)
2 quarts ginger ale
1 quart tomato juice (4 quarts,
 if serving brunch)
2 quarts orange juice
2 dozen cans diet cola, or
 desired type
3 limes (5 limes in summer), 3
 lemons, and olives
 cocktail onions (optional)

1 large pitcher of water
 bottle opener
 corkscrew
 knife (for cutting lemon and
 lime peels and pieces)
 small cutting board
48 cocktail napkins
24 9-ounce balloon wineglasses
 (Serve all drinks in the same
 glass or the combination of
 your choice.)
 ice bucket
 cooler for storing ice
 ice: 1 pound of ice per
 person, plus 10 extra pounds
 lined wastepaper basket near
 the bar area for the bartender

If serving twenty-four or more, half-gallon bottles of liquor and wine can
be purchased to economize.

Service Help

Hiring help to tend the bar, serve the dinner or buffet, and clean up is a
great help in cooking for crowds. Many hosts and hostesses I know would
never dream of hiring help; instead they organize well and play their roles
throughout a dinner.

Friends can also lend a hand; it's a matter of your own taste, the cost,
surroundings, and circumstances.

For groups of sixteen and over, it is extremely helpful to have a bartender and one or two helpers.

Hiring good experienced help can often be more troublesome than expensive. Rely on friends' recommendations or reliable firms for service help.

When hiring help, arrangements should be made several weeks ahead of time. Have those you've hired come to your home early enough to go over exactly what duties they will be expected to perform. Familiarize them with the kitchen, serving area, bar, etc. Give as many instructions before the dinner as possible.

Refrigerator and Freezer Space

Before any shopping and advance preparation of food, the refrigerator and freezer spaces must be checked and cleared.

If you are going to cook several quantity dishes ahead of time, such as hors d'oeuvres, a casserole, sauce, or desserts, storage space must be available in the freezer.

Refrigerator space must also be available for storing vegetables, bags of cleaned and dried lettuce for the salad, fruit, soup, an aspic, or a partially prepared main course—and the white wine and beer.

If you don't have room for the wine and beer in the refrigerator, store them in tubs or coolers of ice several hours before the event.

Unless you are planning a last-minute affair, which would give you little time for any freezing, three weeks ought to be enough time to allow you to use up food in the freezer and clear the refrigerator—and give you an excuse to dine out.

The Shopping Lists

Read through each recipe you are using, carefully listing the ingredients required. Separately list the ingredients and all other items under stores and shops to be visited.

Make sure to include the garnishes you plan to use, and check your larder for ingredients you might already have, such as herbs, spices, condiments, canned products, and all staples. Also check the freezer for stock, meat, poultry, or other foods which can be utilized. Go over the liquor and wine supply you have on hand, too.

At the *supermarket* buy all groceries, canned goods, staples, sodas, juices, some dairy products, etc., up to a week to four days before the event.

The *liquor store* purchases can be made a week or more before the event, but storage might be a problem, so gauge this accordingly.

Speciality shops for cocktail napkins, colored or plastic toothpicks, wooden skewers, candles, etc., can be bought and checked off the list immediately.

Place orders with the *butcher shop* and/or *fish market* for special cuts and large amounts a week in advance.

Orders for the *florist* for flowers and/or plants should be made a week before the event. They can be delivered or picked up the day before or the day of the dinner.

The *greengrocer* stop for vegetables and fruits should be made the day before the event.

Bakery orders for bread and rolls should be made a few days in advance and picked up the morning or afternoon of the party.

Rental stores must be contacted as soon as possible if you are renting tableware, tables, chairs, special oversized grills, or other cooking equipment.

Go over the lists several times, making certain that nothing has been forgotten.

Equipment

It is surprising how well we can cook for a crowd using equipment and utensils we have in our own kitchens, by cooking in batches, advance preparation, and freezing. Some special oversized cooking equipment will be required, but let the recipes dictate what you will actually need. Three pieces of equipment are, however, extremely helpful time-savers in cooking for crowds: a blender, food processor, and electric mixer. ,

The size of the group must first be determined, and specific sizes, if extremely large, such as a 38-quart pot for cooking soup for fifty, must be borrowed, rented, or purchased. Most dishes requiring large pots or pans can be cooked in batches. Soup for fifty can be cooked in two 20-quart pots, for example.

Here are a few items that will be required: several very large mixing bowls—8- to 20-quart capacity, an extra-large strainer and colander, two or three large baking sheets—16 by 20 inches, a 1-quart liquid measuring cup, 10- and 12-inch tart pans, large broiling and roasting pans (Inexpensive heavy duty reusable aluminum pans are available in all shapes and sizes. The 18- by 13-inch size is an excellent roasting pan for quantity baking or roasting.), 14- to 16-quart pots for boiling pasta and vegetables, potatoes, or rice, ragouts, stews, or chili recipes are often required. Heavy cast-iron enamel-covered 9- to 12-quart pots with tight-fitting lids are excellent for cooking for crowds. And 13- to 14-inch deep-dish pizza pans, 14- to 16-inch paella pans, and large woks are excellent, too.

Inexpensive plastic storage boxes (16 by 10¾ by 3¾ inches) store easily in the refrigerator and hold large amounts.

Advance Food Preparation

Many dishes can be totally prepared in advance and frozen for up to a few weeks: hors d'oeuvres, main courses, such as casseroles, lasagne, crêpes, strudel, cakes, or pastry, for example.

Salad dressing can be made and stored in the refrigerator and a sauce will often hold for a day or two. Bean and lentil dishes, ragouts, soups, and stews will actually improve in flavor overnight in the refrigerator.

Vegetables can be peeled and cut or chopped several hours before using them and meat can be cut into small pieces in advance and wrapped and refrigerated. Salad greens can be washed, dried, and refrigerated.

Before your dinner, orchestrate as much advance food preparation as you possibly can, according to the menu you have selected.

Working with Large Quantities of Food

Working with large quantities of food obviously calls for careful planning and organization, and it *will* take more time and require a little patience at first.

Thirty-six chicken breasts waiting on the kitchen counter to be stuffed can be an awesome sight. However, all the breasts can be stuffed, put into the roasting pans, and cooked in about 2 hours. When the stuffed breasts are cooked and ready to be served, a pleasant sense of surprise at the ease with which the whole procedure was accomplished will come over you. That sense of relief brings great satisfaction, and, psychologically, is a giant step toward fearless cooking for crowds. You'll quickly learn it really just isn't that difficult.

Because there isn't space here to give full detailed instructions and advice on time-saving steps for each recipe, I've included a list of twelve general tips and guidelines as checkpoints to be used when cooking for crowds. These suggestions apply to all categories of food and dishes.

I've also added a recipe for Boneless Baked Chicken Breasts with Tarragon Stuffing for 36, along with detailed directions, and a suggested menu with a coordinating time plan. This example can be used as a general guide for the other recipes in the book.

1. When planning your menu, be sure to orchestrate the meal; that is, select several dishes that can be made in advance. Follow a time plan for the meal so that all dishes in the menu will be ready at serving time—they will be cold, warm, or hot, as called for, and ready to be served on schedule. Don't keep guests waiting while the crostini is being toasted and the other food is getting cold.

2. When your menu requires cooking serveral dishes at one time, be sure the cooking methods vary. There will not be enough room to bake a vegetable dish and a meat or seafood entrée for twenty-four in the oven at the same time, and temperatures vary, too. Keep this in mind where desserts are concerned. Most desserts can be prepared in advance. If serving a hot baked dessert, select other cooking methods for the balance of the meal, such as sautéing, frying, poaching, or braising for the entrée, vegetables, and/or starches.

3. Read thoroughly the recipe that you will be using. Make certain that you have all the ingredients required, and that any frozen food is thawed. If a recipe calls for a preheated oven, but the advance preparation of the recipe, because of the volume of food, will take about an hour, wait to preheat the oven until about ten minutes before actually beginning to cook the dish.

4. Make space available so that your work area is cleaned and cleared. Make plenty of freezer and refrigerator space available, too, if it will be needed.

5. Don't begin working until the garbage can is emptied and lined with a fresh plastic bag. Place it close to the work area. In cooking for crowds there are enormous amounts of scraps, such as potato and other vegetable and fruit peels, bones, jars, bottles, cans, and other containers. Have plastic bags handy in which to store prepared ingredients. If making a green salad for thirty-six, storing it in a large plastic bag in the refrigerator works perfectly. Clean up as you work.

6. And now, the *mise en place* . . . a French phrase meaning to put everything in its place. Assemble utensils, knives, measuring spoons and cups, wooden spoons, proper-sized whisks, colanders, strainers, bowls, pots and pans, and cooking equipment such as a blender, food processor, or meat grinder.

7. Collect all the ingredients for the recipe in the work area.

8. Follow the amounts called for in individual recipes when measuring them. Don't eliminate or double an ingredient because you don't like it or do like it. For example, too much wine or garlic can spoil the texture and flavor of a dish if over- or underused. Also use the size and shape or cut of an ingredient called for in the recipe. For example, don't slice or quarter a large onion if the recipe says to finely chop it.

9. *Mise en place* also includes completing any necessary procedure before actually beginning to cook a dish. In cooking for crowds this is particularly important. Peel, slice, cube, dice, chop, seed, shell, grate, shred, or grind ingredients in advance. Melt butter, chill an ingredient, or have anything that must be marinated already prepared.

10. If working with highly perishable foods, such as chicken, pork, seafood, cheese, and vegetables, such as lettuce or certain fruits, in large amounts, refrigerate them until called for. Work in batches and refrigerate the part not being worked with until called for. This particularly applies to chicken, pork, and seafood.

11. Working at a steady, even pace, as fast as possible without rushing, is vital when cooking in large quantities. This is as much a matter of saving your own time as saving the crispness and freshness of any food. Peeling six pounds of carrots can take twenty minutes or one hour.

12. Many recipes include suggestions for cooking in batches, and many of the recipes can be doubled, which will also require cooking in batches. This is because home kitchens are not set up for quantity cooking. Our range tops won't hold several 20-quart pots at once. Cooking in batches is an extremely efficient method for cooking for crowds.

SUMMER MENU FOR THIRTY-SIX

Sesame Shrimp Streamers
Crudités with Creamy Blue Cheese Dressing with Bacon and Horseradish
Boneless Baked Chicken Breasts with Tarragon Stuffing
Italian Green Beans alla Positano
Mixed Green Salad with Vinaigrette Dressing
Emily McCormack's "In a Pinch" Chocolate Chocolate Cake with Vanilla Ice Cream

All of the dishes in the menu, except for the chicken and green beans can be prepared in advance. (See the index for the recipes.) These dishes only need last-minute mixing or arranging on serving platters or dishes just before serving them. Lots of refrigerator space is needed.

Before beginning to prepare the chicken, the other dishes in the menu should be ready as follows:

Sesame Shrimp Streamers: The shrimp has been cooked and the sauce prepared. Both are covered and in the refrigerator.

Crudités with Creamy Blue Cheese Dressing with Bacon and Horseradish: The vegetables are cut and stored in the refrigerator in plastic bags. The dressing is made, covered, and also in the refrigerator.

Italian Green Beans alla Positano: The beans are trimmed and stored in a plastic bag or bags in the refrigerator. Thirty minutes before serving time, the water for the beans can be brought to a boil in the proper-sized pot. The chopping of the other ingredients in the recipe, and other procedures can be accomplished quickly just before cooking the beans . . . 10 minutes before serving time.

Mixed Green Salad with Vinaigrette Dressing: The lettuce has been washed and dried and stored in plastic bags in the refrigerator. The dressing is made and stored in a jar in the refrigerator, as well.

Emily McCormack's "In a Pinch" Chocolate Chocolate Cakes (three of them) have been made and wrapped and are resting at room temperature. One gallon of vanilla ice cream is in the freezer.

Serving dishes for all the recipes should be put out.

BONELESS BAKED CHICKEN BREASTS WITH TARRAGON STUFFING

◊ ═══════════════════════════════════════ ◊

SERVES 36

36 medium-sized boned chicken breasts
Salt and freshly ground black pepper

¾ cup (1½ sticks) butter, melted, plus extra for greasing pans
½ cup fresh lemon juice
Paprika

STUFFING

1 cup finely chopped shallots	4 cups fresh bread crumbs
3 tablespoons dried tarragon	1 cup (2 sticks) butter, melted
1½ cups chopped fresh parsley leaves	Salt and freshly ground black pepper

1. Season the chicken breasts with salt and pepper.

2. Combine the stuffing ingredients well.

3. Separate the skin from the meat on each side of each chicken breast. Do not separate the skin over the very center of the breast.

4. Put the stuffing under each side of the breast between the meat and the skin in equal amounts. Replace the skin over the meat. Fold each side of the breast under, making a neat chicken package. Put the breast in 1 of 2 large well-greased roasting pans.

5. Continue stuffing the remaining chicken breasts in the same manner, and putting them side by side, touching, but not pressed together in the two pans.

6. Preheat the oven to 350 degrees.

7. Combine the melted butter and lemon juice, and brush it over the breasts. Sprinkle lightly with salt, pepper, and paprika. (At this point the chicken can be covered and refrigerated for 1 hour.)

8. Put one pan on the lower oven shelf and one pan on the middle shelf of the oven. Bake for 30 minutes; then reverse the pans on the shelves, and bake for 30 minutes. Serve immediately.

The chicken recipe will take about one hour to prepare, and one hour to cook. The prepared chicken can rest in the refrigerator for one hour before cooking it, as indicated in the recipe. This hour will give you time to organize the other elements of the meal. If your party is called for 8 o'clock, at 7:30 you can arrange the hors d'oeuvres on platters and put the chicken in the oven at 7:50. You should serve dinner no later than one hour after the appointed time of the party.

1. Make space for the two roasting pans in the refrigerator if you are going to hold the prepared chicken for 1 hour before cooking it.

2. Read the recipe thoroughly.

3. Check that the wastebasket is emptied and lined with a fresh plastic bag and is near the work area.

4. Put all the equipment, utensils, pots, pans, and equipment in the work area: one 20-quart bowl or colander or both, juice squeezer, 1-quart measuring cup, medium-sized saucepan, one small bowl, one large bowl,

chopping knife, measuring spoons, two large roasting pans, and a food processor for making the crumbs.

5. Assemble all the ingredients for the recipe: 36 boned chicken breasts, salt and pepper, 3½ sticks of butter, plus a little extra for greasing the roasting pans, lemons, paprika, shallots, dried tarragon, parsley, and bread for the crumbs.

6. Arrange the ingredients in two separate groups: one for the chicken and one for the stuffing.

7. Do the *mise en place* for the stuffing: chop the shallots, measure the tarragon, chop the parsley, make the bread crumbs, and melt the butter and pour it into a bowl.

8. Now melt the butter to baste the chicken with. Squeeze the lemon juice and add it to the butter, mix and set it aside.

9. Grease the roasting pans with a little butter.

10. Season the chicken breasts with salt and pepper. (This can be done on the counter surface, in a large colander or bowl, transfering the seasoned breasts from one to the other, and vice versa when separating the skin from the meat.)

11. Combine the stuffing ingredients in the large bowl.

12. Separate the skin from the meat from each chicken breast. (If it is a very warm day, you can refrigerate half of the chicken breasts while stuffing the other half. When one roasting pan is filled with the first half of stuffed breasts, refrigerate it, and continue stuffing the remaining half of the breasts.)

13. With your fingers press down the stuffing mixture lightly and draw a crisscross over the top of it. This sectioning will help to measure equal amounts of stuffing for each breast. Each measured quarter must stuff 9 breasts.

14. Stuff the breasts and place them side by side in the two large roasting pans. Baste the chicken and season it with salt, pepper, and paprika. If you are going to cook the chicken immediately, preheat the oven to 350 degrees about 10 minutes before you've finished stuffing the breasts and basted and seasoned them. If you're going to cover and refrigerate the chicken for 1 hour, preheat the oven 10 minutes before cooking time begins.

15. Cook the chicken as directed for 30 minutes, one pan on the lower oven shelf, and the other one on the midddle shelf. Rotate the pans on the shelves and cook them for another 30 minutes. During the last half hour of cooking time, the green beans can be prepared and the salad tossed.

16. The chicken breasts can be served directly from the roasting pans, or transferred to two large serving dishes or platters.

Table Settings

Make a list of the number of dinner plates, glasses, dessert plates, cups, and saucers, and how many place settings of flatware you will need. Go over the menu and select the serving dishes, platters, bowls, and serving forks and spoons, trivets, and bread baskets you will need. When entertaining crowds, large bowls, platters, and dishes are necessary. You may own many of these items, or they can be borrowed, purchased, or rented. There are many inexpensive and attractive ceramic, plastic, and stainless steel bowls and platters available. I normally try to buy these items on sale.

Select colorful tablecloths, place mats, runners, and napkins. Remember to consider attractive sheets and large pieces of fabric for big tables. Select plain white or any combinations of colors and prints you desire, as long as they are harmonious.

Flowers for the dining tables and buffet can be beautiful small arrangements or single flowers in small vases, pitchers, bottles, or teapots. This will depend on what you have on hand. There is usually no need to make special purchases, unless you want to.

Food centerpieces can also be extremely attractive—a cornucopia basket with fall gourds and fruit with autumn leaves or a basket of red and green apples are lovely for the fall. Palm fronds with tropical fruit always look stunning in the summer. It will all depend on the season, event, and your budget and imagination.

For each table or on the buffet table, salt cellars and pepper shakers, and a butter dish and knife may be called for. Napkins will be needed to line bread baskets.

Candles are always a beautiful touch and are sometimes necessary for lighting. They can be thick, free-standing ones placed on saucers and surrounded by fresh flower wreaths, or a single candlestick.

Do remember that flowers or candle arrangements should never interfere with the sight lines—guests should be able to see one another easily.

Coffee and Tea

The coffee maker and teapots, sugar, creamers, and lemon slices can be set up before dinner, but brewing the coffee and tea should be left until the last minute.

Do offer guests the choice of brewed decaffeinated coffee.

Large electric coffee makers are wonderful for crowds. They are inexpensive to buy if you don't already have one. However, they can be borrowed or rented.

Cleanup

If you have help during the dinner, they can collect the dirty dishes and utensils and keep the kitchen straightened as the meal progresses.

However, if you are in charge of cleanup, collect and stack the dishes in as orderly a manner as possible and wait until the last guest has left before washing the dishes or turning on the dishwasher or using the garbage disposal.

Before the event begins, remember to empty all wastebaskets and garbage pails and line them with fresh plastic bags.

Hot and Cold
Hors d'Oeuvres

◇ ═══════════════════ ◇

Hors d'oeuvres are the overture, designed to wake up the appetite for the meal ahead. In cooking for crowds, they are doubly important because they also often take the place of a first course. Nevertheless, hors d'oeuvres should never overwhelm hungry guests; therefore, they should be limited to three or four of each variety per guest.

Because they require last-minute heating, it isn't practical or desirable to serve only hot hors d'oeuvres. Serve two cold and one hot hors d'oeuvres for parties of eight to sixteen. Large parties, naturally, require more of a selection, but never more than five or six different types. Two hot hors d'oeuvres are always enough.

Whichever hors d'oeuvres are selected, they should complement each other in flavor, texture, and color. Try to vary the ingredients: For example, if a selection of three hors d'oeuvres is sufficient, serve one seafood, one cheese, and one meat.

For large groups, balance the cost with one or two expensive hors d'oeuvres and two or three inexpensive ones, preparing as many ahead of time as possible.

The presentation of hors d'oeuvres is extremely important. Beautiful tray arrangements can be great fun. Use interesting dishes, platters, baskets, trays, and bowls, and include a variety of materials—glass, ceramic, stainless steel or silver, straw, or wood.

Garnish platters with fresh greens, such as parsley or watercress, sprouts, whole small leaves of radicchio, bibb lettuce, arugula, or sorrel. Tiny bouquets or sprigs of fresh herbs, such as thyme, dill, sage, and tarragon, are lovely accents. Use miniature colorful peppers (both red and yellow), cherry tomatoes, crab apples, lady apples, radishes, or green or black olives.

Accents of brightly colored flowers or single blossoms are beautiful, too, but they musn't be overdone so the food won't be upstaged.

Fluted lemons, limes, and oranges, topped with a pinch of parsley, a sprinkling of paprika, capers, or sliced black or green olives, are always attractive.

Crudités and fresh fruit make wonderful hors d'oeuvres, and you should definitely consider them. They are not included here because, by now, they are familiar to us all. At the end of this chapter, there is a section devoted to dips, spreads, and fillings; many of these suggestions can be served with crudités.

Also at the end of this chapter are some quick and easy hors d'oeuvres that are all proven crowd-pleasers—and host-pleasers, too.

I once attended a large dinner party where the only hors d'oeuvre offered was sautéed blanched almonds, sprinkled lightly with salt, served still warm in small gleaming silver bowls placed around the room—with champagne, the combination seemed perfect.

LOBSTER MOUSSE WITH PIMIENTO-MOUSSELINE SAUCE

SERVES 8

1½ pounds raw lobster meat
4 egg whites
1 whole egg
2 teaspoons salt
1 teaspoon dried tarragon

1 cup heavy cream
½ cup dry white wine
Softened butter for greasing the molds

PIMIENTO-MOUSSELINE SAUCE

1 cup chopped pimiento
1 tablespoon fresh lemon juice
1 cup mayonnaise

½ cup heavy cream, whipped
Salt and freshly ground black pepper to taste

1. Purée the lobster meat in a food processor until it is very smooth. Add the egg whites, egg, salt, and tarragon and purée.

2. Through the feed tube, with the machine running, add the cream and white wine.

3. Preheat the oven to 325 degrees.

4. Butter a 2-quart rectangular mold. Turn the mixture into the mold and smooth the top. Cover the mold tightly with a lid or aluminum foil.

5. Put the mold in a larger pan and pour hot water to come halfway up the side of the mold. Bake for 1 hour.

6. Remove the mold from the oven and cool; then chill thoroughly.

7. To make the sauce, purée the pimientos with the lemon juice and mayonnaise in a food processor or blender. Turn into a bowl and fold in the whipped cream. Season with salt and pepper and serve with the mousse.

More Servings
To serve 16, double the recipe and bake the mousse in two molds.

JAMBON PERSILLÉ

SERVES 8
(PREPARATION BEGINS THE DAY BEFORE)

3 tablespoons unflavored gelatin
3 cups canned chicken consommé
1½ cups dry white wine
2 pounds cooked ham, cut into bite-sized cubes

1 teaspoon finely minced garlic
2 tablespoons fresh lemon juice
Freshly ground black pepper to taste
1½ cups chopped fresh parsley leaves

1. Soften the gelatin in ½ cup cold water.

2. Meanwhile, combine the consommé and white wine in a large saucepan. Add the ham, garlic, lemon juice, and pepper. Stir and simmer for 10 minutes.

3. Transfer the ham to a bowl with a slotted spoon. Cool, cover, and refrigerate.

4. Off the heat, stir the softened gelatin into the liquid and cool. Refrigerate for about 30 minutes, or until the gelatin begins to set.

5. Stir the parsley and ham into the gelatin mixture and turn into a 2-quart glass or ceramic bowl. Cover and refrigerate overnight.

6. Unmold the Jambon Persillé and serve with sliced French bread and sweet butter.

More Servings
The recipe can be doubled to serve 16 and made in one 4-quart bowl or two 2-quart bowls.

GRAY'S STANDING CRAB MEAT RUMAKI

SERVES 8 · MAKES ABOUT 40 RUMAKI

1 6-ounce can crab meat, drained and flaked with fork
1½ cups fresh bread crumbs
⅓ cup freshly grated Parmesan cheese
⅓ cup tomato juice
¼ cup chopped fresh parsley leaves

1½ tablespoons minced shallots or onion
1 large egg, lightly beaten
¼ teaspoon celery seeds
Freshly ground black pepper to taste
1 pound bacon, cut in half crosswise

1. Preheat the oven to 400 degrees.
2. Combine the first 9 ingredients well in a bowl.
3. With your fingers, press together about a rounded teaspoon of the mixture and put it at one end of a halved strip of bacon. Fold the bacon over the mixture, and fold again. Press the rumaki flat. Continue filling the remaining bacon strips in the same manner. (The filled rumaki can be wrapped and frozen at this point, if desired.)
4. Put the rumaki in a large roasting pan, seam side down, and bake for 10 minutes.
5. Turn the rumaki gently and bake for about 10 minutes, or until golden brown all over. Drain.
6. Stick a toothpick into the center of each rumaki and arrange in rows on a serving platter.

More Servings
The recipe can be doubled to serve 16 and make 80 rumaki. Bake in two pans.

Cooking Instructions for Frozen Rumaki
Put the rumaki in a roasting pan and bake in a preheated 400-degree oven for 15 minutes. Turn the rumaki and cook for 10 minutes, or until golden brown.

Variation
A delightful hors d'oeuvre called pot stickers can be made with the crab meat stuffing. Cut 40 wonton wrappers into circles with a 3½-inch biscuit cutter. Fill each wonton with 1 teaspoon of the crab meat mixture. Brush half of the inside edge of the wonton with water, and fold the wonton over. Press to secure the edges together. Make the remaining pot stickers in the same manner. Sauté the pot stickers in about ⅓ inch of peanut or vegetable oil in a large frying pan until crisp and brown on each side. This will only take a few minutes. Drain on paper towels and serve.

CURRIED GROUND LAMB KEBABS WITH LIME MAYONNAISE

SERVES 8 · MAKES ABOUT 32 KEBABS

2 pounds ground lamb
2 tablespoons curry powder
1 large egg
⅓ cup finely chopped scallions
1 tablespoon soy sauce
3 dashes of Tabasco sauce

Salt and freshly ground black pepper to taste
All-purpose flour
3 large eggs, lightly beaten
3 cups fresh bread crumbs
Peanut oil

LIME MAYONNAISE
1½ cups mayonnaise
1 cup sour cream
3 tablespoons confectioner's sugar

2 tablespoons fresh lime juice
1 tablespoon grated lime rind
1 tablespoon poppy seeds

1. Put the lamb, curry powder, 1 egg, scallions, soy sauce, Tabasco sauce, and salt and pepper into a bowl. Mix well.

2. Using rounded tablespoons, shape the mixture into 1½-inch-long ovals. The mixture will make about 32. Dust each with flour and roll in the 3 lightly beaten eggs; then coat lightly with the bread crumbs.

3. Heat 1½ inches of oil in a deep wide pan and cook the lamb ovals, as many as will fit comfortably into the pan at one time, until they are golden brown all over and thoroughly cooked. Drain on paper towels.

4. Combine the sauce ingredients with a wire whisk.

5. Put each lamb oval on the end of a 5- to 6-inch-long wooden skewer and serve with the sauce.

More Servings
Double the recipe to serve 16 or to make 64 kebabs.

ITALIAN SWEET SAUSAGE-AND-MOZZARELLA-STUFFED FRIED WONTONS

SERVES 8 · MAKES ABOUT 48 WONTONS

¾ pound Italian sweet sausages, removed from the casings and crumbled
1 medium-sized onion, minced
1 pound mozzarella, shredded

¼ cup chopped fresh parsley leaves
1 pound wonton wrappers
Peanut oil for deep-frying

1. Cook the sausage with the onion in a large frying pan until the sausage is thoroughly cooked but not brown. Cool completely.

2. Combine the cheese and parsley with the sausage mixture.

3. Put 1 rounded teaspoon of the mixture into the center of a wonton wrapper. Brush a little water along two inside edges of the wonton. Fold the wonton over and press slightly to seal well. Bring the two pointed ends of the wonton up over the stuffed center and press together. Assemble the remaining wontons in the same manner.

4. Heat 2 inches of peanut oil in a deep pot to about 370 degrees. Fry the wontons, about six at a time, until they are golden brown all over. Drain on paper towels. Serve the wontons immediately, or keep warm

in a low oven. The wontons can also be cooled, wrapped in aluminum foil, and frozen. To reheat them, place on a baking sheet in a preheated 350-degree oven for about 15 minutes.

More Servings
Double the recipe to serve 16 or to make 96 wontons.

CAPONATA

◇ ══════════════ ◇

Caponata is a wonderfully refreshing hors d'oeuvre. But it can also be served as a condiment, a vegetable dish, or be used as a stuffing for an omelet. It's superb as a side dish for roast chicken, or cold sliced turkey, roast beef, or fish.

SERVES 12
(PREPARATION BEGINS THE NIGHT BEFORE)

½ cup olive oil
2½ pounds eggplant, cut into ¾-inch cubes with the skin
2 large sweet red peppers, diced
1 large onion, chopped
2 large garlic cloves, minced
1½ cups thinly sliced celery
1 6-ounce can tomato paste
Water
1 cup homemade or canned tomato sauce
8 dashes of Tabasco sauce
3½ ounces capers (from Madagascar, if possible)
⅓ cup red wine vinegar, or to taste

1 teaspoon sugar
Salt and freshly ground black pepper to taste
2 7¼-ounce cans pitted large black olives, chopped
1 4½-ounce jar pitted green olives, sliced crosswise
½ cup pine nuts (optional)
⅓ cup chopped fresh parsley leaves
1 tablespoon chopped fresh basil leaves, or 1 teaspoon dried basil

1. In an 8- to 9-quart heavy-bottomed pot, heat the olive oil. Add the eggplant, red peppers, onion, and garlic and cook over medium-high heat for 5 minutes, stirring often.

2. Add the celery, tomato paste, 1 can of water (using the tomato paste can), and tomato sauce. Simmer for 20 minutes, stirring often.

3. Add the remaining ingredients, stir, and simmer for 15 minutes.

4. Remove from the heat, cool completely, cover, and refrigerate overnight. Serve cold or at room temperature with crackers or toasted Italian or French bread.

Variation
One-half cup of chopped sun-dried tomatoes can be stirred into the hot cooked mixture.

MALLORCAN MARINATED MUSSELS ON THE HALF SHELL

SERVES 12

7 dozen mussels, well scrubbed and with beards removed
1 bottle dry white wine
2 cups virgin olive oil
3 large garlic cloves, coarsely chopped
¾ cup chopped fresh parsley leaves
½ cup fresh lemon juice
2 teaspoons salt, or to taste
Freshly ground black pepper to taste
6 drops Tabasco sauce

1. Put the mussels in a large pot with the wine and 4 cups of water. Cover and bring to a boil. Stir, cover again, and cook over high heat for 6 minutes.

2. Remove the mussels and drain them in a large colander or the sink. Discard any mussels that have not opened. Cool.

3. Put the remaining ingredients in a blender or food processor and purée for 1 minute. Taste for seasoning.

4. Break off the empty mussel shell halves. With the tip of a small sharp knife, release each mussel from its shell. Arrange the mussels on one or two large serving platters in concentric circles, with the pointed ends of the mussel shells pointing out.

5. Spoon about a scant tablespoon of the oil mixture over each mus-

sel. Cover and marinate at room temperature for 1 hour. At serving time, put empty bowls for the shells in the serving area along with plenty of cocktail napkins.

More Servings
To serve 24, double the recipe and cook the mussels in two batches. Make the sauce in two batches in the blender or food processor.

FRUIT KEBABS WITH CURRIED CREAM CHEESE AND CHUTNEY DIP

SERVES 12 · MAKES 36 KEBABS

2 medium-sized cantaloupes, halved, seeded, peeled, and cut into 1-inch cubes or balls
36 small strawberries, hulled

6 medium-sized firm ripe bananas, peeled and cut into ¼-inch-thick slices
36 seedless green grapes

CURRIED CREAM CHEESE AND CHUTNEY DIP

1 8-ounce package cream cheese, softened
1½ cups chutney

1 tablespoon curry powder
1 tablespoon fresh lemon juice
1 cup heavy cream, whipped

1. On each of 36 toothpicks, make kebabs of 1 piece of cantaloupe, a strawberry, a banana slice, and a grape.
2. In a food processor or blender, combine the cream cheese, chutney, curry powder, and lemon juice.
3. Turn the mixture into a bowl and fold in the whipped cream.
4. Arrange the kebabs on a large serving platter with a bowl of the dip in the center or at one end. Serve at once.

More Servings
Double the recipe to serve 24. Make the dip in two batches in equal amounts in a food processor or blender for the first part of the recipe. Turn the mixtures into one large bowl and fold in the whipped cream.

CHERRY TOMATOES STUFFED WITH ORZO PRIMAVERA

◇ ══════════════════════════════ ◇

SERVES 12

48 cherry tomatoes (about
   2 pints)
1 cup orzo (rice-shaped pasta)
   Salt
½ cup minced scallions
½ cup minced sweet red pepper
¼ cup chopped fresh parsley
   leaves

½ teaspoon dried oregano
1 teaspoon dried basil
½ teaspoon dried thyme
   Freshly ground black pepper
   to taste
   Olive oil
   White wine vinegar
1 bunch parsley sprigs

1. Cut ¼ inch off the bottom of the cherry tomatoes—the ends opposite the stem end. (This will allow the tomatoes to stand up easier.) Scoop out the tomato pulp with a small melon-ball scoop. Turn the tomatoes upside down on paper towels to drain.

2. Meanwhile, cook the orzo in 1 quart of rapidly boiling water to which 2 teaspoons of salt have been added. Cook until tender, about 6 minutes. Drain very well.

3. In a bowl, combine the scallions, red pepper, parsley, and herbs. Add the orzo and season well with salt and pepper. Add enough oil and vinegar, in equal amounts, to just moisten the mixture. Taste for seasoning.

4. Fill the cherry tomatoes with the mixture. Serve immediately, or cover and chill. Serve the stuffed tomatoes within the next 2 hours on a bed of parsley—again, to enable them to stand up easier.

More Servings
Double the recipe to serve 24.

TART FLAMBÉE CANAPÉS

◊ ═══════════════════════════════════ ◊

An Alsatian Tart Flambée resembles a large pizza in shape and size. Traditionally, the flat open-faced pie or tart is cooked in an open oven over a wood-burning fire.

Transformed into canapés, the tiny Tart Flambées make savory hors d'oeuvres.

SERVES 12 · MAKES 48 CANAPÉS

2 cups crème fraîche (see Note)
1 8-ounce package cream cheese, softened
Salt and freshly ground black pepper
Freshly ground nutmeg
8 strips bacon, cooked crisp and crumbled

48 2-inch circles of firm white bread
4 small onions, very thinly sliced and separated into rings
Olive oil

1. Combine the crème fraîche and cream cheese in a food processor. Transfer to a large bowl and season well with salt, pepper, and a few gratings of nutmeg. Fold in the bacon.

2. Spread about a rounded teaspoon on each circle of bread. Top with a few onion rings and press them lightly into the cheese.

3. Preheat the oven to 425 degrees.

4. Put the canapés side by side on one or two large baking sheets. Sprinkle each canapé with a drop or two of the olive oil. Bake for 6 minutes. Pass quickly under the broiler until golden brown and serve immediately.

More Servings
The recipe can be doubled to serve 24 or to make 96 canapés. The canapés must be cooked in several batches and served as soon as they are removed from the broiler.

NOTE: To make crème fraîche, whisk together 2 cups of heavy cream with 4 tablespoons of buttermilk; then transfer to a jar. Cover tightly and let stand at room temperature for 8 hours. Whisk, cover again, and refrigerate overnight. The recipe can be doubled to make about 1 quart. It will keep for a week.

SCALLOP AND LEEK EGG ROLLS

MAKES 12 EGG ROLLS

Peanut oil
1 pound sea scallops, coarsely chopped
3 large leeks (white parts only), well washed and thinly sliced
1 cup fresh bean sprouts
3 cups finely shredded celery cabbage (sometimes called Chinese lettuce)
½ cup minced water chestnuts
2 tablespoons dry sherry
1 teaspoon grated fresh gingerroot

3 tablespoons light soy sauce, or to taste
2 teaspoons Oriental sesame oil
Freshly ground black pepper to taste
12 egg roll wrappers
1 large egg, lightly beaten
1½ cups Chinese plum or sweet and sour sauce
½ cup Chinese hot mustard

1. Heat 3 tablespoons of peanut oil in a wok or large frying pan with curved sides (a seasoned paella pan is also good). Stir-fry the scallops for about 3 minutes. Transfer the scallops to a dish. Add 3 more tablespoons of oil to the pan and cook the leeks, stirring, for about 4 minutes. Add the next 7 ingredients (through the sesame oil) and stir-fry until the cabbage begins to wilt. Add the scallops and season with pepper. Drain the mixture and transfer it to a shallow bowl to cool completely.

2. Put an egg roll wrapper on a work area in front of you, with one corner pointing toward you. Spoon about 2 heaping tablespoons of the scallop mixture into the center of the wrapper. Fold the bottom third of the wrapper up over the filling. Brush a ½-inch border edge of the 3 remaining corners of the wrapper lightly with the beaten egg. Fold in the sides of the wrapper and roll up. Put the roll on a plate, sealed side down, and keep covered with a dish towel. Continue making the remaining egg rolls.

3. Heat about 2 inches of peanut oil in a wok or deep pan or pot to about 370 degrees. Cook 6 egg rolls at a time until they are golden brown all over. Remove the egg rolls with tongs or chopsticks and drain them on paper towels. Cook the remaining 6 egg rolls. Serve immediately with the plum sauce and Chinese mustard, or cool, tightly wrap, and freeze the egg rolls. To reheat the egg rolls, put them on a baking sheet in a preheated 350-degree oven for about 20 minutes.

More Servings
Double the recipe to make 24 egg rolls.

Variation
Add 1 tablespoon of curry powder to the ingredients after cooking the leeks; mix thoroughly for curry-flavored egg rolls.

PORK SATES WITH SPICY PEANUT SAUCE

SERVES 12 · MAKES 48 SATES

3 pounds small pork tenderloin strips, cut into ¾-inch cubes
1 cup soy sauce
¼ cup dry sherry
⅓ cup Oriental sesame oil
¼ cup honey

3 tablespoons fresh lemon juice
¼ cup grated onion
2 large garlic cloves, crushed
¼ teaspoon cayenne pepper (optional)

SPICY PEANUT SAUCE

1½ cups chunky peanut butter
3 tablespoons Oriental sesame oil
2 tablespoons chili paste with garlic (available in Oriental markets)

¾ cup cream of coconut
3 tablespoons fresh lemon juice
2 tablespoons soy sauce
½ cup hot water, or as needed

1. Arrange 3 pork cubes on each of 48 toothpicks. Put the sates in a large shallow baking dish.
2. Combine the next 8 ingredients (through the cayenne pepper) and pour the mixture over the sates. Turn to coat evenly; then cover and refrigerate for at least 3 hours.
3. Cook the pork sates in broiler pans under a hot broiler until they are golden brown and thoroughly cooked on each side. This will take about 6 minutes per side.

4. Combine the sauce ingredients in a heavy saucepan and cook, stirring constantly, until thoroughly combined and hot.

5. Serve the sates on a large platter with a bowl of the peanut sauce.

More Servings
Double the recipe to serve 24 or to make 96 sates. Cook the satés in several batches. Serve as soon as they are cooked.

SHRIMP AND HOISIN SAUCE CANAPÉS

◊ ══════════════════ ◊

SERVES 16 · MAKES ABOUT 78 CANAPÉS

1 1-pound loaf firm white
  sandwich bread
2 cups hoisin sauce (available in
  many supermarkets or
  Oriental markets)

2 pounds medium-sized
  shrimp, shelled, deveined,
  boiled for 6 minutes, and
  then drained and chilled
2 bunches scallions, cut into
  ½-inch lengths

1. Toast the bread and cut it into 78 1½-inch circles, using a scalloped pastry cutter.

2. Spread about a teaspoon of the hoisin sauce over each piece of toast.

3. Put a shrimp in the center of each and stick a piece of scallion in the center of the shrimp. Serve at once.

More Servings
Double the recipe to serve 32 or to make 156 canapés.

CHICKEN AND RED PEPPER ROLLS

SERVES 12

4 slices firm white bread
½ cup milk
4 medium-sized skinned and boned chicken breasts, cut into 1½-inch pieces
2 large sweet red peppers, seeded and finely diced
3 tablespoons chopped fresh chives

½ cup chopped fresh parsley leaves
6 tablespoons butter, softened
Salt and freshly ground black pepper to taste
All-purpose flour
3 large eggs, lightly beaten
Plain dry bread crumbs
Peanut oil

1. Soak the bread in the milk in a bowl for 5 minutes.

2. Meanwhile, grind the chicken in a food processor or grinder and turn it into a bowl.

3. Squeeze out the milk from the bread and add the bread to the chicken along with the peppers, chives, parsley, and butter. Season well with salt and pepper and combine thoroughly.

4. Divide the mixture into six portions and shape into 1-inch-thick sausages. Dust each with flour and coat with the beaten eggs and then the bread crumbs.

5. Heat ½ inch of oil in a large frying pan and cook the rolls until they are golden brown all over and thoroughly cooked.

6. Drain the rolls on paper towels and cut them into ¼-inch-thick slices. Arrange on a platter. Serve at once or cover and chill until ready to serve.

BELGIAN ENDIVE LEAVES STUFFED WITH CRAB MEAT AND DIANE YOUNG'S ALOHA SAUCE

Diane Young bakes the superb cheesecake served in Hotel 1829 restaurant in St. Thomas. She won't part with her cheesecake recipe, but she shared her uncommonly delicious and easy sauce recipe with me. It was given to her as a wedding present by a relative.

SERVES 12 · MAKES 48 HORS D'OEUVRES

DIANE YOUNG'S ALOHA SAUCE

1½ cups mayonnaise	2 tablespoons fresh lemon juice
3 tablespoons honey	1½ tablespoons curry powder
2 tablespoons minced scallions	3 tablespoons ketchup
8 drops Tabasco sauce	
2 pounds crab meat, coarsely chopped	48 Belgian endive leaves (about 7 large endives)
	8 red radishes, finely diced

1. Combine the sauce ingredients in a large bowl. (The sauce can be made a day in advance.) Add the crab meat and combine thoroughly.

2. Spoon about a tablespoon of the mixture onto the base of each endive leaf and sprinkle with diced radish.

3. Arrange the stuffed leaves on a large serving platter and serve immediately.

More Servings
Double the recipe to serve 24.

WEST INDIAN MEAT PATES

◊ ═══════════════════════════════ ◊

West Indian meat pates are envelopes of soft pastry dough stuffed with a spicy ground beef filling (saltfish is also popular) which are fried until golden brown. In a complimentary way, they are to the Caribbean what hot dogs are to the States. Meat pates are savory meat pies. Like other meat pie cousins from cuisines around the world, such as the Cornish pasty, the Spanish empanada, Italy's calzone, and Indian samosas, they are held in the hand and eaten: an enclosed sandwich really.

I have queued up to many pate wagons and stands in St. Thomas for a deliciously satisfying lunch of hot steaming pates.

Small pates make superb hors d'oeuvres, and they can be made in advance and frozen.

Doris Farrington of St. Thomas, who makes pates for Carnival every year, recently shared her pastry dough recipe with me. The filling is my own combination.

Do keep in mind that this recipe will make 12 to 14 regular-sized pates, which are about four times as large as the amounts given for the dough and filling given for the pates in the following recipe.

SERVES 16 · MAKES 48 PATES

PATE PASTRY DOUGH

6 cups unsifted all-purpose flour
2 tablespoons baking powder
2 teaspoons salt
1½ tablespoons sugar
6 tablespoons vegetable shortening
½ cup evaporated milk
¾ cup water, or as needed

MEAT FILLING

2 pounds ground beef
¾ cup minced onion
3 large garlic cloves, minced
1 large sweet green pepper, seeded and diced
½ teaspoon dried thyme
2 teaspoons salt
1 6-ounce can tomato paste
⅓ cup red wine vinegar
1 tablespoon all-purpose flour
½ cup water
½ teaspoon Tabasco sauce, or to taste
Peanut oil for deep-frying

1. Put the dry ingredients for the pate dough into a large bowl and cut in the shortening until the mixture resembles course crumbs.

2. Combine the milk and water and work the mixture into the

dough. The dough should be soft and easy to knead with the hands. Add a little extra water, if necessary. Knead for 5 minutes, cover with a dish towel, and let rest for 30 minutes.

3. Meanwhile, in a large frying pan, cook the crumbled ground beef with the onion, garlic, and green pepper until the meat is no longer pink, stirring often.

4. Add the thyme, salt, tomato paste, and vinegar and stir. Simmer for 5 minutes. Sprinkle with the flour and stir. Cook 1 minute. Add the water and Tabasco sauce. Stir and cook until thickened.

5. Transfer the mixture to a bowl and cool.

6. To make each pate, flatten a piece of dough the size of a walnut between the palms of your hands. With a rolling pin, roll the dough out to about a 4-inch circle on a marble or formica surface (no flour will be needed).

7. Put 1 rounded teaspoon of the meat filling in the center of the dough and fold it over into a half-circle. Press the edge of the dough with your thumb to completely seal it. Using your thumb, pull up about ½ inch of the dough and press it over. Continue this procedure all along the sealed edge of the dough, making an attractive scalloped edge. Cover the shaped pate with a dish towel and make the remaining pates.

8. Heat 2 inches of oil in a large heavy Dutch oven to about 370 degrees. Add about 8 pates and cook on both sides until they are golden brown. Drain on paper towels. Then fry the remaining pates.

More Servings
Double the recipe and make two batches to serve 32 or to make 96 pates.

Freezing Instructions
Cool the cooked pates and put them in several plastic bags; close the bags tightly. Freeze for up to 2 weeks. To cook the frozen pates, put them on baking sheets in a preheated 350-degree oven and bake for about 20 minutes.

LUGANEGHE WITH FONTINA CHEESE SAUCE

Luganeghe is the marvelous thin sausage made with pork and parsley and sometimes cheese. It comes in a long coil and is available in Italian butcher shops.

SERVES 16

4 pounds luganeghe, cut into
   1½-inch lengths

FONTINA CHEESE DIP

2½ cups milk
 1 pound Fontina cheese,
   shredded
 2 tablespoons cornstarch

1 large sweet red pepper,
   seeded and diced
2 scallions, thinly sliced

1. Cook the sausage in batches in a large frying pan until it is golden brown and thoroughly cooked.

2. Meanwhile, prepare the sauce: Bring the milk to a boil. Toss the cheese with the cornstarch and stir it into the milk.

3. Add the red pepper and scallions and simmer for a few minutes.

4. Stick a 6-inch wooden skewer three quarters of the way into each sausage link and arrange on a large serving platter with a bowl of the sauce. Serve immediately.

FRANCES BANGEL'S "FAUX CRAB MEAT" ARTICHOKE BAKE

Frances Bangel's Artichoke Bake has become my favorite quick hors d'oeuvre. There is never any left over when it's served to company. (For variety, ³/₄ cup diced ham or crisp cooked chopped bacon can be mixed with the other ingredients.)

SERVES 16

3 14-ounce cans artichoke
hearts, well drained and
finely chopped
3 cups mayonnaise
2½ cups freshly grated Parmesan
cheese
1 tablespoon Worcestershire
sauce

1 medium-sized onion, finely
chopped
1 medium-sized sweet red
pepper, seeded and diced
½ teaspoon freshly ground
black pepper
64 plain crackers or toast points

1. Preheat the oven to 350 degrees.

2. Combine all the ingredients and turn the mixture into a shallow ovenproof 14-inch au gratin dish or baking dish.

3. Bake for exactly 30 minutes. Serve immediately with crackers and/or toast points.

More Servings
Make the recipe in two batches in two dishes to serve 32.

FILLET AND SHRIMP KEBABS WITH GREEN MUSTARD SAUCE

SERVES 24 · MAKES ABOUT 100 KEBABS

1 4-pound beef fillet, roasted
(see recipe page 136) and
chilled

3 pounds medium-sized
shrimp, boiled, shelled,
deveined, and chilled

GREEN MUSTARD SAUCE
1½ cups Dijon mustard
½ cup chopped fresh parsley
leaves
¾ cup chopped fresh watercress
leaves

1 teaspoon dried basil
1 teaspoon dried tarragon
1½ cups mayonnaise

1. Cut the fillet into 1-inch cubes.

2. Put 1 shrimp and 1 piece of beef on each of about 100 5- to 6-inch wooden skewers. Cover and chill.

3. Purée the mustard, parsley, watercress, and herbs in a food processor or blender. Transfer to a bowl and fold in the mayonnaise; then cover and chill. Serve the kebabs on a large platter with the sauce.

More Servings
Double the recipe to serve 48.

COLOSSAL BLACK OLIVES STUFFED WITH PESTO-CREAM FILLING

SERVES 24 · MAKES 96 STUFFED OLIVES

2 8-ounce packages cream cheese, softened
¾ cup packed coarsely chopped fresh basil leaves (Do not use dried basil in this recipe.)
3 large garlic cloves, minced
2 tablespoons fresh lemon juice
½ teaspoon freshly ground black pepper
Salt to taste
96 colossal pitted black olives (about five 15-ounce cans), well drained and patted dry

1. Purée all the ingredients, except the olives, in a food processor. Taste for seasoning.

2. Spoon the mixture into a pastry bag fitted with a round tip and pipe into the olive cavities.

3. Pile up the stuffed olives in an attractive bowl, cover, and chill until serving time.

More Servings
Double the recipe to serve 48 and purée the mixture in two batches in a food processor in the original amounts given in the recipe.

Sliced Smoked Turkey Canapés with Tonnato Sauce and Fried Capers

SERVES 24 · MAKES 96 CANAPÉS

TONNATO SAUCE

2 12½-ounce cans solid white meat tuna, drained

1 8-ounce package cream cheese, softened

2 tablespoons fresh lemon juice

12 anchovy fillets, drained and coarsely chopped

1 cup olive oil

Freshly ground black pepper

Peanut or vegetable oil for deep-frying

96 large capers (about 1½ 3-ounce jars)

2 pounds skinned smoked turkey, thinly sliced

96 pieces Melba toast

1. Combine one can of the tuna, the cream cheese, lemon juice, and anchovies in a food processor. In a slow drizzle, with the machine running, add ½ cup of the olive oil through the feed tube. Season with the pepper. Transfer to a bowl and purée the other can of tuna with the remaining ½ cup of oil. Combine the two purées and mix well.

2. Heat 1 inch of oil in a large deep frying pan and cook the capers, stirring, until the blossoms open up. Drain on paper towels.

3. Use a cookie or pastry cutter to cut the turkey into circles the same size as the Melba toast. Put a slice of turkey on each piece of toast.

4. Spoon about a rounded teaspoon of the sauce onto the center of the turkey and top with a fried caper. Serve within 30 minutes.

More Servings
Double the recipe and make the Tonnato Sauce in two batches to serve 48 or to make 192 canapés.

MARY EUSTIS'
CHINESE CHICKEN WINGS
◇ ══════════════ ◇

This recipe has become a favorite of mine for the best of all culinary reasons: It's inexpensive, easy to make, and delicious. The mahogany-colored wings make a beautiful presentation, too. Because the wings are sticky, be sure to have plenty of cocktail napkins handy, as well as two empty bowls to hold the bones.

SERVES 24 · MAKES 72 HORS D'OEUVRES

36 chicken wings	½ cup granulated sugar
1 cup soy sauce	1 cup packed dark brown sugar

1. Preheat the oven to 325 degrees.
2. Cut off the wing tips (pinions) and wrap and freeze them for stock-making. Cut each of the chicken wings into two pieces, separating them at the joint.
3. Put 36 parts in each of two large shallow roasting pans. Combine the soy sauce and sugars and pour the mixture over the chicken in each pan.
4. Bake for 30 minutes.
5. Remove the pans and turn each piece of chicken over using tongs. Return the pans to the oven for 30 minutes.
6. Turn the wings again and cook for about 20 minutes longer, or until mahogany colored and very tender.
7. Transfer the chicken wings to a large warm platter and garnish with a bouquet of parsley with a yellow flower in the center.

More Servings
Double the recipe to serve 48 and bake in two batches. Serve the batches as they are cooked.

ITALIAN STUFFED MUSHROOMS

SERVES 24 · MAKES 96 HORS D'OEUVRES

96 medium-to-large fresh mushrooms

½ pound bulk pork sausage, crumbled

3 tablespoons butter

½ cup finely chopped onion

1 large garlic clove

½ cup finely chopped pimientos

¼ cup diced black olives

¼ cup dry sherry

¾ cup plain dry bread crumbs

3 tablespoons chopped fresh parsley leaves

1 teaspoon dried oregano

½ teaspoon dried thyme

Salt and freshly ground black pepper to taste

Freshly grated Parmesan cheese

1. Wipe the mushrooms clean with a damp cloth and remove the stems. Trim off the stem ends and finely chop the stems. Set the caps and chopped stems aside separately.

2. Cook the sausage in a large frying pan until it is no longer pink. Drain and transfer to a large bowl.

3. Pour off the fat from the frying pan and add the butter. Cook the onion and garlic until the onion is transparent. Transfer to the bowl with the sausage. Add the chopped mushroom stems and all the remaining ingredients, except the cheese. Combine well.

4. Stuff the mushroom caps with the mixture.

5. Preheat the oven to 400 degrees.

6. Put the stuffed mushrooms onto one or two large baking sheets and sprinkle them lightly with the cheese. Bake for 6 minutes. Quickly pass under the broiler until the tops of the stuffing are golden brown. Serve immediately.

More Servings

Double the recipe to serve 48 and bake in two batches. Serve each batch as soon as it is done.

MINIATURE FICELLE PIZZAS NIÇOISE

SERVES 24

3 cups homemade or canned
  tomato sauce
2 long *ficelle* (thin loaves of
  French bread), cut into
  ⅓-inch-thick slices
1 cup minced red onion
½ cup well-drained capers

1 cup minced pitted black
  olives
1 2-ounce can anchovy fillets,
  drained and finely chopped
1 pound mozzarella, shredded
  Freshly grated Parmesan
  cheese

1. Spread a heaping teaspoon of the tomato sauce over each slice of bread.

2. Combine the onion, capers, black olives, and anchovies. Mix well. Spoon the mixture in equal amounts over the bread and top with a good pinch of mozzarella. Sprinkle each pizza lightly with Parmesan cheese.

3. Cook under the broiler on one or two large baking sheets for a few minutes, or until the cheese melts and is golden brown. Serve immediately.

Fewer Servings
Cut the recipe in half to serve only 12.

APPLE SLICES
WITH GORGONZOLA SPREAD

SERVES 24

GORGONZOLA SPREAD
2 8-ounce packages cream
  cheese, softened
½ pound Gorgonzola cheese at
  room temperature

½ cup sour cream
3 tablespoons Cognac

8 large Granny Smith apples,
  cored and thinly sliced

1. Combine the spread ingredients well.

2. Spread the mixture lightly on the apple slices and arrange them on a large serving platter.

More Servings
Double the recipe to serve 48.

COUNTRY PÂTÉ LOAF

SERVES 36
(PREPARATION BEGINS THE NIGHT BEFORE)

3 pounds ground beef
1 pound ground veal
2 pounds ground pork
1 pound bulk pork sausage
4 large eggs
1 teaspoon dried tarragon
1 teaspoon dried thyme
¼ cup chopped fresh parsley
　 leaves

2 cups fresh bread crumbs
¼ cup green peppercorns
　 Salt and freshly ground black
　 pepper to taste
¾ cup grated onion
⅓ cup brandy
6 strips bacon
3 cups cornichons
3 cups Dijon mustard

1. Preheat the oven to 350 degrees.

2. In a large bowl, combine all the ingredients, except for the bacon, cornichons, and mustard, well with your hands.

3. Shape the mixture into a loaf that will conform in shape to fit into a 4-quart casserole or crock, oval in shape, if possible.

4. Cover the top of the pâté with the bacon strips lengthwise, tucking the ends behind the pâté. Cover the pâté with foil and bake in a roasting pan filled with hot water coming halfway up the side of the casserole.

5. After 1 hour of cooking, remove the foil and drain off the fat that has accumulated in the dish.

6. Return the pâté to the pan with the water and bake for 1 hour.

7. Drain off the juices in the casserole and cool completely.

8. Put a double sheet of heavy duty aluminum foil over the casserole and put a weight on top, such as a brick. Refrigerate overnight.

9. To serve, cut the pâté into ½-inch-thick slices and then cut into bite-sized cubes. Serve with toothpicks on a platter, and accompany with the cornichons and mustard.

PANINI

◊ ══════════ ◊

SERVES 36 · MAKES 72 PANINI

72 small soft rolls
1 cup (2 sticks) butter, softened
2½ pounds boiled ham, thinly sliced
2½ pounds Genoa salami, thinly sliced
2½ pounds mortadella, thinly sliced
2½ pounds Provolone, thinly sliced

1. Cut the rolls open and generously butter each cut side.

2. Cut the meat and cheese into pieces the same size as the rolls. On the bottom half of each roll place 1 slice each of the ham, salami, mortadella, and Provolone. Cover with the tops of the rolls. Serve immediately, or cover with plastic wrap and serve within 3 hours.

More Servings
Double the recipe to serve 72.

Sesame Shrimp Streamers

◇━━━━━━━━━━━━━━━━━◇

SERVES 36 · MAKES 144 HORS D'OEUVRES

72 large shrimp, shelled,
deveined, and cut in half
lengthwise
1 lemon, quartered and seeded
1/2 cup Oriental sesame oil
1/2 cup dry sherry

2 tablespoons light soy sauce
3 tablespoons rice wine vinegar
(available in Oriental
markets)
1 cup peach preserves, puréed
1/2 cup thinly sliced scallions

1. Cover the shrimp with water in a large saucepan and squeeze the juice of the lemon quarters into the water; then add the lemon pieces.

2. Slowly bring the water to a boil, stirring occasionally. Immediately lower the heat to a low boil and cook for exactly 4 minutes. Drain the shrimp and cool them. Discard the lemon pieces.

3. Spear each piece of shrimp lengthwise with a 5- to 6-inch wooden skewer. Put the skewers into a large glass baking dish with the wooden ends of the skewers resting up on the side of the dish.

4. Combine the remaining ingredients, except the scallions, and pour the mixture over the shrimp in a slow steady stream. Cover and chill.

5. When ready to serve, spoon the sauce over the shrimp again, and let the excess drip off into the dish. Arrange the shrimp on a large serving platter and sprinkle with the scallions.

More Servings
Double the recipe to serve 72, using two large dishes for marinating. Serve on two large platters.

CHICKEN GOUJONETTES
WITH APRICOT-GINGER SAUCE

SERVES 36

APRICOT-GINGER SAUCE

3 cups apricot preserves, puréed in a blender or food processor

¾ cup canned chicken broth

¼ cup dry sherry

3 tablespoons soy sauce

½ cup rice wine vinegar (available in Oriental markets)

2 tablespoons grated fresh gingerroot

12 large boned and skinned chicken breasts, halved
Salt and freshly ground black pepper
All-purpose flour

6 large eggs, beaten

5 cups plain dry bread crumbs

¾ cup sesame seeds
Peanut oil

1 bunch scallions, thinly sliced

1. Combine the sauce ingredients in a large bowl. Set aside until needed.

2. Flatten each chicken breast half between two sheets of wax paper to a ¼-inch thickness.

3. Cut each flattened chicken breast half into ¼-inch-wide strips.

4. Season the strips with salt and pepper.

5. Dust each strip with flour; then roll them in the eggs and coat them with the combined bread crumbs and sesame seeds.

6. Heat 1 inch of the peanut oil in a large frying pan. Cook the chicken in batches, until golden brown all over. Drain the chicken on paper towels. Add more oil and reheat as needed.

7. Put the cooked goujonettes onto one or two large baking sheets or roasting pans and reheat in a preheated 350-degree oven for about 10 minutes. Pile the goujonettes onto one or two large platters and sprinkle with the scallions. Serve with a bowl of the sauce.

OPEN-FACED REUBEN CANAPÉS

SERVES 36 · MAKES 72 CANAPÉS

RUSSIAN DRESSING

2 cups mayonnaise
½ cup ketchup
2 tablespoons Dijon mustard

⅓ cup minced sweet gherkin pickles

72 slices cocktail rye bread (about 2 loaves)
2 pounds corned beef, thinly sliced and cut into 2-inch squares

1 pound sauerkraut at room temperature, well drained but not rinsed
2 pounds Muenster cheese, thinly sliced and cut into 2-inch squares

1. In a bowl combine the Russian Dressing ingredients.

2. Spread 1 slice of bread lightly with the dressing. Put 1 slice of the corned beef on the bread and spoon about 1 rounded teaspoon of sauerkraut over the corned beef. Pat down evenly. Put 1 slice of the cheese on top of the canapé. Assemble the remaining canapés in the same manner.

3. On a baking sheet, arrange as many canapés as will fit comfortably. Put them under the broiler for about 5 minutes, or just until the cheese melts and is golden brown.

4. Transfer the canapés to a serving platter and cook the remaining canapés in the same manner. After the first batch of canapés is cooked, serve them and continue cooking the second batch.

More Servings
The recipe is easily doubled to serve 72 or to make 144 canapés.

MINIATURE SWEET AND SOUR SPARERIBS

SERVES 36

8 pounds Canadian baby back
  spareribs

SAUCE

1 cup (8 ounces) frozen orange
  juice concentrate
1 cup dry sherry
1 cup soy sauce
1 cup pineapple juice
¾ cup red wine vinegar
3 tablespoons Oriental sesame
  oil

1½ cups packed dark brown
   sugar
2 cups tomato sauce
¼ cup Worcestershire sauce
2 teaspoons ground ginger
¾ cup grated onion

1. Have the butcher cut the rib sides in half crosswise. Cut the ribs into individual pieces.

2. Combine the sauce ingredients in a large bowl.

3. Preheat the oven to 325 degrees.

4. Divide the ribs between two large roasting pans and pour half of the sauce over each pan of ribs. Turn the ribs to coat them evenly. Bake in the oven for 30 minutes.

5. Turn the ribs and bake for 30 minutes longer.

6. Remove the pans from the oven and put as many of the ribs as will fit comfortably onto a broiling pan.

7. Cook them under the broiler until they are golden brown. Serve at once and continue cooking the remaining ribs in batches.

WILLIAM AND DANIELS STUFFED CHICKEN BREAST PÂTÉ SLICES WITH MUSTARD SAUCE

◇ ═══ ◇

Daniel Rospond, owner/chef of the charming William and Daniels restaurant in St. Thomas has also run the D&R Catering Company for six years. Born in Glen Ridge, New Jersey, where his mother had a small catering business, food has always played an important role in his life: past, present, and future.

Daniel advises those cooking for crowds "not to panic: Never be afraid of the numbers, and get as much preparation done in advance as possible. In the end, the main thing is to enjoy your own party. Being confident about what you're serving allows you to relax."

William and Daniels restaurant opened in December of 1984. I attended a large celebration cocktail party, where I sampled many of Daniel's specialities. He graciously shared this recipe with me. He says it can easily be doubled several times to serve hundreds.

SERVES 50

(PREPARATION BEGINS THE DAY BEFORE)

1½ pounds Swiss cheese, shredded

1½ pounds cooked smoked ham, cut into 1-inch pieces

17 large chicken breasts, boned but left whole

Butter for greasing the pan

Salt and freshly ground black pepper

Paprika

MUSTARD SAUCE

2 pounds (four 8-ounce packages) cream cheese, softened

2 cups Dijon mustard

1. Combine the Swiss cheese and ham in a food processor, 1½ cups of each at a time; then transfer to a large bowl.

2. Combine the mixture well and divide it into 17 equal-sized portions. Press and shape each portion into a 1½-inch-thick roll, the shape of an Italian sausage, matching the length of a chicken breast, crosswise.

3. Preheat the oven to 350 degrees.

4. Put 1 cheese and ham roll, crosswise, onto the center of a chicken

breast. Wrap each side of the chicken breast around the roll and put it in one or two large greased roasting pans. Continue assembling the remaining chicken in the same manner, placing the stuffed breasts side by side in the pan or pans, so that they fit snugly together. Season the tops of the chicken with salt, pepper, and paprika.

5. Bake in the oven for about 45 minutes, or until the chicken rolls are golden brown on top.

6. Remove from the oven and cool completely. Drain off and discard the fat and pan juices that have accumulated in the pans. Cover the pans and refrigerate overnight.

7. Shortly before serving, combine half the cream cheese and half the mustard in a food processor. Blend until smooth. Transfer to a large bowl. Repeat with the remaining cream cheese and mustard. Combine. Cover until ready to serve.

8. Skin the chicken breasts.

9. Cut each breast, crosswise, into thin slices, about 10 per breast, and arrange in layers on a large serving platter or two. (Use the end pieces for chicken salad.) Garnish the platter with a bouquet of parsley and a fluted lemon, if desired, and serve with the Mustard Sauce.

More Servings
Double the recipe to serve 100 and cook in two batches.

ROAST BEEF TURBANS
WITH CREAMY ROQUEFORT SAUCE

SERVES 50 · MAKES 200 HORS D'OEUVRES

CREAMY ROQUEFORT AND HORSERADISH DRESSING

4 cups sour cream
3 cups mayonnaise
1 pound Roquefort cheese, crumbled

3 tablespoons drained bottled horseradish

8 pounds rare roast beef, thinly sliced

1. Combine 1 cup of the sour cream, 1 cup of the mayonnaise, the Roquefort, and horseradish in a food processor. Blend until smooth. Turn the mixture into a large bowl and fold in the remaining sour cream and mayonnaise thoroughly. Cover and chill.

2. Cut about 8 stacked slices of the roast beef, lengthwise, into 4 equal-sized strips. Continue cutting the beef in stacks of 8 slices until all the beef has been cut.

3. Wrap 1 slice of the beef around the tip of a 6-inch wooden skewer, sticking the point of the skewer through one end of the piece of meat. Continue making the turbans on about 199 skewers. Cover and chill. Serve the turbans on a large platter or two, with a bowl of the Roquefort sauce.

More Servings
Double the recipe to serve 100.

SHRIMP TOAST

◇ ══════════ ◇

Shrimp Toast variations appear in several of my previous cookbooks. It is included here in a slightly different version, because Shrimp Toast is the perfect hot hors d'oeuvre for a crowd. It is so delicious that there will never be any left over.

Shrimp Toast freezes beautifully, so it can be prepared well in advance of a party. Instructions for reheating frozen Shrimp Toast follow the recipe.

SERVES 50 · MAKES 160 HORS D'OEUVRES

2½ pounds raw shrimp, shelled and deveined
½ bunch scallions, minced
½ cup minced water chestnuts
1 egg, lightly beaten
2 tablespoons soy sauce
2 tablespoons cornstarch
1 tablespoon Oriental sesame oil

1 teaspoon salt
1 teaspoon grated fresh ginger-root, or ½ teaspoon ground ginger
40 slices firm white bread with crusts trimmed
Peanut or vegetable oil for deep-frying
2 lemons, quartered and seeded

1. Purée the shrimp in three batches in a food processor or blender. The mixture should only just be puréed but not pasty. Transfer the shrimp to a large bowl and add the next 8 ingredients (through the ginger). Mix well.

2. Spread one side of each slice of the bread evenly with about 1 rounded tablespoon of the mixture.

3. Heat about 1½ inches of oil in a large frying pan with high sides to about 370 degrees. Fry the toast, shrimp side down, a few slices at a time until golden. Turn and cook on the other side until golden brown. The total cooking time is about 5 minutes.

4. Drain the cooked toasts on paper towels. Cook the remaining toast in the same manner, adding more oil as needed to keep a level of 1½ inches. When adding more oil to the pan, be certain to reheat the oil before adding more toast. Cut each piece of toast in half diagonally, twice, to make four triangles.

5. Reheat the cooked toast pieces on baking sheets in a preheated 350-degree oven for about 10 minutes before serving. Arrange the toast attractively on a large platter and garnish with the lemon quarters.

More Servings
Double the recipe to make 320 hors d'oeuvres to serve 100.

Freezing Instructions
Wrap the cooled cooked Shrimp Toast in several layers in packages of aluminum foil; about 50 per package. To reheat frozen Shrimp Toast, put them on baking sheets in single layers in a preheated 350-degree oven for about 20 minutes.

SYLVIA PUTZIGER'S PEANUT BUTTER AND BACON HORS D'OEUVRE ROLLS

Sylvia Putziger has been coming to St. Thomas since 1948. "I've survived many a war," she said, meaning cocktail parties, with her delectable hors d'oeuvre. It is always on the menu at her annual New Year's Day party.

The original recipe was given to Sylvia many years ago in New York by a Swedish friend, Dagne Rundstrom. Here is Sylvia's version.

SERVES 50 · MAKES 225 HORS D'OEUVRES
(PREPARATION BEGINS THE DAY BEFORE OR EARLIER)

3 12-ounce jars crunchy or
smooth peanut butter
1½ cups (3 sticks) butter, melted
1 teaspoon Worcestershire
sauce
3 dashes Tabasco sauce

4 pounds bacon strips, cut in
half crosswise
3 1-pound, 8-ounce loaves fresh
soft white bread, such as
Wonder Bread

1. Put the peanut butter, still in the jars, in a large saucepan. Pour water into the pan to come 1½ inches up the side of the jars. This will soften the peanut butter and make it easier to spread. Set aside.

2. In a saucepan, melt the butter and combine it with the Worcestershire sauce and Tabasco sauce.

3. Cut the crusts off each slice of bread. With a rolling pin flatten each slice of the bread.

4. To assemble each hors d'oeuvre, brush 1 slice of flattened bread lightly with the butter mixture and spread lightly with peanut butter. Roll up the coated slice of bread, jelly roll fashion. Stretch 1 slice of the bacon and fold it over the end of the roll, and wrap it up around the bread in a spiral. Fold the end of the bacon strip over the top of the roll and secure it with a toothpick. Make the remaining rolls in the same manner.

5. Wrap up the rolls tightly in plastic wrap and foil and freeze them overnight or for several weeks before cooking.

6. When ready to cook the rolls, preheat the oven to 350 degrees. Remove the toothpicks from the frozen rolls and cut each one into 3 equal-sized lengths, crosswise. Place the rolls in two large roasting pans. Bake for about 20 minutes, or until golden and crisp, turning at least once during the cooking time. It may be necessary to bake the rolls in two batches, depending on the size of the pans used and the oven space. Drain on paper towels and serve at once.

More Servings
Double the recipe to make 450 rolls to serve 100 and bake in several batches.

Robbie Robinson's Fresh Hot Sausage Balls

SERVES 50 · MAKES 200 SAUSAGE BALLS

4 6½- to 7-pound fresh ham shoulders
½ cup whole fennel seeds
3 tablespoons dried hot pepper flakes (omit if desired)

1 tablespoon canned ground black pepper
2 tablespoons salt, or as desired
Vegetable oil

1. Trim the fat off of the pork shoulders and cut the meat into 2-inch pieces. Grind the pork twice through the fine blade of a meat grinder. The butcher can do this procedure for you.

2. In a very large bowl, combine the pork with the fennel seeds, hot pepper flakes, pepper, and salt.

3. Cover the sausage and refrigerate overnight.

4. Shape the sausage into 200 generous 1-inch balls.

5. Heat a ¼-inch layer of the oil in a large frying pan and cook the sausage balls in batches until golden brown all over and thoroughly cooked. Refrigerate the sausage balls that are not being cooked until the next batch is ready to go into the pan. Add oil as needed.

6. Drain the cooked sausage balls and continue cooking the rest in batches.

7. The sausage balls can be served hot or refrigerated and reheated in a 350-degree oven for about 10 minutes. The balls can also be frozen cooked and reheated in a 350-degree oven for about 20 minutes.

QUICK AND EASY HORS D'OEUVRES

WARM BRIE IN FILO LEAVES WITH ALMOND SLICES

SERVES 8

Preheat the oven to 350 degrees. Arrange 6 overlapping sheets of filo pastry leaves, brushed liberally with melted butter (about 1 stick) over a dinner plate. Put a 1-pound wheel or wedge of Brie in the center of the filo, and fold the leaves over it. Tear away the extra bunch of leaves collected in the center and discard.

Turn the wrapped Brie over and put it in a buttered shallow baking dish. Brush the top with butter and sprinkle ½ cup of almond slices over the top.

Bake for about 20 to 25 minutes, or until the filo leaves and almonds are golden brown.

Remove and let stand for 30 minutes before serving.

SHRIMP WRAPPED IN PROSCIUTTO

SERVES 8

Wrap 36 medium-sized cold boiled shrimp with 1½-inch-wide and about 4-inch-long thin slices of prosciutto (about ¾ pound). Put on a platter, seam side down (no toothpick is necessary). Cover the platter with plastic wrap and chill until ready to serve. Garnish with lemon or lime wedges. Any number of dips can be served with the shrimp. I particularly recommend Diane Young's Aloha Sauce (page 36), but just a splash of lemon or lime juice is sufficient for this delicacy.

Prosciutto can also be wrapped around melon balls or cubes, pieces of fresh figs, peaches, apples, papaya, or mango, cold cooked artichoke hearts, or marinated small mushrooms. It is delicious when used to cover small cubes of cheese, such as Fontina or bel paese. Toothpicks are necessary to serve all these suggestions.

FILLET OF BEEF CANAPÉS WITH TARRAGON MUSTARD

SERVES 12

Lightly toast 48 ¼-inch-thick slices of ficelle (long thin French bread loaf). Spread one side of each piece of toast lightly with tarragon mustard. You'll need about ¾ cup.

Top each with a ¼-inch-thick slice of chilled rare roast fillet of beef, cut to just fit over the toast, about 2 pounds will be required. (See recipe page 136.)

Garnish each slice of beef with a pinch of chopped fresh parsley leaves.

More Servings
Double the recipe to serve 24.

SAUTÉED CASHEW NUTS WITH CURRY

SERVES 12

Sauté 2 pounds of raw cashew nuts in a large frying pan in two or three batches in ¼ inch of vegetable oil until they are golden brown. Turn often. Drain on paper towels and sprinkle lightly with salt, curry powder, and freshly ground black pepper; then toss.

More Servings
Double the recipe to serve 24.

ARTICHOKE HEARTS WITH CURRIED LEMON DIP

SERVES 16

4 14-ounce cans artichoke
hearts, drained and cut in
half lengthwise

CURRIED LEMON DIP

2 cups mayonnaise
1 cup sour cream
3 tablespoons fresh lemon juice
1/4 cup chopped scallions

1 tablespoon curry powder
1/2 teaspoon ground tumeric
Salt and freshly ground black
pepper to taste

1. Put the artichoke heart halves on a large serving platter.
2. Combine all the dip ingredients in a bowl with a wire whisk and
turn into a serving bowl. Put the bowl on the platter with the artichoke
hearts before serving.

More Servings
Double the recipe to serve 32 and serve on two platters with a bowl of
the dip on each.

BRIE WITH GRANNY SMITH APPLE SLICES AND WALNUTS

SERVES 24

1 4-pound wedge ripe Brie at
room temperature

8 large Granny Smith apples,
cored and cut into 12 slices
each
1 pound halved walnuts

Place the Brie on a wooden cheese board or platter and serve with the apple slices and walnuts.

More Servings
Double the recipe to serve 48. Two cheese boards or platters can be used.

Dried Fruit with Toasted Coconut and Nuts

SERVES 36

Toast 2 cups of coconut on a large baking sheet under the broiler, stirring often, until it is golden brown. Cool. Put in a bowl with 3 pounds of Spanish peanuts, 1 pound shelled pumpkin seeds (pepitas), 2 pounds unsalted whole almonds, and 2 pounds mixed dried fruit. Serve in two or three attractive bowls.

More Servings
Double the recipe to serve 72.

Shirley Petrofsky's Curried Herring with Dill

SERVES 50 TO 60

4 cups (1 quart) mayonnaise
1/4 cup dried dill
3 tablespoons curry powder, or
   to taste
4 1-pound loaves cocktail
   pumpernickel

8 12-ounce jars herring tidbits
   in wine, lightly drained
   (include the onions in dish)

1. Combine the mayonnaise, dill, and curry powder thoroughly in a large bowl. Add the herring and onions and mix well. Cover and refrigerate until serving time.

2. Serve the curried herring in one large bowl or two smaller ones, accompanied by the pumpernickel bread.

More Servings
To serve 100 to 125, double the recipe, but use only 1 quart plus 3 cups of mayonnaise.

Extras
If any herring is left over, it makes excellent open-faced Danish sandwiches.

FRIED WONTON WRAPPER STICKS

One pound of wonton wrappers will serve 8 people; multiply according to number of guests.

Cut stacks of wonton wrappers into ½-inch-wide strips. Heat 2 inches of oil in a deep heavy pot. Fry a handful of the separated strips at a time until they are crisp (this will take under a minute), stirring constantly. Serve with a sweet-and-sour dip, if desired.

SUPER NACHOS

SERVES 12

3 tablespoons vegetable oil
1 pound ground beef
1 medium-sized onion, chopped
1 tablespoon chili powder
½ cup thinly sliced scallions

1 cup finely chopped green chili peppers
2 cups shredded Monterey Jack cheese
2 cups shredded Cheddar cheese
2 7½-ounce packages tortilla chips

1. Preheat the oven to 400 degrees.
2. Heat the oil in a large frying pan. Add the beef, onion, and chili powder and cook, stirring often, until the beef is no longer pink. Drain.
3. Arrange each bag of chips across two large heatproof au gratin pans. Sprinkle with the beef mixture, scallions, chili pepper, and combined cheeses.
4. Bake for 15 minutes, or until the cheese melts and is golden brown. Pass under the broiler briefly, if necessary. Serve immediately.

More Servings
Double the recipe to serve 24 and cook in four dishes or pans in two batches.

GRILLED CHÈVRE CANAPÉS

SERVES 16 · MAKES 64 CANAPÉS

1½ pounds firm white sandwich
　　bread
2½ pounds 1½-inch-thick rolls
　　chèvre, chilled

Olive oil
½ cup chopped fresh chives

1. Toast the bread very lightly and cut the slices into 64 2-inch circles using a pastry cutter.
2. Cut the well-chilled cheese into ⅛-inch-thick slices and put one on each piece of toast.
3. Put the canapés on a large baking sheet and brush lightly with olive oil. Run under the broiler until the tops are golden brown; this will only take a minute or two. Garnish each canapé with a pinch of the chives.

More Servings
Double the recipe to serve 32 or to make 128 canapés. Cook in two or four batches.

ANCHOVY AND
PARMESAN CHEESE CROSTINI

◊ ════════════════════════════════ ◊

Crostini make wonderful, easy hors d'oeuvres, and they also can serve as bread with any pasta dish that doesn't include anchovies in its ingredients. For those dishes, make plain Parmesan Cheese and Butter Crostini, eliminating the anchovies.

SERVES 24 · MAKES 72 HORS D'OEUVRES

10 anchovy fillets, drained and finely chopped
1 cup (2 sticks) sweet butter, softened
1 long French baguette, cut into 72 $\frac{1}{4}$-inch-thick slices
Freshly grated Parmesan cheese

1. Preheat the oven to 350 degrees.

2. Mix together the anchovies and the butter well. Lightly spread the mixture on one side of each slice of the bread. Sprinkle Parmesan cheese very lightly over the top.

3. Put half of the bread side by side on a large baking sheet and bake on the lower shelf of the oven for 5 minutes. Immediately turn on the broiler and place the baking sheet on a shelf about 5 or 6 inches from the heat and cook for a few minutes, just until the crostini are golden brown. Watch very carefully, because this happens quickly.

4. Transfer to a serving platter; then bake the remaining crostini in the same manner.

More Servings
Double the recipe to serve 48 and cook in several batches.

Variation
Two minced garlic cloves and/or 2 tablespoons chopped fresh basil leaves can be added to the butter and anchovy mixture.

ITALIAN SWEET SAUSAGES WITH RED PEPPER MUSTARD

◇ ══════════════════════════ ◇

SERVES 36

Cut each of 36 Italian sweet sausages in half. Grill or bake them at 350 degrees in a roasting pan until they are golden brown and thoroughly cooked, turning them frequently. (Drain if cooked in a roasting pan.)

Meanwhile, combine 2 cups of Dijon mustard with 1 large minced sweet red pepper and ½ chopped fresh parsley leaves.

Insert a 6-inch wooden skewer lengthwise into each sausage half, and serve hot on a large platter with a bowl of the mustard.

(Another excellent and easy hors d'oeuvre can be made from 144 sautéed tiny smoked sausages, frankfurters, or bratwurst, or a combination of all three. Serve with the red pepper mustard or plain Dijon or whole grain German mustard or a variety of three or four mustards, such as lemon, tarragon, shallot, or herb.)

SAUTÉED KIELBASA SLICES WITH HONEY MUSTARD

◇ ══════════════════════════ ◇

SERVES 50

10 pounds kielbasa, cut into ¼-inch-thick slices	Peanut or vegetable oil

HONEY MUSTARD

6 cups Dijon mustard at room temperature	2 tablespoons grated orange rind
1 cup honey	3 tablespoons Grand Marnier

1. Cook as many kielbasa slices as will fit comfortably in a large frying pan with 2 tablespoons of oil at a time until golden brown on each side. Put the cooked sausage in a large roasting pan, standing the slices up

in rows. Cook the remaining slices in the same manner in several batches, adding a little oil as needed.

2. Just before serving, reheat the kielbasa in the roasting pan in a pre-heated 325-degree oven for 15 minutes.

3. To prepare the Honey Mustard, combine the ingredients well, cover, and refrigerate until ready to serve. Stir before serving. Place the kielbasa slices on a large serving platter, with or without toothpicks, but with a bowl of the dip.

More Servings
Double the recipe to serve 100 and reheat in two or three batches.

Fewer Servings
Cut the recipe in half to serve 25.

SAUCES, DIPS, AND SPREADS

EL INVERNADERO'S SALSA CHIMICHURRY

Angel Noño Ramirez of El Invernadero restaurant in Mexico City gave me this unusually delicious recipe. The sauce is excellent with roast or grilled chicken or pork or paillards of veal or chicken. It's also excellent as a sauce served with plain cheese nachos or chalupas (see recipe page 220).

MAKES ABOUT 3 CUPS

½ cup white wine vinegar
1 cup extra virgin olive oil
½ cup dry red wine
3 tablespoons Worcestershire sauce
3 tablespoons Bovril
3 large garlic cloves, minced
1 cup minced onion
1 large sweet red pepper, seeded and cut into fine dice

4 large bunches cilantro (coriander), washed and finely chopped (about 4 cups)
1½ cups chopped fresh parsley leaves
Salt and freshly ground black pepper to taste

1. Put all the ingredients into a large heavy saucepan and simmer for about 15 minutes.
2. Transfer to a bowl and cool. Cover and chill thoroughly.

MEXICAN SALSA

◊ ══════════════════════ ◊

This is excellent as a dip for tortilla chips or served with cold roast chicken.

MAKES ABOUT 4 CUPS

2½ cups finely chopped peeled and seeded tomatoes
2 large garlic cloves, minced
½ cup chopped scallions
½ cup chopped fresh cilantro (coriander) or parsley leaves
½ cup minced mild green chilies

½ cup minced sweet green pepper
½ teaspoon dried oregano
½ teaspoon hot pepper flakes, if desired
1 teaspoon salt
2 tablespoons olive oil
1 tablespoon fresh lemon juice

Combine all the ingredients in a large bowl. Cover and chill for several hours before serving. Must be used within two days.

CREAMY BLUE CHEESE DRESSING WITH BACON AND HORSERADISH

◊ ══════════════════════ ◊

MAKES ABOUT 6½ CUPS
(PREPARATION BEGINS THE NIGHT BEFORE)

12 strips bacon, cooked crisp and crumbled
2½ cups mayonnaise
1½ cups sour cream
2 tablespoons Dijon mustard
1 tablespoon Worcestershire sauce

2 tablespoons grated fresh white horseradish
Salt and freshly ground black pepper to taste
Crudités

1. Combine the ingredients well in a large bowl using a wire whisk or electric mixer.
2. Turn the mixture into a large jar and cover tightly. Chill overnight. Serve with crudités.

LIGHT GUACAMOLE DIP

MAKES ABOUT 4 CUPS

4 large ripe avocados, halved, pitted, and peeled
½ cup finely chopped onion
3 tablespoons finely chopped cilantro (coriander), optional

3 tablespoons fresh lemon juice
Salt and freshly ground black pepper to taste
Chili powder

1. Put the avocado pulp into a large shallow bowl. Mash the avocado with a potato masher or fork until it is creamy, although some small bits of the avocado should remain. (This is not a puréed version.)

2. Add the onion, cilantro, lemon juice, and salt and pepper and combine thoroughly. Sprinkle with the chili powder. Serve immediately or turn into a bowl and press a sheet of plastic wrap onto the surface of the Guacamole. This will keep it from turning brown. Refrigerate the Guacamole until ready to serve. Mix it again before serving and sprinkle lightly with chili powder. (The Guacamole will keep in the refrigerator for one day.) Serve with taco or corn chips, cucumber slices, or other vegetables. This is also excellent as a filling for cherry tomatoes.

RED SALMON CAVIAR
AND GREEN PEPPERCORN DIP

This dip is especially good served with cucumber slices, endive leaves, or fennel or celery sticks. It's also an excellent filling for finger sandwiches.

MAKES ABOUT 5½ CUPS · SERVES 24

3 cups sour cream
1 8-ounce package cream cheese, softened
6 ounces red salmon caviar (Red lumpfish caviar can also be used.)

3 tablespoons green peppercorns with a little liquid from the can (Use peppercorns from Madagascar, if possible.)
⅓ cups minced fresh chives

Beat together the sour cream and cream cheese until smooth. Fold in the remaining ingredients. Cover and chill. The dip will keep for two days in the refrigerator. Stir before serving.

More Servings
Double the recipe to make about 2¾ quarts to serve 50.

Fewer Servings
Cut the recipe in half to serve 12 or to yield about 2¾ cups.

TUNA TARRAGON DIP OR SPREAD

MAKES ABOUT 9 CUPS · SERVES 36

4 12½-ounce cans solid white meat tuna, drained
3½ 8-ounce packages cream cheese, softened
⅓ cup fresh lemon juice
1 cup thinly sliced scallions
¼ cup dried tarragon
1 teaspoon freshly ground black pepper

In a large mixing bowl, combine the tuna, cream cheese, and lemon juice thoroughly. Add the scallions, tarragon, and pepper and mix well. Cover and chill.
Serve in bowls as a dip for crudités, or on toast points, pumpernickel bread, or crackers as a canapé.

More Servings
Double the recipe to make 4½ quarts to serve 72. Make two batches, if necessary.

Fewer Servings
Cut the recipe in half to make about 4½ cups to serve 18.

CURRIED CHICKEN AND BLACK SESAME SEED SPREAD

MAKES ABOUT 2½ CUPS

1½ cups coarsely chopped cooked chicken breast

1 8-ounce package cream cheese, softened

1½ tablespoons curry powder

1 teaspoon Oriental sesame oil

2 tablespoons soy sauce

2 tablespoons chopped fresh chives

1 tablespoon black sesame seeds (available in Oriental markets)

Salt and freshly ground black pepper to taste

1. Put the chicken, cream cheese, curry powder, sesame oil, and soy sauce in a food processor. Blend until smooth.

2. Turn into a bowl and mix in the chives, sesame seeds, and salt and pepper. Spread on crackers, toast, or cucumber slices for canapés, sprinkling the top lightly with additional black sesame seeds.

More Servings
Double the recipe to make about 5 cups.

HUMMUS WITH MINT

MAKES ABOUT 6 CUPS · SERVES 16 TO 20

2 16-ounce cans chick-peas, drained

4 large garlic cloves, minced

1 cup tahini (sesame seed paste)

½ cup fresh lemon juice

¾ cup olive oil, or as needed

Salt and freshly ground black pepper to taste

¼ cup chopped fresh mint leaves, or 1 tablespoon dried mint

1. Purée half of the chick-peas, garlic, tahini, and lemon juice in a food processor or blender. Add half of the oil in a slow drizzle through the feed tube of the processor or the opening in the lid of the blender.

The mixture should be smooth and spreadable; if not, add a little more oil. Season with salt and pepper and turn into a bowl.

2. Purée the remaining half of the ingredients in the same manner, and season. Then blend the two mixtures together.

3. Combine the mixture with the mint and taste for seasoning. Serve with cucumber slices, endive leaves, breadsticks, toast, or pita bread. Also very nice spooned onto individual chilled cooked artichoke leaves.

More Servings
The recipe can be doubled to serve 32 to 40 and made in four batches.

Smoked Salmon and Caper Spread

MAKES ABOUT 5½ CUPS · SERVES 16 TO 20

½ pound smoked salmon, coarsely chopped
2 8-ounce packages cream cheese, softened
3 tablespoons fresh lemon juice
2 cups sour cream
4 tablespoons well-drained capers
Freshly ground black pepper

1. Purée the smoked salmon, cream cheese, and lemon juice in a food processor.

2. Turn the mixture into a large bowl and mix in the sour cream thoroughly.

3. Spoon the mixture into an attractive bowl and smooth the top. Make a border with the capers. Grind pepper over the center. Serve with crackers, pumpernickel bread, toast points, cucumber slices, or endive leaves.

DIANE YOUNG'S
PECAN AND PINEAPPLE SPREAD

MAKES ABOUT 5½ CUPS · SERVES 12

2 cups chopped pecans
2 8-ounce packages cream cheese, softened
½ cup chopped sweet green pepper
3 tablespoons finely chopped onion

1 teaspoon seasoned salt
1 8-ounce can crushed pineapple, well drained
¾ cup chopped fresh parsley leaves

1. Mix all the ingredients, except the parsley, thoroughly.

2. Form into a round cake or disk, about 1 inch thick and 6 inches wide.

3. Put about ¼ cup of the parsley on a sheet of wax paper. Lay the cake on the parsley to coat the bottom. Then coat the side and top with the remaining parsley. Cover and chill until ready to serve. Serve with crackers or toast.

SYLVIA SHAPIRO'S TUNA MOLD SPREAD

SERVES 24

1 10-ounce can tomato soup
1 tablespoon Worcestershire sauce
4 drops Tabasco sauce
1 8-ounce package cream cheese, softened
1 tablespoon unflavored gelatin
¼ cup lukewarm water
1 cup finely chopped celery
1 medium-sized onion, finely chopped

1 whole pimiento, finely chopped
2 6½-ounce cans tuna, drained and flaked
1 teaspoon paprika
1 teaspoon salt
¼ teaspoon freshly ground black pepper
1 cup mayonnaise
1 tablespoon fresh lemon juice

1. Heat together the tomato soup, Worcestershire sauce, Tabasco sauce, and cream cheese until the cheese melts, stirring constantly.

2. Dissolve the gelatin in the water and let stand for 5 minutes.

3. Remove the soup mixture from the heat and stir in the dissolved gelatin. Set aside to cool. Add the celery, onion, pimiento, and tuna and mix very well. Stir in the remaining ingredients.

4. Turn into a lightly oiled 8-cup mold, cover, and chill thoroughly.

5. Unmold and serve with toast, crackers, or cut up fresh vegetables.

Soups

◇ ═══════════════════════════════════════ ◇

Soup is both a practical and economical course at large gatherings.

Because many soups can be made well in advance, they need only last-minute reheating to be served piping hot, or taken well-chilled straight from the refrigerator.

Hot or cold, soup is easily transported in large thermos jugs or coolers, and is excellent as part of a menu for picnics, tailgate and beach parties, boat trips, or any outing.

Seafood Minestrone Casalinga with Fine Egg Noodles, Thick Russian Cabbage Soup, or Mexican Black Bean Soup as the main-course for a crowd, along with a salad, makes a particularly pleasing winter buffet. To complete the meal, serve a selection of warm garlic bread, black bread, and cornsticks with plenty of sweet butter.

FRENCH RED ONION SOUP

The strength of yellow onions are required for a good French onion soup, and the addition of red onions adds a sweetness and complementing dimension.

SERVES 8

6 tablespoons butter
6 medium-sized yellow onions, thinly sliced
6 medium-sized red onions, thinly sliced
1 large garlic clove, minced
3 tablespoons all-purpose flour
8 cups (2 quarts) homemade beef stock or canned broth

1 tablespoon Worcestershire sauce
¼ cup Cognac
Salt and freshly ground black pepper to taste
8 1-inch-thick slices French bread, lightly toasted
1 cup grated Gruyère cheese

1. Melt the butter in a large heavy pot. Add the onions and garlic and cook over low heat, stirring often, for about 20 minutes, or until the onions are light golden brown.

2. Sprinkle the flour over the onions and stir it in. Cook for about 3 minutes, stirring constantly.

3. Add the stock, Worcestershire sauce, and Cognac. Bring to a boil, lower the heat, and simmer for 30 minutes. Season with salt and pepper.

4. Ladle the soup into eight individual ovenproof crocks and top each with a slice of the toasted French bread. Sprinkle each piece of bread with equal amounts of the cheese. Put the crocks on a large baking sheet. Put in the broiler about 5 inches from the broiler element. Cook until the cheese melts; then serve immediately.

FRESH CREAM OF VEGETABLE SOUP

SERVES 8

6 tablespoons butter
6 leeks (white parts only), well cleaned and thinly sliced
1 pound carrots, scraped and thinly sliced
4 parsnips, peeled and thinly sliced
4 celery stalks, sliced
4 medium-sized Idaho potatoes, peeled and cubed
1 teaspoon paprika

1 teaspoon chopped fresh thyme leaves, or ½ teaspoon dried thyme
¼ cup chopped fresh parsley leaves
8 cups (2 quarts) homemade chicken stock or canned broth
1½ cups heavy cream
Salt and freshly ground black pepper to taste
2½ cups fried croutons

1. Melt the butter in a large heavy pot. Add the leeks, carrots, parsnips, and celery and stir. Cover and simmer for 10 minutes.

2. Add the potatoes, paprika, thyme, parsley, and chicken stock. Stir and bring to a boil. Immediately lower the heat to a simmer and cook for 40 minutes, stirring occasionally.

3. A few cups at a time, purée the mixture in a blender or food processor. Put the puréed mixture into a clean pot. Add the heavy cream, mix well, and season with salt and pepper. Heat thoroughly. If a thinner consistency is desired, add a little more broth or cream. Garnish individual servings with the crisp fried croutons.

More Servings
Double the recipe to serve 16.

Variation
To make Curried Cream of Vegetable Soup, add 2 tablespoons of curry powder with the paprika.

CURRIED CHICKEN AND LEEK SOUP WITH RICE

◇══════════════════════════════════════◇

SERVES 12

6 tablespoons butter
1½ cups finely chopped leeks
  (white parts only)
2 large garlic cloves, minced
4 tablespoons curry powder
½ teaspoon ground turmeric
10 cups (2½ quarts) homemade
  chicken stock or canned broth

2 cups finely chopped cooked
  chicken breast
1 cup long-grain rice
1 cup heavy cream
  Salt and freshly ground black
  pepper to taste

1. Melt the butter in a 5-quart Dutch oven. Add the leeks and garlic. Cook over medium heat, stirring often, for 5 minutes. Stir in the curry powder and turmeric.

2. Add the chicken stock. Bring to a boil and add the chicken and rice. Stir, cover, and simmer for 30 minutes.

3. Add the cream, stir, and season with salt and pepper. Heat thoroughly and serve immediately.

More Servings
The recipe can be doubled to serve 24, using an 8- to 9-quart pot.

MARGOT BACHMAN'S KALLALOO WITH FUNGI

◇══════════════════════════════════════◇

Margot Bachman, editor and publisher of St. Thomas This Week, *the island's indispensable weekly paper, has lived in St. Thomas for over twenty-five years.*

On a sunny Sunday afternoon before Carnival week, Margot made her delicious Kallaloo. Kallaloo is prepared by every serious cook at holiday time, especially Old Year's Eve (which is what St. Thomians call New Year's Eve) and for Carnival. It is said to bring good luck.

Margot says, "Almost every West Indian island has its own version of Kallaloo, more often a soup, sometimes a stew. If it's a stew, fungi is also served; if it's a soup, small fungi balls can be added. (They are made from a cornmeal mixture similar in texture and flavor to Italy's polenta.) Because many of the ingredients are indigenous to the islands, such as dasheen and the herb papalolo, I've worked out a supermarket version—and blended it, which is the way I once had it in Martinique."

Kallaloo has an assertive fish flavor that I find addictive. The soup can be served hot or cold.

SERVES 12

1 ham bone
12 cups (3 quarts) homemade chicken stock or canned broth
1 pound grouper or snapper fillets
½ pound crab meat
2 medium-sized onions, coarsely chopped
2 large garlic cloves, minced
2 celery stalks with leaves, chopped
1 small fresh hot pepper, chopped (West Indian peppers are extremely hot. A jalepeño pepper or ¼ teaspoon Tabasco sauce can be substituted.)

5 parsley sprigs
2 10-ounce packages frozen chopped spinach
1 10-ounce package frozen cut okra
1 teaspoon dried thyme
2 tablespoons red wine vinegar
Grated rind of 1 lemon
Salt and freshly ground black pepper to taste

FUNGI
2½ cups water
1¼ cups cornmeal

1 teaspoon salt
1 tablespoon butter

1. Put the ham bone in a large heavy pot with the chicken stock and bring to a boil. Lower the heat and simmer for 30 minutes.

2. Skim the top of the stock and add the remaining ingredients, except the vinegar, lemon rind, and salt and pepper. Bring to a boil again, lower the heat, and simmer for 40 minutes.

3. Meanwhile, prepare the Fungi. Bring the water to a rolling boil in

a saucepan. Add the cornmeal, salt, and butter, stirring constantly. Turn the heat very low, cover, and cook for exactly 5 minutes.

4. Remove the pan from the heat and turn the cornmeal mixture into a bowl. When cool enough to handle, make 36 small balls by rolling the mixture between the palms of your hands. Cover and set aside.

5. Add the vinegar, lemon rind, and salt and pepper to the soup. Discard the ham bone and purée the soup, 2 cups at a time, in a blender. Add a little water or dry white wine to the soup if the mixture needs thinning. Reheat. Garnish each bowl of soup with 3 Fungi balls and serve immediately.

CHILLED CELERY BISQUE

SERVES 16

6 tablespoons butter
9 cups chopped celery with some leaves
1½ cups chopped onion
12 cups (3 quarts) homemade chicken stock or canned broth

3 cups heavy cream
Salt and freshly ground white pepper to taste
Freshly grated nutmeg
Chopped fresh parsley leaves for garnish

1. Melt the butter in a 9-quart stainless steel pot, and sauté the celery and onion over medium-low heat for 8 minutes, stirring often.

2. Add the stock and bring to a boil. Immediately lower the heat and simmer for 30 minutes.

3. Purée the soup, a few cups at a time, for about 30 seconds, or until very smooth. Transfer the puréed soup to a large bowl or jar. Stir in the cream and season with salt and pepper. Add a few gratings of nutmeg and combine. If desired, strain the soup through a fine strainer.

4. Chill thoroughly. When serving, garnish each bowl with chopped fresh parsley leaves.

More Servings
Double the recipe to serve 32 and cook in a 15- to 18-quart pot.

BOB CONNORS' CORN CHOWDER

Entertaining crowds is second nature to Bob and Midge Connors from Boston, Massachusetts. At least once a month they cook for crowds ranging from eight to three hundred. Their sizable kitchen is stocked with restaurant equipment, including huge pots, pans, and baking dishes.

Every year for a family Easter for about sixty, Bob cooks the same menu—Bob's Corn Chowder, Roast Beef, Fresh Asparagus, Baked Potatoes, and gallons of fresh strawberries and ice cream. Midge is in charge of logistics.

The Connors' meals are always sit-down affairs. The tables are made of six-foot by four-foot pieces of plywood balanced on saw horses. Attractive sheets are the tablecloths. They own sixty folding chairs, but often have to rent more for their larger parties.

Weather permitting, they eat in the backyard, or in several rooms of their spacious home.

Bob's tasty chowder is a quick recipe, but it can be made a day or two in advance to save last-minute cooking time for the balance of the menu.

SERVES 16

4 tablespoons butter	1 13-ounce can evaporated milk
1½ cups finely chopped onion	1 13-ounce can water
4 cups peeled and diced boiling potatoes	1 13-ounce can fresh milk
3 cups water, or just enough to cover the potatoes	Salt and freshly ground black pepper to taste
2 17-ounce cans creamed corn	3 tablespoons chopped fresh parsley leaves
2 10-ounce packages frozen corn kernels	

1. Melt the butter in a 6- to 7-quart pot. Cook the onion for 5 minutes over medium heat, stirring often.

2. Add the potatoes and 3 cups water and bring to a boil. Cook over medium-high heat for about 15 minutes, or until the potatoes are tender.

3. Add the remaining ingredients, except the parsley, and bring to a boil. Lower the heat and simmer for 5 minutes.

4. Purée half of the soup, a few cups at a time, in a blender and return to the pot. Stir well. Garnish each bowl of soup with a little parsley.

More Servings
Double the recipe to serve 24 and cook in an 8- to 9-quart pot.

Variations
Add 1½ cups of diced smoked ham and/or 1 large chopped sweet green pepper when cooking the onion.

SEAFOOD MINESTRONE CASALINGA WITH FINE EGG NOODLES

SERVES 24

¼ cup olive oil

1½ cups chopped onion

2 large garlic cloves, minced

3 medium-sized zucchini, cut into ½-inch cubes

3 cups diced peeled and seeded fresh or canned tomatoes

2 cups drained canned chick-peas

1 pound medium-sized shrimp, chopped

2 cups chopped fresh clams

½ pound sea scallops, cut into ½-inch cubes

1 teaspoon dried thyme

24 cups (6 quarts) homemade beef stock or canned broth

8 ounces fine egg noodles

¼ cup chopped fresh parsley leaves

Salt and freshly ground black pepper to taste

2 cups freshly grated Parmesan cheese

1. Heat the oil in a 12-quart stock pot. Add the onion and garlic and cook for 5 minutes, stirring.

2. Add the next 7 ingredients (through the stock). Slowly bring to a boil; then lower the heat and simmer for 10 minutes.

3. Stir in the egg noodles and parsley and simmer for about 15 minutes. Season with salt and pepper. Serve sprinkled with the Parmesan cheese.

COLD BUTTERMILK BORSCHT WITH DILL

SERVES 24

3 quarts buttermilk
4 16-ounce cans sliced beets, including liquid
1 cup coarsely chopped onion
¼ cup fresh lemon juice
1 6-ounce can tomato paste

3 tablespoons sugar
½ cup chopped fresh dill, or 3 tablespoons dried dill
Salt and freshly ground black pepper to taste
2½ cups sour cream

Purée the beets with the liquid from each can, one can at a time, in a blender. Pour the purée into a large bowl. To the last can, add the onion and 1 cup of the buttermilk and purée. Add this mixture to the bowl with the remaining 2¾ quarts of buttermilk and the remaining ingredients, except the sour cream. Mix well with a large wire whisk. Cover and chill thoroughly before serving. Garnish each serving with a dollop of sour cream.

More Servings
The recipe can be doubled to serve 48.

COLD CREAM OF BROCCOLI SOUP

This soup is excellent hot, too.

SERVES 36

20 cups (5 quarts) homemade chicken stock or canned broth
4 20-ounce packages frozen chopped broccoli
2 cups chopped onion

1 tablespoon dried oregano
1½ quarts heavy cream
Salt and freshly ground black pepper to taste
Freshly grated nutmeg
5 cups crisp fried croutons

1. Bring the chicken stock to a boil in a 12-quart pot. Add the broccoli, onion, and oregano and return to a boil. Simmer for 10 minutes.

2. Purée the mixture, a few cups at a time, in a blender until very smooth. Pour the purée into a large bowl.

3. Stir in the cream and season with salt and pepper and nutmeg. Chill thoroughly. Garnish each bowl of soup with croutons.

MEXICAN BLACK BEAN SOUP

SERVES 36

4 pounds dried black beans, sorted and rinsed
2 large onions, chopped
1 tablespoon minced garlic
1 bunch cilantro (coriander), washed and chopped
2 bay leaves
3 large sweet green peppers, seeded and chopped
4 jalapeño peppers, chopped (optional)

1 tablespoon salt
3 tablespoons chili powder
1 tablespoon ground cumin
1 cup dry sherry
½ cup olive oil
4 cups (1 quart) sour cream
3 large sweet green or red peppers, diced

1. Cover the beans with water and soak them overnight.

2. Drain the beans and put them into an 8-quart pot. Add the next 11 ingredients (through the olive oil) and about 32 cups of water, or enough to cover the beans by at least 3 inches. Stir well and bring to a boil. Immediately lower the heat and simmer for about 2½ hours, or until the beans are tender. Taste for seasoning.

3. Purée 4 cups of the beans with a little liquid, a few cups at a time, in a blender and return the purée to the pot. If the soup is too thick, add a little extra water. Taste for seasoning. Garnish each bowl of soup with a large dollop of sour cream and diced sweet green or red pepper, if desired.

THICK RUSSIAN CABBAGE SOUP

◇ ════════════════════════════════ ◇

With thanks to Nadia Cossman and Barbara Cossman

SERVES 50

6 pounds flanken, short ribs, and/or any meaty beef bones
6 cups (4 quarts) homemade beef stock or canned broth
28 cups (7 quarts) water
5 pounds cabbage, coarsely chopped
4 cups coarsely chopped onion
4 cups peeled and chopped parsnips
7 cups thinly sliced celery
2 28-ounce cans imported Italian whole tomatoes, including liquid, chopped

1 cup tomato paste
Juice of 7 lemons
⅓ cup sugar
¾ cup chopped fresh dill, or ⅓ cup dried dill
¾ cup chopped fresh parsley leaves
3 tablespoons salt, or to taste
1 teaspoon freshly ground black pepper
4 cups (1 quart) sour cream
5 loaves black bread or pumpernickel bread
Sweet butter

1. Put the beef, stock, and water into a 38-quart pot. Cover and bring to a boil. Lower the heat and simmer for 30 minutes.

2. Skim the foam from the top of the soup and add the next 12 ingredients (through the black pepper). Stir and bring to a boil, covered. Lower the heat, partially cover, and simmer for 1½ hours, stirring occasionally.

3. Add the lemon juice, sugar, dill, and parsley. Stir and simmer, partially covered, for 1 hour.

4. Remove the beef and cool it. Shred the meat, discarding the bones, or cut the meat into small pieces and return it to the soup. Taste for seasoning. Garnish each bowl with a dollop of sour cream and serve with black bread and sweet butter.

Cheese and Egg Dishes

◇ ═══════════════════════════════ ◇

The cheese and egg dishes that follow represent only a fraction of the hundreds of main-course possibilities for each of these food categories. Sole and Gruyère Tart, Spanakopita, Feuilleté au Roquefort, and Ricotta, Mushroom, and Sun-Dried Tomato Strudel can each serve as a pièce de résistance, around which to build a sensational menu.

The variety and versatility of cheese, and the economy and ease of preparing egg dishes make them both excellent choices when cooking for crowds, especially for brunches, weekend entertaining, light suppers, or informal relaxed dinners any time.

A splendid menu for entertaining a large crowd, can be made up of a cheese board which includes Brie, Explorateur, Pont l'Evêque, Port Salut, Bucheron, and Blue de Bress, or other favorites. The cheeses can be accompanied by platters of cold sliced baked ham, veal, and turkey, served with small bowls of freshly made herb mayonnaise, and a selection of mustards. Add crisp French bread, sweet butter, a tossed green salad, an assortment of seasonal fruit, and cookies, and both a dry red and a crackling cold white wine to round out a marvelous meal.

To entertain a large group with minimal effort and cost, serve a basic egg salad, enhanced with chopped fresh dill, snipped fresh chives, and crisp bacon strips, on thin slices of black bread. Add a cold pasta and vegetable salad, or ratatouille, and Double Chocolate Brownies and French vanilla ice cream for dessert and help your guests enjoy themselves.

SOLE AND GRUYÈRE TART

SERVES 8

1 pastry shell for 10-inch tart (see recipe page 289)
1 cup dry white wine
1 tablespoon minced shallot
2 tablespoons chopped fresh parsley leaves

1 tablespoon fresh lemon juice
1½ pounds sole fillets, halved and cut into 3-inch pieces
4 tablespoons butter
½ pound finely chopped fresh mushrooms

SAUCE

3 tablespoons butter
3 tablespoons all-purpose flour
1¾ cups milk, heated
Reduced liquid from fish

⅓ pound Gruyère cheese, grated
Salt and freshly ground black pepper to taste

1. Preheat the oven to 400 degrees. Line a 10-inch tart pan with the pastry. Fit a sheet of aluminum foil a little larger than the pan into the shell. Fill the foil with 2 cups of dried beans. Bake for about 15 minutes, or until the pastry begins to brown. Remove the foil and beans, and bake the pastry for about 5 minutes more, or until it is golden brown. Cool.

2. Meanwhile, combine the wine, shallot, parsley, and lemon juice in a large frying pan. Bring to a simmer. Add the sole, cover, and simmer for 10 minutes.

3. Transfer the fish to a plate using a slotted spoon. Reduce the liquid in the pan to ⅓ cup.

4. In another pan, melt the butter and cook the mushrooms over high heat until all the butter has been absorbed. Set the mushrooms aside.

5. Prepare the sauce by melting the butter in a saucepan. Whisk in the flour and cook for 1 minute, stirring. Whisk in the hot milk and stir until the sauce boils and thickens. Add the reduced liquid from the fish and the cheese. Stir until the cheese melts. Season with salt and pepper.

6. To assemble the tart, spread the mushrooms over the bottom of the pastry shell. Cover with the pieces of sole. Spoon the sauce over the fish. Pass quickly under the broiler until the top is golden brown. Serve at once.

More Servings
Double the recipe to serve 16 and make two tarts. Bake both at the same time.

AVOCADO HALVES
WITH CURRIED SCRAMBLED EGGS

I often serve this refreshing and quick dish to weekend guests for Sunday lunch. French baguette sandwiches of butter and ham accompany the avocado and eggs. For dessert, there are always fresh fruit and cookies.

SERVES 8

4 large ripe avocados, halved and pitted
2 tablespoons fresh lemon juice
5 tablespoons butter
½ cup thinly sliced scallions
1 tablespoon curry powder

12 large eggs, lightly beaten
Salt and freshly ground black pepper to taste
16 thin strips jarred roasted red pepper, well-drained

1. Brush the cut surfaces of the avocados with lemon juice and set them aside.
2. Melt the butter in a large frying pan and add the scallions. Cook over medium heat, stirring, for 2 minutes.
3. Add the curry powder and stir well. Pour in the eggs, which have been seasoned with salt and pepper. Cook the eggs over medium heat, stirring with a wooden spoon, until they are set but not dry.
4. Spoon the eggs in equal portions into the center of the avocado halves.
5. Garnish the top of each with a crisscross of two red pepper strips. Serve immediately.

SPANAKOPITA

I've made this delectable Greek dish into a giant pie. It's easily cut into twelve wedges and makes a very special lunch or supper when served with a tossed green salad, sliced tomatoes, and hot crusty French bread.

SERVES 12

4 10-ounce packages frozen
chopped spinach
1 pound large-curd cottage
cheese
1 8-ounce package cream
cheese, softened
1 pound feta cheese, drained
and crumbled
½ cup thinly sliced scallions
6 large eggs, lightly beaten

⅓ cup chopped fresh parsley
leaves
¼ cup chopped fresh dill, or 1½
tablespoons dried dill
Salt and freshly ground black
pepper to taste
1½ cups (3 sticks) butter, melted
1 pound filo pastry leaves
(available in specialty food
stores—see Note)

1. Cook the spinach following package directions. Drain it well, pressing out the excess water with the back of a large spoon.

2. In a large bowl, combine the cottage cheese, cream cheese, and feta cheese well. Add the scallions, eggs, parsley, dill, and drained spinach. Season with salt and pepper and mix well.

3. Preheat the oven to 350 degrees.

4. Brush butter on the bottom and sides of a 14-inch deep-dish pizza or paella pan. Arrange 6 overlapping sheets of buttered filo leaves over the bottom of the pan, one at a time, with about one quarter of the leaves hanging over the edge of the pan. Work quickly as the filo breaks easily. (Be sure to keep the filo leaves that you are not working with covered with a damp towel to keep them from drying out.)

5. Turn the spinach mixture into the pan over the filo leaves and spread it out evenly. Brush another sheet of filo with butter and place it on top of the spinach mixture. Leave about one quarter of the leaf hanging over the side. Repeat this procedure with five more buttered leaves.

6. Carefully tuck all the edges under the pie. The pastry will break a little when this is done.

7. Bake for about 45 minutes, or until the top of the pie is golden brown.

8. Cool the Spanakopita for 10 minutes before cutting it into 12 wedges.

More Servings
Double the recipe and make two pies to serve 24.

NOTE: Only 12 filo leaves are needed, so remove these and immediately rewrap the rest tightly in plastic wrap and refreeze them for use at another time.

BOBBE HART'S BRUNCH SOUFFLÉ

When the wind blows in the right direction, from the southeast, aromatic breezes often reach our home in St. Thomas from our neighbors, Bobbe and Donn Hart. These food winds, as I called them as a child, can make the mouth water even if one isn't hungry. The most satisfying aspect of a food wind is recognizing the aroma: bacon cooking, bread baking, chicken frying, or a roast roasting. The most frustrating food wind is one for which you can't determine the source, only that it piques the senses: One stops, alert, like an animal on the scent of something.

On a late Sunday morning last year, just before a brunch at the Hart's, I detected such a wind, and was eager to find out its source. It was Bobbe's Brunch Soufflé, which satisfied the sense of taste as much as the sense of smell.

Bobbe serves her delectable and easy soufflé with sliced baked ham and warm sweet rolls.

SERVES 12

¼ cup butter	¼ cup freshly grated Parmesan cheese
18 eggs, lightly beaten	
1 cup sour cream	½ cup thinly sliced scallions
1 cup milk	¼ cup chopped fresh parsley leaves
1 teaspoon salt (optional)	

1. Preheat the oven to 350 degrees.
2. Melt the butter in a 9- by 13- by 2-inch baking pan in the oven.
3. Put the remaining ingredients in a large bowl and combine them well. Pour the egg mixture into the hot pan. Bake for 35 minutes, or until the dish is golden brown and puffed up. Cut into 12 squares and serve immediately.

More Servings
Make two soufflés in two batches to serve 24 and bake in the oven at the same time.

FEUILLETÉ AU ROQUEFORT

◇ ══════════════════════════════ ◇

SERVES 16

16 frozen puff pastry patties,
thawed
All-purpose flour
2 8-ounce packages cream
cheese, softened and cut into
8 pieces each

1 pound Roquefort cheese,
crumbled
½ cup chopped fresh parsley
leaves
½ cup finely chopped shallots
2 eggs, lightly beaten

1. Preheat the oven to 425 degrees.

2. For each individual feuilleté, roll a patty into a 6-inch circle on a lightly floured surface. Place 1 piece of the cream cheese in the center of the dough. Spread it out slightly. Sprinkle one sixteenth of the Roquefort, 1 teaspoon of the parsley, and 1 teaspoon of the shallots over the dough. Fold the dough over and seal and crimp the edges. Put on one of two ungreased large baking sheets. Continue making 7 more patties. Brush each with a little egg and bake the first batch for about 18 minutes.

3. Make the remaining feuilletés.

4. Remove the first batch and bake the second. Serve immediately.

REFRIED BEANS AND CHEESE BURRITOS WITH SOUR CREAM AND TOMATOES

◇ ══════════════════════════════ ◇

This is an easy crowd-pleaser for an informal gathering. Balance out the rest of the menu with a large mixed green salad, sangria, and ice cream with Double Chocolate Brownies (page 300).

Canned refried beans are used in this recipe as a suitable time-saver, but if you have the time (about 3½ hours), cook 6 cups of kidney beans and refry, following the instructions for refried black beans on page 222. Refried black beans can be used in this recipe, too.

SERVES 24

6 16-ounce cans refried beans
1½ cups chopped canned green chilies
2 cups mild taco sauce
24 10-inch flour tortillas
1½ pounds Cheddar cheese, shredded
1½ pounds Monterey Jack cheese, shredded

5 cups (1¼ quarts) sour cream
6 large firm ripe tomatoes, diced
1 large bunch scallions, thinly sliced
1 16-ounce can pitted large black olives, quartered lengthwise

1. Preheat the oven to 350 degrees.

2. Combine the refried beans, green chilies, and taco sauce in a large bowl.

3. Spoon equal amounts of the beans on the center of each tortilla and smooth with the back of a spoon.

4. Sprinkle the top of the beans with equal amounts of the combined cheeses. Fold the bottom of each tortilla up over the filling. Fold in the two sides and roll up the tortilla.

5. Place the prepared burritos side by side, seam side down, in two large roasting pans. Bake for about 20 minutes, or until the burritos are heated through.

6. Serve each burrito topped with a heaping tablespoon of sour cream and a little of the tomatoes, scallions, and olives.

More Servings
Double the ingredients in the recipe and bake in two or three batches to serve 48.

SALMON CROQUETTES
WITH GORGONZOLA FILLING

◊ ══════════════════════════════ ◊

SERVES 36

6 15-ounce cans salmon, well-drained, with skin and bones removed

10 cups (2½ quarts) mashed potatoes (Instant mashed potatoes are fine for this purpose.)

1 cup chopped onion

1 cup minced celery

⅓ cup fresh lemon juice

8 large eggs

Salt and freshly ground black pepper to taste

1¼ pounds Gorgonzola cheese, chilled and cut into 36 equal-sized pieces

All-purpose flour

8 large eggs, beaten

4 cups plain dry bread crumbs, or as needed

Peanut oil

1. Combine the salmon, mashed potatoes, onion, celery, lemon juice, 8 eggs, and salt and pepper in a very large bowl. Mix well.

2. Shape the mixture into 36 equal-sized balls with a piece of the cheese in the center.

3. Dust each croquette with flour; then roll in the beaten eggs and coat lightly with the bread crumbs. Lay on baking sheets or platters, cover, and refrigerate for 1 hour.

4. Heat 1 inch of oil in a large frying pan and cook the croquettes, as many as will fit comfortably into the pan, until golden brown all over, adding and reheating oil as needed.

RICOTTA, MUSHROOM, AND SUN-DRIED TOMATO STRUDEL

This delicious strudel dish is made in advance and frozen, so that all that's required is cooking it at the last minute. Although easy to make, preparing and assembling the ten strudels will take some time, about an hour and fifteen minutes, working at a steady pace.

Ricotta, Mushroom, and Sun-Dried Tomato Strudel can be the highlight of a meal for fifty. To complete the menu, add a Salade Verte with Vinaigrette Dressing (page 204), sliced smoked chicken or turkey, salamis, a mild horseradish dressing, a selection of breads, and Lemon-Poppyseed Cakes (page 302).

SERVES 50

1½ cups (3 sticks) butter

3 pounds fresh mushrooms, wiped clean and coarsely chopped

7 pounds ricotta

1 quart sun-dried tomatoes packed in oil, drained and chopped

3 cups thinly sliced scallions

1 tablespoon dried rosemary

1½ cups freshly grated Parmesan cheese

Salt and freshly ground black pepper to taste

4 pounds packaged filo pastry leaves

4 cups (8 sticks) butter, melted

4 cups plain dry bread crumbs

1. Melt 1 stick of the butter in a large frying pan and cook 1 pound of the mushrooms over medium-high heat for 5 minutes, stirring often. Transfer to a colander in the sink. Then cook the remaining mushrooms in two batches using a stick of butter for each pound of mushrooms.

2. Squeeze the mushrooms dry in a dish towel or two and put them into a very large bowl. Add the ricotta, sun-dried tomatoes, scallions, rosemary, and Parmesan cheese and combine thoroughly. Season with salt and pepper.

3. Put a dish towel on the counter or work area, and lay a sheet of filo dough on it. (Keep unused filo leaves covered with a damp towel at all times to prevent them from drying out and cracking.) Brush the filo leaf with melted butter and sprinkle lightly with bread crumbs. Repeat this procedure until you have four layers.

4. Spoon about 2 cups of the mushroom mixture along one of the long sides of the layered leaves. Lift up the towel edge on the side closest

to you and carefully roll up the strudel. The roll will actually be flat, about 3½ inches wide. Fold the ends of the roll underneath and, with the help of two spatulas, place it on a small baking sheet or pan and brush it with butter.

5. Put the baking sheet in the freezer.

6. Make nine more strudels in exactly the same way.

7. When all the strudels have been made, remove them from the freezer and wrap each of them in plastic wrap and aluminum foil. Then freeze them.

8. When you are ready to cook the strudels, preheat the oven to 350 degrees.

9. Unwrap the strudels and place them on two or three large baking sheets. Bake the strudels on two or three shelves of the oven for about 45 minutes, or until they are golden brown. Rotate the baking sheets, so that each is on the lower shelf for at least 15 minutes. The strudels can also be baked in two batches. When the first batch is done, let it cool, while baking the second batch. Reheat the first batch in the oven for about 10 minutes while serving the second batch.

Fish and Shellfish

◇ ══════════════════════════ ◇

Few main courses can compare with a perfectly cooked fresh fish or shellfish dish; and because fish and shellfish take little cooking time, they are great assets when cooking for crowds. Shellfish and some fish in quantity can be expensive these days; however, balancing the rest of the menu with reasonably priced seasonal vegetable dishes, a salad, a rice or potato dish, and a fruit dessert can help make cooking seafood for a crowd affordable.

Modern transportation and storage has made it possible for every area of the country to enjoy fresh fish and shellfish of the finest quality. Geography is no longer an obstacle to serving dishes like Grilled Swordfish with Mustard Mayonnaise, Red Snapper with Bananas and Feta Cheese Baked in Filo Leaves with Beurre Blanc, or Sliced Sea Scallops with Orange Sections in Cream Sauce.

Fish and shellfish casseroles are excellent and reasonably economical selections even for the most special celebrations. And today's diet-conscious guests will welcome seafood.

GRILLED SWORDFISH
WITH MUSTARD MAYONNAISE

Swordfish, brushed with mustard mayonnaise and quickly grilled, remains moist and delicately tender. I first tasted this miracle of simplicity in Falmouth, Massachusetts, at the home of Emily and Edward McCormack. Emily rounded out the meal with corn on the cob, fresh steamed string beans, and sliced tomatoes topped with a mixture of chopped basil, red onions, oil, and vinegar. We had strawberries and blueberries with vanilla ice cream for dessert. Emily's menu is an example of first-rate honest American cooking.

SERVES 8

1 cup mayonnaise
2 tablespoons Dijon mustard
2 tablespoons fresh lemon juice
Freshly ground black pepper
to taste

8 6- to 7-ounce swordfish
steaks
8 lemon wedges, seeded

1. Combine the mayonnaise, mustard, and lemon juice. Season the mixture with pepper.

2. Spread one side of the fish with half of the mayonnaise mixture and cook coated side down, on a grill over hot coals for about 6 minutes. Brush the remaining mayonnaise on the top of the steaks, turn and cook about 6 minutes longer, or until the fish is just tender and cooked through. Serve each swordfish steak with a lemon wedge.

More Servings
Double the recipe to serve 16. It will be necessary to cook in two batches on the grill. Keep the cooked swordfish warm in a covered serving dish.

SOLE CAROLINA À LA HARRY'S BAR

SERVES 8

½ cup olive oil
2 large ripe tomatoes, peeled,
 seeded, and diced
3 tablespoons drained capers
3 tablespoons fresh lemon juice
3 tablespoons chopped fresh
 parsley leaves

Salt and freshly ground black
 pepper
3 pounds sole fillets
All-purpose flour
Butter
Peanut oil

1. Heat the olive oil in a saucepan. Add the tomatoes, capers, lemon juice, and parsley. Season well with salt and pepper. Stir and simmer over very low heat for 10 minutes.

2. Meanwhile, season the sole fillets with salt and pepper and dust them with flour.

3. Heat 2 tablespoons of butter and 2 tablespoons of peanut oil in a large frying pan. Cook several pieces of the sole at a time, until they are golden brown on both sides. Transfer to a warmed serving platter. Continue cooking the remaining sole, adding small equal amounts of butter and oil when necessary.

4. Spoon the tomato mixture evenly over the fillets and serve at once.

More Servings
The recipe can be doubled to serve 16. Cook in two pans.

FULVIA SESANI'S VENETIAN SAOR

Each year that I have the good fortune to return to Venice, I discover something new. Last year it was saor. *I spent an October afternoon in the kitchen of Fulvia Sesani's Venetian palazzo observing one of her cooking demonstrations. It was there that I was introduced to* saor, *an ancient and typical Venetian fish dish.*

Signora Sesani told us, "The most Venetian of dishes, which, together with the fireworks, is the real protagonist of the Redentore feast is saor *or marinated fish.*

"The Venetian word saor means taste, flavor, relish, and in truth, the oil, wine vinegar, onions, raisins, and pine nuts combine to evoke the memory of the long Venetian civilization. The possibility of keeping the fish for long periods, of eating it in the hot months without having to toil over the stove, of buying the fish when plentiful and, therefore, inexpensive—these are the advantages of the saor."

Saor *still provides an extraordinarily good summer dish.*

SERVES 8

3 pounds small sole fillets
Salt and freshly ground black pepper
All-purpose flour
Olive oil
6 medium-sized onions, thinly sliced

½ cup white wine vinegar
¾ cup pine nuts
¾ cup golden raisins
2 tablespoons chopped candied citron peel
4 whole bay leaves

1. Season the fillets with salt and pepper. Dust them with flour and cook them, a few at a time, in a large frying pan in olive oil that just covers the bottom of the pan, until they are golden brown on each side. Add a little oil as needed to cook all the fillets. Drain them on paper towels.

2. Heat about 1 cup of oil in the frying pan and cook the onions over medium-low heat, stirring often, just until they begin to turn golden brown, about 10 minutes.

3. Add the vinegar, pine nuts, raisins, citron, and ¼ cup of water and cook the mixture over medium-high heat for 5 minutes, stirring often.

4. Make a layer of half of the fish fillets in a shallow 10-inch dish. Spoon half of the onion mixture over the fish. Top with the remaining fillets and finally the remaining onion mixture. Press the onion mixture down slightly and put the bay leaves on top at equal distances. Cover and refrigerate for 24 hours.

More Servings
Double the recipe to serve 16 and use a large gratin dish or two 10-inch dishes.

Steven Gregor's Red Snapper with Bananas and Feta Cheese Baked in Filo Leaves with Beurre Blanc Sauce

Steven Gregor, a 1976 Culinary Institute graduate and award-winning chef, created this spectacular recipe.

SERVES 12

24 filo pastry leaves
 1 cup (2 sticks) butter melted, or as needed
12 4-ounce red snapper fillets
 Salt and freshly ground black pepper to taste

 6 medium-sized firm ripe bananas, peeled and cut in half lengthwise
 1 pound feta cheese, cut into 12 slices
 1/4 cup chopped fresh parsley leaves

BEURRE BLANC SAUCE
 1/2 cup finely chopped shallots
 1/2 cup white wine vinegar
 3/4 cup dry white wine

 2 cups (4 sticks) butter, cut into tablespoon-sized pieces
 Salt and freshly ground black pepper to taste

1. Have all the ingredients in the working area. Keep the filo leaves covered at all times, except when working with one.
2. Season the fish with salt and pepper.
3. Brush one sheet of filo with butter and top with another sheet. Brush with melted butter. Put one snapper fillet in the center and top with half of a banana. Top with a slice of feta cheese and a little sprinkle of parsley. Fold the sides in over the filling; then fold the top and bottom sides over and under the filling, making a square package. Put the package on a large ungreased baking sheet and continue making the remaining packages in the same manner.
4. Preheat the oven to 425 degrees.
5. Bake the fish packages for 15 to 20 minutes, or until they are puffed and golden brown.
6. Meanwhile, prepare the sauce. Combine the shallots, vinegar, and wine in a saucepan. Reduce over high heat to two-thirds the original amount. Over low heat, whisk in the butter, a tablespoon at a time. Season with salt and pepper. Serve with the fish immediately.

More Servings
The recipe can be doubled, cooking the fish in two batches. Reheat the first batch on the middle shelf of the oven during the last 5 minutes of cooking time for the second batch. It will also be necessary to make two batches of beurre blanc.

SLICED SEA SCALLOPS WITH ORANGE SECTIONS IN CREAM SAUCE

SERVES 12

1 cup (2 sticks) sweet butter, or as needed
3 pounds sea scallops, cut crosswise into 3 slices each
1/3 cup finely chopped shallots
1/3 cup fresh lemon juice
1 cup dry white wine
4 cups (1 quart) heavy cream
1 tablespoon grated orange rind

Freshly ground nutmeg
Salt and freshly ground black pepper to taste
6 navel oranges at room temperature, peeled (including white pith) and separated into sections with seeds removed
1/4 cup snipped fresh chives

1. Melt the butter in a large frying pan. Simmer one third of the scallops in the butter for about 4 minutes on each side. Using a slotted spoon, transfer the scallops to a plate and keep them warm. Cook the remaining scallops, which are really poached, in the butter, until they are cooked. Add more butter if necessary.

2. Combine the shallots, lemon juice, and wine in a heavy saucepan and cook over high heat until the liquid is reduced by half.

3. Meanwhile, boil the cream in a non-metallic saucepan or pot until it thickens. Stir in the reduced shallot mixture, orange rind, and a few gratings of nutmeg. Season with salt and pepper.

4. For each serving, arrange a portion of scallops on a dinner plate and spoon some sauce over them. Arrange about 6 orange sections between the scallops and sprinkle with the chives.

More Servings
Double the recipe to serve 24, using only 7 cups (1³/₄ quarts) of cream.

JOELLE BURROWS' BAKED HADDOCK WITH SOUR CREAM AND DILL

Joelle Burrows, who was born in Cape Elizabeth, Maine, says, "Fresh Maine haddock is an exquisite fish, especially in the late fall and early winter, when the Atlantic is very cold. The best way to cook haddock is to bake it. Haddock is delicious poached in a seasoned milk bath, too, but it is even better smothered in sour cream and sprinkled with fresh dill after baking."

Requiring only 30 minutes cooking time, Joelle's dish enables you to come home after work and give an elegant dinner party for twelve.

Haddock is a member of the cod family. If fresh Maine haddock is unavailable, scrod or cod can be substituted successfully.

SERVES 12

4 pounds fresh Maine haddock fillets
3 tablespoons fresh lemon juice
Salt and freshly ground black pepper

4 cups (1 quart) sour cream
6 tablespoons chopped fresh dill (don't substitute dried dill), plus 10 sprigs fresh dill for garnish

1. Preheat the oven to 350 degrees.

2. Put the haddock fillets in a large gratin dish or two. Sprinkle the lemon juice over the fish and season it well with salt and pepper. Spoon the sour cream over the fish and spread it out evenly. Bake for 30 minutes.

3. Remove from the oven and sprinkle the top of the fish with the chopped dill and surround it with a wreath of the dill sprigs. Serve at once.

More Servings
Double the recipe to serve 24 and bake in two or three large baking dishes. Bake on two oven shelves, alternating baking dishes halfway through the baking time, which will take 8 to 10 minutes longer.

BROILED SCROD STEAKS WITH BACON AND TARRAGON SAUCE

SERVES 16

16 strips bacon
16 thick 6-ounce scrod fillets
¼ cup butter, melted, plus extra butter for greasing the pan

2 tablespoons fresh lemon juice
¼ cup dry white wine
   Paprika

TARRAGON SAUCE

1½ cups mayonnaise
1½ cups sour cream
¼ cup chopped fresh tarragon leaves, or 1 tablespoon dried tarragon

¼ cup chopped fresh parsley leaves
2 tablespoons fresh lemon juice
   Salt and freshly ground black pepper to taste

1. Wrap a piece of the bacon around each scrod fillet and secure it with a toothpick.

2. Put the fillets on a large greased broiler pan or two.

3. Combine the butter, lemon juice, and wine and brush the mixture over the tops of the fillets. Sprinkle with the paprika.

4. Cook 6 inches under the broiler for 8 minutes on each side.

5. Meanwhile, prepare the sauce by combining all the ingredients thoroughly.

6. Remove the toothpicks from the bacon. Serve the fish with the sauce.

More Servings
The recipe can be doubled to serve 32, but the fish must be cooked in two batches, unless you have two broilers.

SHRIMP STUFFED WITH SCALLOP AND CRAB MEAT MOUSSE

SERVES 16

64 jumbo shrimp, shelled and carefully deveined (Don't cut through the flesh too much.)
1½ pounds sea scallops, chopped
6 large egg whites
3 cups heavy cream

2 teaspoons salt
½ cup chopped fresh parsley leaves
1 pound crab meat, chopped
Butter for greasing the pan

1. Butterfly each shrimp, cutting halfway through the shorter side of the shrimp (the underside).
2. Purée the scallops in a food processor. Add the egg whites and 1 cup of the heavy cream. If necessary, do this in two batches.
3. Turn the mixture into a large bowl and beat in the remaining cream and the salt and parsley. Fold in the crab meat.
4. Preheat the oven to 400 degrees.
5. Spoon equal amounts of the mixture into each shrimp, and put the stuffed shrimp in a large buttered roasting pan. Bake for 15 minutes. Serve at once.

More Servings
The recipe can be doubled to serve 32, but it must be baked in two pans (the sauce must also be puréed in two or more batches). Alternate pans on lower and middle shelves after 10 minutes cooking time, and cook for 10 minutes longer.

BRUCE THOMAS'
STUFFED FLOUNDER WITH CREOLE SAUCE

For Bruce Thomas, the chef of Dobson's restaurant in New York City, cooking for crowds is second nature. "Cooking for large groups is simply a matter of getting used to working with larger quantities. After that, it's easy. There's no great mystery involved; it's certainly no cause for fear. And, cooking for many is so much more rewarding than cooking for only a few people."

Bruce's savory recipe takes about an hour to prepare. For side dishes, he suggests small boiled potatoes and fresh string beans or broccoli, which can be cooked while the fish is baking.

SERVES 16

CREOLE SAUCE

2 cups chopped onion
2 cups chopped sweet green pepper
1 tablespoon minced garlic
2 cups diced celery
2 cups sliced mushrooms
½ cup vegetable oil
6 cups chopped peeled and seeded tomatoes (Drained canned tomatoes can be used.)

2 cups homemade or canned tomato sauce
2 teaspoons salt
1 teaspoon freshly ground black pepper
¼ cup dry sherry
½ teaspoon cayenne pepper
1 tablespoon sugar
1 cup sliced pimiento-stuffed green olives
3 bay leaves

CRAB MEAT STUFFING

1 pound bacon, diced
1½ cups diced onion
1½ cups diced celery
16 slices soft bread with crusts trimmed, cubed
1 pound crab meat

3 large eggs, slightly beaten
3 tablespoons ketchup
2 teaspoons dry sherry
Salt and freshly ground black pepper to taste

16 6- to 7-ounce flounder fillets

Butter for greasing the pan

1. To prepare the Creole Sauce, cook the onion, green pepper, garlic, celery, and mushrooms in the oil in a large saucepan for 5 minutes.

2. Add the remaining ingredients, stir, and bring to a boil. Immediately lower the heat and simmer the sauce for 45 minutes, stirring often.

3. Meanwhile, prepare the stuffing: Cook the bacon in a large frying pan until it is crisp. Drain the bacon on paper towels. Discard half of the fat in the pan. Add the onion and celery and cook for about 5 minutes.

4. Preheat the oven to 350 degrees.

5. Remove the frying pan from the heat and transfer the onion and celery to a large bowl. Add the bacon and remaining ingredients and combine thoroughly.

6. Spread equal amounts of the stuffing evenly across the skinned side of each fillet. Roll up the fillets and place in a large greased baking dish or two.

7. Bake the fish for about 20 minutes, or until it flakes easily.

8. Carefully transfer the fish rolls to a large serving platter or dish. Spoon some of the sauce over each and serve the remaining sauce in a bowl.

GRILLED SWORDFISH AND SALMON KEBABS

SERVES 24

2½ cups olive oil
¾ cup fresh lemon juice
¾ cup finely chopped onion
2 teaspoons dried dill, tarragon, or thyme

Salt and freshly ground black pepper to taste
3½ pounds swordfish steaks, cut into 1½-inch cubes
3½ pounds salmon steaks, cut into 1½-inch cubes

1. Combine all the ingredients, except the fish, in a large bowl. Add the fish cubes, cover, and marinate in the refrigerator for 3 hours.

2. Thread alternating cubes of salmon and swordfish on each of 24 8-inch dampened wooden or metal skewers. Grill about 5 minutes per side on open grill 6 inches over the coals.

More Servings
Double the recipe to serve 48, marinating the fish in two bowls and grilling in as many batches as necessary.

SCALLOP AND VEGETABLE RAGOUT

SERVES 24

1 cup (2 sticks) butter
4 pounds sea scallops, cut in half crosswise
½ cup chopped shallots
⅓ cup fresh lemon juice
3 cups dry white wine
4 cups (1 quart) heavy cream
Salt and freshly ground black pepper to taste

2 pounds carrots, scraped and cut into julienne strips, then parboiled for 4 minutes and drained
2 cups peeled, seeded, and diced tomatoes
3 tablespoons snipped fresh chives

1. Melt half the butter in a large Dutch oven. Add the scallops and turn gently. Cover and *simmer* for 5 minutes. Remove the pan from the heat and let stand, covered.

2. Cook the shallots in a large non-metallic heavy saucepan with the lemon juice and wine over high heat until the mixture is reduced to 1½ cups. Stir in the cream and boil until thickened. Add the juice that has accumulated in the pan with the scallops and the remaining butter, 1 tablespoon at a time. Season with salt and pepper.

3. Add the sauce to the scallops and combine gently with the vegetables. Season with salt and pepper and sprinkle with the chives. Serve immediately.

PENELOPE JAGO'S CHILEAN CHUPE

Serve this dish with a tossed green salad and crusty French bread and butter.

SERVES 36

½ cup olive oil
3 large onions, chopped
5 large sweet green peppers, seeded and chopped

6 pounds potatoes, peeled and diced
14 cups (3½ quarts) homemade chicken stock or canned broth

2 pounds haddock, cubed
3 pounds medium-sized
   shrimp, shelled and deveined
3 8-ounce packages cream
   cheese, cut into 6 pieces each
3 cups heavy cream

3 dashes Tabasco sauce
½ cup chopped fresh parsley
   leaves
Salt and freshly ground black
   pepper to taste

1. In a 12-quart stock pot, heat the oil and cook the onions and peppers for 10 minutes, stirring often.

2. Add the potatoes and stock and bring to a boil. Lower the heat and simmer for about 20 minutes, or until the potatoes are tender.

3. Stir in the haddock and shrimp and cook for 3 or 4 minutes. Add the remaining ingredients, seasoning well with the pepper. Heat thoroughly.

SEAFOOD GUMBO

SERVES 50

¾ cup vegetable oil
¾ cup all-purpose flour
4 large onions, chopped
4 large sweet green peppers,
   seeded and chopped
10 celery stalks, sliced
8 large garlic cloves, minced
5 large ripe tomatoes, peeled,
   seeded, and diced
2 tablespoons Worcestershire
   sauce
½ teaspoon Tabasco sauce
2 bay leaves
36 cups (9 quarts) boiling water

1 cup chopped fresh parsley
   leaves
1½ teaspoons dried thyme
6 cups sliced fresh okra
2 tablespoons salt, or to taste
1 teaspoon freshly ground
   black pepper
8 pounds raw small shrimp,
   shelled and deveined
2 pounds crab meat
4 tablespoons filé powder
   (made from sassafras leaves, a
   flavoring and thickening
   agent found in specialty food
   stores)

1. In a heavy 15- to 18-quart kettle, mix together the oil and flour with a wooden spoon. Cook over very low heat, stirring constantly, for

about 25 minutes, or until the mixture is a rich dark brown in color. Do not let the roux burn.

2. Add the onions, peppers, celery, and garlic. Simmer for 10 minutes, stirring often.

3. Stir in the remaining ingredients, except the seafood and filé powder. Bring to a boil; then immediately lower the heat to a simmer and cook over very low heat for 30 minutes.

4. Add the seafood and simmer for 20 minutes longer.

5. Remove from the heat and let the gumbo stand, stirring occasionally, for 10 minutes.

6. Stir in the filé powder and let stand for 5 minutes. Stir again and check the seasoning. Serve with hot cooked rice (see chart for cooking rice on page 259) and bottled hot red pepper sauce.

Poultry

◇ ══════════════════════════════════ ◇

When cooking for a large group with varying tastes and eating habits, you can always rest assured that poultry, especially chicken, is safe.

Chicken is prepared imaginatively in all the cuisines of the world. Chicken is nutritious and low in fat and calories; it is probably the most economical main course that can be served to crowds.

In cooking for crowds, boneless chicken breast is often selected because it represents the choicest part of the bird. If time is no object, you can reduce costs by boning chicken breasts in advance of meal preparation. Then you can freeze the bones and skins for stock-making—an added bonus.

Duck and Cornish game hens make superb dishes for crowds, and turkey allows you a wide range of serving options from a whole roast turkey, to grilled paillards, to a turkey salad for sixteen.

ROAST CHICKEN WITH CREAMY RASPBERRY VINEGAR SAUCE

SERVES 8

2 4-pound roasting chickens
Salt and freshly ground black pepper
3 tablespoons butter, softened
¾ cup raspberry vinegar

¼ cup finely chopped shallots
2 cups heavy cream
¼ cup framboise (raspberry liqueur)

1. Preheat the oven to 400 degrees.
2. Season the chickens inside and out with salt and pepper. Rub each chicken with 1½ tablespoons of butter. Tie the legs together and fold the wings back.
3. Put the chickens, breast side up, into a large roasting pan. Roast for 1 hour and 10 minutes, or until the chickens are golden brown and tender. Remove from the oven and let stand for 10 minutes.
4. Meanwhile, combine the raspberry vinegar with the shallots in a medium-sized heavy saucepan. Cook over high heat until the mixture is reduced by half. At the same time bring the cream to a boil in a non-metallic pan. Cook it over high heat, whisking constantly until it thickens, about 5 minutes.
5. Stir the vinegar and shallots and the framboise into the cream. Season with salt and pepper to taste.
6. Quarter the chickens, discarding the backbones and arrange on a large serving platter. Serve with the sauce.

More Servings
Double the recipe to serve 16 and roast the chicken in two roasting pans.

ITALIAN CHICKEN WITH PEPPER AND SAUSAGE

SERVES 8

5 Italian sweet sausages
3½ pounds skinned and boned chicken breasts, cut into bite-sized pieces
Seasoned salt
8 tablespoons butter
4 tablespoons olive oil
1 large onion, halved and cut into thin slivers
1 teaspoon minced garlic
2 large sweet green peppers, seeded and cut into 1-inch squares
2 large sweet red peppers, seeded and cut into 1-inch squares
2 large carrots, scraped and diced

1 28-ounce can imported Italian tomatoes with liquid, chopped
1½ teaspoons paprika
1 teaspoon dried basil
½ teaspoon dried oregano
1 bay leaf
2 tablespoons red wine vinegar
1 teaspoon sugar
1 cup dry white wine
2 chicken bouillon cubes
4 tablespoons all-purpose flour
Salt and freshly ground black pepper
3 tablespoons chopped fresh parsley leaves
1½ cups freshly grated Parmesan cheese

1. Prick each sausage with the point of a small sharp knife. Simmer the sausages in water to cover for 10 minutes. Drain and cool.

2. Meanwhile, season the chicken pieces lightly with seasoned salt. Heat 2 tablespoon of the butter and 2 tablespoons of the olive oil in a seasoned paella pan or 5-quart heavy pot and cook and brown the chicken pieces, a few at a time, turning them often with a wooden spoon. Transfer the cooked chicken cooked pieces to a large bowl as they brown. Halfway through cooking the chicken, add 2 tablespoons more of both butter and oil, and continue browning the chicken. Leave the remaining 4 tablespoons of butter out to soften.

3. Cut the sausages into ¼-inch-thick slices and brown them in the fat in the pan. Add the sausages to the bowl with the chicken.

4. Add the onion, garlic, and peppers to the pan, and pour the accumulated juices from the bowl with the chicken into the pan. Cook over medium heat for about 8 minutes, stirring often. Add the next 10 ingredi-

ents (through the bouillon cubes). Mix well and cook over high heat for 10 minutes, stirring occasionally.

5. Make a beurre manié by mashing together the remaining 4 tablespoons of softened butter with the flour. Stir into the chicken mixture, and cook until the sauce thickens slightly, about 5 minutes. Season with salt and pepper. Sprinkle with the parsley and serve with the cheese.

More Servings
Make in two batches to serve 16. Reheat the first batch during the last 5 minutes of the cooking time of the second batch.

CRISP ROAST DUCK WITH CRANBERRY AND CHUTNEY SAUCE

SERVES 8

1/2 cup honey
2 4 1/2-pound ducks, fat removed from cavity area
Salt and freshly ground black pepper

1 cup whole cranberry sauce
1 1/2 cups Mango and Date Chutney (recipe page 175)
1 tablespoon grated orange rind

1. Preheat the oven to 400 degrees.
2. Heat the honey with 8 cups of water in a Dutch oven and bring to a boil. Turn off the heat and roll the ducks, one at a time, in the honey water. Drain well.
3. Put a roasting pan with 2 inches of water in it on the floor of the oven.
4. Prick each duck with the sharp point of a small knife in several areas, but not on the breast.
5. Put the ducks side by side, but not touching, on a clean oven rack directly over the pan of water. (The pan collects the dripping fat.) Roast for 1 hour and 20 minutes, or until the ducks are very brown and tender.
6. Meanwhile, combine the cranberry sauce, chutney, and orange rind and set aside.

7. Remove the ducks and let rest for 10 minutes. Carve each into quarters, discarding the backbones. Scrape away any fat from under the breast, leg, and thigh skin with a small sharp knife; then replace the skin. Serve the duck with the sauce.

POLLO ALLA VENEZIANA

SERVES 12

Butter
Olive oil
2 large onions, halved crosswise and cut into thin slivers
3 tablespoons chopped fresh sage, or 1½ teaspoons dried sage
7 large chicken breasts, skinned, boned, and cut into ¼-inch-thick slices about 1½ inches long

Salt and freshly ground black pepper
All-purpose flour
½ cup dry white wine
¼ cup chopped fresh parsley leaves

1. Heat 3 tablespoons each of the butter and oil in a large wok, paella pan, or frying pan. Cook the onions over medium-low heat for 10 minutes, stirring often. Transfer the onions to a large bowl and toss with the sage.

2. Season the chicken pieces with salt and pepper and dust them with flour.

3. Heat 2 tablespoons each of butter and oil in the pan and cook one third of the chicken at a time, stir-frying for about 5 minutes. Transfer the cooked chicken to the bowl with the onions and sage. Continue cooking the chicken, in two more batches, adding a little butter and oil as needed.

4. Put the cooked chicken, onions, and juices that have collected in a large pot with the wine and bring to a boil. Sprinkle with the parsley and season with salt and pepper. Serve at once.

BONELESS BREAST COQ AU VIN

SERVES 12

1 cup (2 sticks) butter
4 tablespoons olive oil
6½ pounds skinned and boned chicken breasts, halved and cut into bite-sized pieces
48 small white onions, peeled but left whole
1 cup chopped onion
1 teaspoon minced garlic
⅓ cup minced shallots
6 tablespoons all-purpose flour
1½ bottles dry red Burgundy wine (the same wine you are going to serve with dinner)
6 cups (1½ quarts) homemade beef stock or canned broth

2 bay leaves
1 teaspoon dried thyme
¼ cup tomato paste
1½ pounds mushrooms, quartered
1 pound lean slab bacon, cut into ½-inch cubes and browned
Salt and freshly ground black pepper to taste
2 cups peeled, seeded, and diced ripe tomatoes
½ cup Cognac or brandy
¼ cup chopped fresh parsley leaves

1. Heat 4 tablespoons of the butter and 2 tablespoons of the olive oil in a 6-quart heavy pot and brown the chicken in four batches (add 4 tablespoons of butter and 2 tablespoons of oil after cooking the second batch of chicken). Transfer the browned chicken to a large bowl as it is cooked.

2. Meanwhile, put the onions in a large saucepan with boiling water to cover. Simmer the onions for about 10 minutes. Drain well.

3. Add the chopped onion, garlic, and shallots to the pot in which the chicken was cooked. Cook over medium heat for 5 minutes, stirring often.

4. Return the chicken and the juices in the bowl to the pot. Sprinkle with the flour and mix gently. Add the next 5 ingredients (through the tomato paste) and mix well. Bring to a boil; then immediately lower the heat and simmer for 20 minutes.

5. Meanwhile, heat 4 tablespoons of the remaining butter in a large frying pan and brown the poached onions, shaking the pan often. Remove the onions to a bowl.

6. Add the remaining 4 tablespoons of butter to the frying pan and cook the mushrooms over medium-high heat for 5 minutes, shaking the pan often. Put the mushrooms in the bowl with the onions.

7. When the chicken has simmered for 20 minutes, transfer it to a dish using a slotted spoon. Strain the sauce into a clean pot. Add the bacon, chicken, onions, and mushrooms. Combine and season with salt and pepper. Simmer for 5 minutes.

8. Stir in the tomatoes and Cognac and cook over medium heat for 5 minutes. Garnish with chopped fresh parsley.

BUTTERMILK BATTER-FRIED CHICKEN

This sensational crunchy fried chicken recipe has evolved over the years from my grandmother's original Texas recipe. Grandmother used more pepper in her recipe, so if you like it spicy, add 1/2 to 1 teaspoon more pepper. Grandmother always used canned pepper, and so do I.

SERVES 12

BATTER

1 cup unsifted all-purpose flour	1 teaspoon paprika
1/2 teaspoon canned black pepper	2 tablespoons poultry seasoning
1 teaspoon salt	1/4 teaspoon Tabasco sauce
1 teaspoon seasoned salt	1 quart buttermilk
8 chicken legs	All-purpose flour for coating the chicken
8 chicken thighs	Peanut or vegetable oil for frying
4 chicken breasts, halved	

1. In a large bowl, prepare the batter (I use a large plastic salad bowl.): Put the flour, pepper, salt, seasoned salt, paprika, poultry seasoning, and Tabasco sauce into the bowl and mix well. Whisk in the buttermilk and let stand for 10 minutes.

2. Add the chicken pieces to the batter and turn the chicken to coat each piece evenly.

3. Place 3 cups of flour in a large bowl and coat each piece of chicken well. Add more flour to the bowl as needed.

4. In two heavy pots or frying pans with 3-inch sides, such as cast iron, heat 1½ inches of oil to 370 degrees. Add 6 pieces of the chicken to each pan and cook until golden brown all over. You'll need to turn the chicken three or four times for even browning. The total cooking time will be about 18 minutes.

5. Drain the cooked chicken on paper towels. Cook the remaining chicken, 6 pieces in each frying pan, in the same manner. It will be necessary to add a little more oil to the pans. Be sure that the oil is reheated to 370 degrees before you add the chicken.

6. Pile the chicken on a large platter and serve it immediately. The chicken is also very good served cold, although it will not be as crisp.

More Servings:
Double the recipe to serve 24 and cook in four batches. Keep the cooked chicken warm in 250-degree oven.

CHICKEN TANDOORI

SERVES 12
(PREPARATION BEGINS THE NIGHT BEFORE)

2½ cups plain yogurt
2 large garlic cloves, minced
1 tablespoon ground coriander
1 tablespoon ground cinnamon
1 tablespoon ground cumin
1 tablespoon ground turmeric
⅛ teaspoon cayenne pepper
1 teaspoon salt
2 teaspoons grated fresh gingerroot

½ cup fresh lime juice
3 3½-pound chickens, quartered, with backbones removed
8 tablespoons butter, melted
Peanut oil for deep-frying
3 cups thinly sliced small yellow onions, separated into individual rings
12 thin lime slices, seeded

1. In a large plastic, glass, or ceramic bowl, combine the yogurt, garlic, spices, salt, ginger, and lime juice. Put the chicken into the bowl and turn the pieces to coat them evenly. (If necessary, use two bowls, dividing the yogurt mixture and chicken evenly between them.) Cover the bowl and refrigerate overnight.

2. Preheat the oven to 375 degrees.

3. Place the chicken, skin side up, in two roasting pans. Drizzle 4 tablespoons of the melted butter over the chicken in each pan. Bake for 1 hour, basting with the pan juices after 30 minutes.

4. Ten minutes before the chicken is done, heat 2 inches of oil in a large heavy saucepan. Add the onions and cook them until they are golden brown, stirring often. Drain on paper towels.

5. Transfer the chicken to a serving platter and top the chicken quarters with equal amounts of the onion rings. Garnish with the lime slices before serving.

More Servings
The recipe can easily be doubled to serve 24, but it must then be cooked in two batches, unless you have two large ovens. To do this, reheat the first cooked batch during the last 10 minutes of the cooking time of the second batch, using the middle shelf of the oven.

BAKED GARLIC CHICKEN LEGS

These chicken legs are such crowd-pleasers, that I recommend cooking two for each guest. If there are any leftover, they are excellent cold.

SERVES 12
(PREPARATION BEGINS THE DAY BEFORE)

MARINADE

1 cup peanut or vegetable oil	1 tablespoon sweet mild paprika
1 cup olive oil	1 teaspoon celery salt
1/4 cup coarsely chopped garlic	1/2 cup red wine vinegar
1 cup chopped onion	1/2 teaspoon Tabasco sauce or
3 tablespoons soy sauce	other hot sauce (optional)

24 medium-sized whole chicken
legs (legs and thighs attached)

1. Combine the marinade ingredients in a large bowl.

2. Prick the skin of the chicken legs in several places with the point

of a sharp knife. Put the chicken in a large non-metallic shallow pan or glass dish. Pour the marinade over the chicken. Turn the legs several times to coat the pieces evenly. Cover tightly with plastic wrap and refrigerate overnight.

3. Preheat the oven to 350 degrees.

4. Wipe off any garlic or onion pieces from the chicken legs and put them side by side in two large roasting pans. If necessary, put one pan on the lower shelf and the other on the next shelf up in the oven. Roast for 30 minutes.

5. Meanwhile, strain the marinade and set it aside.

6. After the chicken has cooked for 30 minutes, turn each piece and brush the chicken liberally with the marinade. Rotate the pans on the shelves. Roast for 30 minutes more, or until the legs are golden brown. Turn again, if necessary. Serve immediately or chill and serve.

More Servings
Double the recipe to serve 24 and roast in two batches. Reheat the first batch for about 8 minutes in a 350-degree oven immediately after taking the second batch out of the oven.

CORNISH GAME HENS AMANDINE

SERVES 12

12 Cornish game hens (fresh if possible)
Salt and freshly ground black pepper
12 shallots, coarsely chopped
2 teaspoons dried thyme
½ cup chopped fresh parsley leaves

6 tablespoons butter, softened
3 tablespoons peanut or vegetable oil
3 tablespoons butter
2 cups blanched almond slivers
½ cup honey
½ cup orange juice, heated

1. Preheat the oven to 400 degrees.

2. Remove the giblets from the hens and freeze the giblets for stock-making or some other use. Season the hens well inside and out with salt and pepper.

3. In a bowl, combine the shallots, thyme, and parsley. Put equal amounts of the mixture into the cavity of each hen. Rub each hen all over with ½ tablespoon of the softened butter. Fold the wings of each hen back and tie the legs together.

4. Put the hens in two large roasting pans. They must not touch each other. Roast for 45 minutes, or until the hens are golden brown and tender. If your oven won't accommodate the roasting pans on one shelf, place one pan on the lower shelf and the other on the next possible higher shelf. Cook the hens for 30 minutes. Rotate the pans and cook for about 30 minutes longer. The hens can be halved when cooked, if desired.

5. Meanwhile, heat the 3 tablespoons of oil and butter in a large frying pan and lightly toast the almond slices, stirring often. Drain on paper towels.

6. Combine the honey and warmed orange juice in a small bowl.

7. Transfer the hens to one or two large serving platters. Brush the hens with the honey mixture and sprinkle them evenly with the almonds. Serve at once.

CHICKEN SALTIMBOCCA

Substituting chicken for veal and working with the other ingredients that constitute a classic saltimbocca recipe produced this uncommonly delicious and easy company dish.

SERVES 16

¾ cup (1½ sticks) butter
½ cup chopped fresh parsley leaves
1½ tablespoons dried sage
1½ tablespoons dried rosemary
1 teaspoon dried oregano
3 tablespoons fresh lemon juice

16 medium-sized skinned and boned chicken breasts, halved
32 thin slices prosciutto or boiled ham
1 cup dry white wine

1. Preheat the oven to 400 degrees.

2. Melt the butter in a saucepan over low heat; then immediately remove it from the heat. Stir in the herbs and lemon juice.

3. Divide the chicken halves between two large roasting pans. Spoon equal amounts of the butter mixture over the chicken in each pan. Turn the chicken pieces to coat them evenly. Working directly over each pan of chicken, roll up a breast half and wrap one slice of the ham around it. Put the rolled chicken back into the pan. Repeat this procedure with the remaining 31 pieces of chicken, 16 per pan.

4. Pour ½ cup of the wine over each pan of chicken. Cover the pans tightly with aluminum foil and bake for 30 minutes.

5. Remove the foil and bake for 30 minutes longer.

6. Carefully transfer the chicken to a large warmed serving dish and spoon the pan juices over the chicken.

More Servings
Double the recipe for 32 servings and cook in two batches. When the first batch of chicken is cooked, cover and let stand until the second batch has cooked for 50 minutes. Put the two pans of the first batch on the middle shelf of the oven over the second batch on the lower shelf and reheat the first batch for 10 minutes.

CHICKEN CUTLETS POJARSKY WITH MUSHROOM-DILL SAUCE

SERVES 16

8 large chicken breasts, skinned, boned, and cut into small pieces

10 slices firm white bread with crusts trimmed, cut into cubes

1 cup heavy cream

¼ cup vodka

1 cup (2 sticks) butter, softened

2 teaspoons salt

Freshly ground white pepper

Freshly ground nutmeg to taste

All-purpose flour

4 large eggs, lightly beaten

Plain dry bread crumbs (about 3½ cups)

½ cup peanut oil, or as needed

½ cup (1 stick) butter, or as needed

MUSHROOM-DILL SAUCE

6 tablespoons butter
1½ pounds mushrooms, coarsely chopped
¼ cup fresh lemon juice
½ cups minced shallots

4 cups (1 quart) heavy cream
¼ cup chopped fresh dill
Salt and freshly ground white pepper to taste

1. Grind the chicken, 2 cups at a time, in a food processor or grinder and transfer to a large bowl.

2. Soak the bread in the combined cream and vodka in another bowl for 5 minutes. Squeeze out most of the liquid and add the bread to the chicken with the softened butter, salt, pepper, and nutmeg. Combine well. Cover and refrigerate for 30 minutes.

3. Meanwhile, make the sauce by melting the butter in a large frying pan. Add the mushrooms and cook over high heat for 10 minutes, stirring often. Drain off the liquid in the pan and reserve it. Put the mushrooms in a bowl.

4. Heat the lemon juice with the shallots in a large non-metallic saucepan and cook over high heat for a few minutes to reduce the juice by half. Add the cream and bring to a boil. Whisk constantly over high heat for 5 or 6 minutes, or until the cream thickens. Stir in the mushrooms, ¼ cup of the mushroom liquid; then season with salt and pepper. Cover the sauce and set it aside.

5. Divide the chicken mixture into 16 equal-sized portions. Form each portion into the shape of a loin lamb chop, about 1 inch thick.

6. Dust each cutlet lightly with flour; then dip the cutlets in the beaten eggs to cover evenly and coat with the bread crumbs.

7. Preheat the oven to 350 degrees.

8. Heat ½ cup of oil and ½ cup of butter in a large frying pan. Cook 5 or 6 cutlets at a time, until they are golden brown on each side. Drain on paper towels. Continue cooking the cutlets, adding small equal amounts of oil and butter when necessary.

9. Transfer the drained cutlets to a large baking sheet. Bake the cutlets for 10 minutes. Meanwhile, reheat the sauce. Arrange the cutlets on an attractive platter, garnished with fluted lemons, if desired, and serve with the sauce in a sauceboat.

More Servings
Double the recipe to serve 32. Prepare the sauce in a non-metallic 4-quart pot.

OUTDOOR PAELLA

*This outdoor paella requires two grills or one very large one. All the prep-
aration is done ahead in the kitchen, and the dish is finished outside just
before serving.*

*I served half of this recipe for eight (the recipe is easily cut in half) and
cooked it on a grill at the Harvard/Yale game a few years back, on the
stadium grounds in New Haven. It was a blustery cold day, and the steaming hot paella was most welcome. Although the crowd that gathers yearly
for the game always serves a different main course, there have been hints
that the paella would be happily accepted again.*

*Outdoor paella is lovely in the summer, too, of course. Served with a
tossed green salad, crusty bread and butter, and red wine, it makes a fine
one-dish meal. Fresh berries with flan is a complementing dessert.*

*For those not so adventurous, the paella can be cooked in the oven,
alternating the two pans on the oven shelves halfway through the cooking
time, which will be about 10 minutes longer.*

SERVES 16

8 Italian sweet sausages
6 large chicken breasts, halved and cut crosswise into 3 pieces each
Salt and freshly ground black pepper
1 cup olive oil
6 pork chops, boned and cut into 1-inch pieces
4 large garlic cloves, minced
2 cups chopped onion
2 large sweet green peppers, seeded and chopped
2½ cups chopped drained canned tomatoes

1 teaspoon powdered saffron
2 teaspoon paprika
¼ teaspoon hot red pepper flakes
9 cups (2¼ quarts) homemade chicken stock or canned broth
5 cups long-grain white rice
1 20-ounce bag frozen green peas, thawed
2 pounds shrimp, shelled and deveined
2 large pimientos, cut into thin strips

1. Prick the sausages in various areas with the point of a small sharp
knife. Simmer the sausages in a large frying pan in 1½ inches of boiling
water for 10 minutes, turning once.

2. Meanwhile, pat the chicken pieces dry and season them with salt
and pepper.

3. Heat ½ cup of the olive oil in a large frying pan and brown the chicken pieces on both sides over medium-high heat. Transfer the browned chicken to a large bowl.

4. Remove the sausages from the boiling water, drain, and cool them on a plate. Then cut the sausages into ¼-inch-thick slices and put them in the bowl with the chicken.

5. Put the remaining ½ cup of oil into a 5-quart heavy pot. Add the pork cubes, garlic, onion, and green pepper. Cook over medium heat for 8 minutes, stirring often.

6. Add the tomatoes, saffron, paprika, and red pepper flakes. Season lightly with salt and pepper. Simmer for 10 minutes.

7. Heat the grill to very hot, or, if cooking in the oven, preheat the oven to 400 degrees.

8. Bring the bowl with the chicken and sausages and the pork mixture to the grill.

9. Put the stock into a saucepan with a cover. Bring it to a boil on the grill or in the kitchen.

10. Put half of the onion and pork mixture into each of two paella pans.

11. Add half the sausages, chicken, rice, and green peas to each pan. Pour 4½ cups of the boiling stock over each pan and combine the mixture in the pans.

12. Press half of the shrimp down into the mixture around the edge of each pan. Cover the pans tightly with heavy duty aluminum foil and cook for about 35 minutes, or until the liquid has been absorbed and the rice is tender. If cooking in the oven, cook for 40 minutes, alternating the pans on the lower and upper shelves after 20 minutes.

13. Remove the foil and garnish the paella with the pimiento strips. Let the paella stand for at least 10 minutes before serving.

ROAST TURKEY WITH PESTO-PASTA STUFFING

◇ ══════════════════ ◇

SERVES 16

1 20-pound ready-to-cook
  turkey
  Salt and freshly ground black
  pepper
4 tablespoons butter, softened
1 pound ditali (small tubular-
  shaped pasta)

2 cups packed chopped fresh
  basil leaves
1 teaspoon minced garlic
1 cup pine nuts
1½ cups olive oil
1 3-ounce package cream
  cheese, softened

1. Season the turkey inside and out with salt and pepper. Rub the butter over the turkey.

2. Cook the pasta in 3½ quarts of boiling salted water until it is *al dente*, or just until tender. Drain well.

3. Meanwhile, combine the basil, garlic, pine nuts, olive oil, cream cheese, and salt and pepper to taste in a large bowl.

4. Add the pasta and toss to combine the mixture.

5. Preheat the oven to 325 degrees.

6. Stuff the turkey body and neck cavities with the mixture. Fold the neck skin over the stuffing to the back and secure it with a small metal skewer or two toothpicks. Tie the legs together.

7. Put the turkey in a large roasting pan and roast for 5 to 6 hours, basting twice.

8. After 3 hours, cover the turkey with a buttered sheet of aluminum foil. Remove the foil 30 minutes before the end of the roasting time. Let the turkey rest for 30 minutes before carving.

PECAN CHICKEN

SERVES 24

24 medium-sized chicken breasts, boned, skinned, and halved
Salt and freshly ground black pepper
3 cups all-purpose flour, or as needed

8 large eggs, beaten
4 tablespoons Dijon mustard
4 cups finely chopped (not ground) pecans
4 cups fresh bread crumbs
1½ cups (3 sticks) butter
1½ cups peanut or vegetable oil

1. Season the chicken pieces well with salt and pepper.

2. Dust each piece with flour and dip in the combined eggs and mustard.

3. Coat the chicken pieces on each side with the combined pecans and bread crumbs, pressing on gently.

4. Heat ½ cup of the butter and ½ cup of the oil in a large frying pan. Cook enough coated chicken pieces as fit comfortably in the pan at one time until they are golden brown on each side. Transfer the chicken pieces to a large baking sheet or two as they are cooked. Add equal amounts of the butter and oil as needed to cook the remaining chicken in batches.

5. Preheat the oven to 350 degrees.

6. Put the chicken on the baking sheets into the oven to reheat for about 10 minutes. Then serve immediately.

SAUSAGE-STUFFED CHICKEN BREASTS WITH CHEESE AND ONIONS

SERVES 24

24 medium-sized chicken breasts, boned
Salt and freshly ground black pepper
½ cup chopped fresh parsley leaves
24 Italian sweet sausages, pricked and simmered in water for 10 minutes

2 cups dry white wine
8 medium-sized onions, thinly sliced and separated into rings
1 pound Cheddar cheese, shredded
2 teaspoons dried thyme
3 cups plain dry bread crumbs
½ cup (1 stick) butter

1. Preheat the oven to 350 degrees.

2. Spread each chicken breast out, skin side down, and sprinkle it with salt and pepper and 1 teaspoon of the parsley.

3. Put 1 sausage link in the center of each chicken breast and roll it up, wrapping each side of the chicken around the sausage. Put the sausage-stuffed chicken breast, seam side down, in one of two large roasting pans. Assemble the remaining breasts and sausage in the same manner and continue putting side by side, in equal numbers, in each pan. Do not press them tightly together, but they should touch.

4. Spread the onions evenly over the top of the chicken rolls and pour the wine over the chicken in equal amounts.

5. Combine the cheese, thyme, and bread crumbs and sprinkle over the chicken. Cut the butter into thin slices and put equal amounts of the butter on top of the chicken in each pan. Bake for 1 hour.

More Servings
The recipe can be doubled to serve 48, but it must be cooked in two batches, unless you have two large ovens. Reheat the first batch for 10 minutes in a 350-degree oven before serving.

COLD POACHED CHICKEN BREASTS WITH FRESH HERB-MAYONNAISE GLAZE

SERVES 24

16 large chicken breasts, skinned, boned, and halved (save the bones and skins)
3 celery stalks, sliced
2 carrots, sliced

1 bay leaf
1 large onion, coarsely chopped
4 cups (1 quart) chicken stock
1 bottle dry white wine

FRESH HERB-MAYONNAISE GLAZE

1 tablespoon unflavored gelatin
½ cup fresh lemon juice
½ cup chopped fresh parsley leaves
1 tablespoon chopped fresh dill
1 tablespoon chopped fresh tarragon

4 cups (1 quart) mayonnaise at room temperature
1 large bunch watercress or parsley

1. Bring the chicken bones and skins, celery, carrots, bay leaf, onion, chicken stock, wine, and 8 cups of water to a boil in an 8-quart pot. Add the chicken breast halves and bring back to a boil slowly. If more water is needed to cover the chicken, add boiling water to just cover the chicken. Immediately lower the heat to a simmer, partially cover the pot, and cook for 15 minutes. Remove the pot from the heat, cover, and let stand for 15 minutes. Drain and cool the chicken breasts. Discard the cooking liquid and vegetables.

2. Soften the gelatin in the lemon juice in a small saucepan for 5 minutes. Heat the mixture until liquid but do not boil.

3. In a large bowl, whip the lemon mixture and herbs into the mayonnaise.

4. Trim each breast evenly and lay them on a wire rack. Spread about 3 tablespoons of the mayonnaise over each breast half.

5. Transfer the breasts to a large baking sheet or dish and refrigerate, uncovered, for several hours.

6. At serving time, arrange the breasts on a large serving platter and garnish with a bouquet of watercress or parsley.

BONELESS BAKED CHICKEN BREASTS WITH TARRAGON STUFFING

◇ ═══════════════════════ ◇

SERVES 36

36 medium-sized whole chicken breasts, boned but not skinned
Salt and freshly ground black pepper

¾ cup (1½ sticks) butter, melted, plus extra butter for greasing the pans
½ cup fresh lemon juice
Paprika

STUFFING

1 cup finely chopped shallots
3 tablespoons dried tarragon
1½ cups chopped fresh parsley leaves

4 cups fresh bread crumbs
1 cup (2 sticks) butter, melted
Salt and freshly ground black pepper

1. Season the chicken breasts with salt and pepper.
2. Combine the stuffing ingredients well.
3. Separate the skin from the meat on each side of each chicken breast. Do not separate the skin over the very center of the breast.
4. Put stuffing under each side of the breast between the meat and the skin in equal amounts. Reshape the skin over the meat. Fold each side of the breast under, making a neat chicken package. Put the breast in 1 of 2 large well-greased roasting pans.
5. Continue stuffing the remaining chicken breasts in the same manner, putting them side by side and touching in the pans, but do not press them together. At this point the chicken can be covered and refrigerated for 1 hour.
6. Preheat the oven to 350 degrees.
7. Combine the melted butter and lemon juice and brush the mixture over the breasts. Sprinkle the chicken lightly with salt, pepper, and paprika.
8. Put one pan on the lower shelf of the oven and the other pan on the middle shelf of the oven. Bake for 30 minutes; then reverse the pans on the shelves and bake for 30 minutes longer. Serve immediately.

GRILLED CHICKEN
AND VEGETABLE KEBABS

*On a recent trip to Venice, I saw a large pan of chicken and vegetable ke-
babs in the window of a butcher shop at the Rialto market. The vivid image
that I took home inspired this recipe.*

*The Rialto market is awe inspiring. It is certainly one of the greatest
markets in the world. Produce stalls neatly stacked with beautiful bouquets
of vegetables, only hours old, are at its center. The produce is surrounded
by butcher shops, pasta and cheese and dairy stores, and, on the west side,
the extraordinary fish market.*

*In the early morning, the market is a main tourist attraction to photo-
snapping visitors who must stand aside as serious home cooks and restaurant chefs busily bargain and fill their baskets. I always regret not having
a kitchen nearby to go to to cook up some of the market's treasures. My con-
solation is that I can always make a batch of Grilled Chicken and Vegetable
Kebabs at home.*

SERVES 36

36 medium-sized chicken
breasts, skinned, boned, and
halved, each cut crosswise
into 3 pieces
9 large sweet green peppers,
seeded and quartered
lengthwise and each quarter
cut into 3 pieces
5 medium-sized onions, cut
into quarters and separated

2 cups olive oil
1 cup white wine vinegar
1 cup dry white wine
1 tablespoon dried rosemary
1 tablespoon dried oregano
1 tablespoon dried sage
Salt and freshly ground black
pepper to taste

1. Assemble each kebab on an 8-inch wooden skewer (you will need
36 skewers in all) by alternating 6 pieces of the chicken with 3 pieces of
green pepper and 2 pieces of onion. Put the kebabs in 1 or 2 large shallow
stainless steel pans or glass dishes.

2. Combine the remaining ingredients well and pour over the chick-
en. Turn the kebabs to coat them evenly. Cover and refrigerate for at
least 3 hours.

3. Cook the chicken kebabs, as many as will fit comfortably, on one

or two grills, about 6 inches over the hot coals, for about 6 minutes on each side, or until the chicken is tender.

More Servings
Double the recipe to serve 72, using several pans to marinate the kebabs. Cook the kebabs on two grills or rent a large commercial one.

POLYNESIAN CHICKEN CURRY WITH CONDIMENTS

A buffet of chicken curry, hot cooked rice, ten condiments, a beautiful fresh tossed green salad, and crusty French bread served with honey butter is a remarkable easy and spectacular meal for a crowd. The curry can be made the day before and refrigerated overnight.

After a meal of the spicy curry, a sherbet with berries is an excellent choice for dessert.

SERVES 50

2 pounds (8 sticks) butter
25 pounds skinned and boned chicken (white and dark meat), cut into bite-sized pieces
4 large onions, finely chopped
8 large garlic cloves, minced
10 tablespoons curry powder, or to taste
Salt and freshly ground black pepper to taste

20 cups (5 quarts) homemade chicken stock or canned broth, or as needed
¼ cup fresh lemon juice
8 cups (2 quarts) heavy cream
Honey Butter (recipe follows)
8 loaves crusty French bread, cut into ½-inch-thick slices

CURRY CONDIMENTS
4 cups (1 quart) chutney
4 cups (1 quart) chopped sweet green and red peppers
4 cups (1 quart) toasted almond slivers

4 cups (1 quart) diced tomatoes
4 cups (1 quart) raisins
4 cups (1 quart) shredded coconut
3 cups sweet pickle relish

2 pounds bacon, cooked crisp
and chopped
4 cups (1 quart) thinly sliced
scallions

3 cups chopped fresh parsley
leaves

1. To prepare the curry, melt the butter in a large deep frying pan, sauté pan, or a seasoned paella pan. Simmer 4-cup batches of the chicken in the butter, stirring to separate the pieces constantly. The chicken is really being poached in the butter. After 10 minutes, transfer it to a large bowl using a slotted spoon and continue cooking the chicken.

2. Pour all but 1 cup of the butter out of the pan and add the onions, garlic, and curry powder. Cook over medium heat, stirring often, for 10 minutes. Do not brown the onions or garlic.

3. Transfer the onions to a 15-quart pot, or two 8-quart pots, dividing the mixture evenly. (If using two pots divide the remaining ingredients between the two pots.) Return the chicken and juice in the bowl to the pot. Season with salt and pepper and add the chicken stock and lemon juice. The stock should just cover the mixture. Add a little more, if necessary.

4. Bring the mixture to a near boil, lower the heat to a *simmer*, and cook for 30 minutes, stirring often. The chicken will begin to shred, which is as it should be.

5. Add the heavy cream, stir, and taste for seasoning. Cook for about 5 minutes, or until thoroughly heated. Serve immediately with hot cooked rice (see chart for cooking rice on page 259), the condiments, bread, and Honey Butter. If serving the curry the next day, cool it completely, cover, and refrigerate. When reheating the next day, it may be necessary to add a cup or two of broth, because the chicken will have absorbed the liquid.

HONEY BUTTER

4 cups (8 sticks) butter,
softened

$\frac{1}{2}$ cup warm honey, or to taste

Combine the butter and honey with a wooden spoon. Turn into a glass bowl, cover, and refrigerate until serving time.

TURKEY TONNATO

This splendid Italian dish can be prepared well in advance of the meal.

The turkey breast can be cooked or bought cooked, depending on how much time and money can be spent on the dish. If you are cooking the turkey breasts yourself, cook two that weigh 7 pounds each, and be sure to cool and chill them completely before slicing them. Cook the breasts following the instructions that come with the turkey.

SERVES 50

12 pounds cooked turkey breast, thinly sliced

1½ cups drained capers

TONNATO SAUCE

6 12½-ounce cans solid white meat tuna, drained

6 cups olive oil

3 2-ounce cans anchovy fillets, drained and coarsely chopped

¾ cup fresh lemon juice
Freshly ground black pepper to taste

1. Arrange the turkey slices on two large platters, cover tightly with plastic wrap, and refrigerate until ready to serve.

2. Purée 1 can of tuna and 1 cup of the olive oil at a time in a food processor or blender. Turn each batch into a large bowl. To the last can of tuna and oil add the anchovies and purée.

3. Whisk in the lemon juice and season with pepper. Cover and refrigerate.

4. At serving time, set out the platters of turkey along with bowls of the sauce and capers. Garnish the platters with parsley and fluted lemons, if desired.

Meat

◇ ════════════════════════════ ◇

We are a country of meat lovers. There is simply no substitute for competently cooked, good-quality meat dishes.

Beef, veal, lamb, and pork offer a multitude of cuts to choose from, both reasonable in cost and expensive.

Meat gives the cook the opportunity to serve succulent ragouts, stews, fricassees, roasts, casseroles, and exotic spiced international dishes, such as Beef Curry with Carrots, Médaillons of Veal with Rosemary-Cream Sauce, Moroccan Lamb Tagine, and Spicy Boneless Pork Roast with Lime and Rum Sauce.

Bobby Connors, a friend and great cook, whose corn chowder is included in this book, recently made a survey of the sixty family members who attend his annual Easter dinner. He asked what main course they all wanted. Prime rib won overwhelmingly, which is what he'd been serving at the event for years.

I have another friend who serves a traditional Christmas Eve dinner of roast beef with Yorkshire pudding, Brussels sprouts with mushrooms and red peppers, flaming plum puddings with hard sauce, followed by Stilton cheese and port. The menu, which is small, never changes, but there's plenty of it, and it is a most satisfying meal.

These two examples, plus my own experience of successfully serving succulent roast fillet, veal, lamb, or pork to large groups, proves that simple roasts are always great crowd-pleasers.

JULIE MCCLENNAN'S ROAST BEEF TENDERLOIN WITH MUSHROOM AND WINE SAUCE

SERVES 8

1 4-pound ready-to-cook beef tenderloin
2 cups dry white wine
2 tablespoons butter, melted

3 tablespoons caraway seeds
Salt and freshly ground black pepper

MUSHROOM AND WINE SAUCE

1 pound mushrooms, thinly sliced
½ cup (1 stick) butter

2 tablespoons chopped fresh parsley leaves
Salt and freshly ground black pepper to taste

1. Put the tenderloin in a glass or ceramic dish and marinate it in the wine for 2 hours at room temperature. Turn the roast often.

2. Preheat the oven to 425 degrees.

3. Remove the roast from the wine (reserve the wine) and pat it dry.

4. Put the roast in a roasting pan and brush it with the melted butter. Press the caraway seeds onto the surface of the roast and season it with salt and pepper. Roast for 20 minutes for rare; roast 5 minutes more for medium-rare.

5. Meanwhile, prepare the sauce. Melt the butter in a large frying pan and cook the mushrooms for 5 minutes, stirring often.

6. In a separate small heavy saucepan, bring the reserved wine to a boil and reduce it to about 1½ cups.

7. Transfer the cooked roast to a carving platter and let it rest for 15 minutes before carving.

8. Pour the reduced wine into the roasting pan and cook over high heat for 2 or 3 minutes. Add the mushrooms, parsley, and salt and pepper.

9. Carve the roast into very thin slices and spoon some of the sauce over each serving.

More Servings
Double the recipe to serve 16, cooking two roasts at the same time.

MÉDAILLONS OF VEAL
WITH ROSEMARY-CREAM SAUCE

SERVES 8

16 veal scallops
   Salt and freshly ground black
   pepper
   All-purpose flour
 4 tablespoons butter
 4 tablespoons vegetable oil

3 tablespoons Dijon mustard
2 tablespoons Cognac or
   brandy
3 cups heavy cream
1 teaspoon dried rosemary

1. Flatten each veal scallop between two pieces of wax paper to a
$\frac{1}{8}$-inch thickness. Season the scallops with salt and pepper and dust them
lightly with flour.

2. Heat 2 tablespoons of the butter and oil in a large frying pan and
quickly cook the scallops, a few at a time, until they are golden brown
on each side. Transfer the scallops to a dish as they are cooked and keep
them warm. After cooking half of the scallops, or when necessary, add
the remaining 2 tablespoons of butter and oil.

3. Stir the mustard and Cognac into the frying pan, scraping up any
browned-on bits in the pan. Whisk in the cream and rosemary and bring
to a boil. Cook, whisking constantly, until the cream thickens. Season
with salt and pepper to taste. Pour a little of the sauce over each serving
of veal.

More Servings
Double the recipe to serve 16, cooking the veal in two large frying pans,
if possible, and making two separate portions of the sauce (one in each
pan).

ROAST BEEF

SERVES 12

2 7½-pound prime rib roasts with bones	6 tablespoons Worcestershire sauce

ROAST BEEF GRAVY

4 tablespoons all-purpose flour	½ cup dry sherry
3½ cups homemade beef stock or canned broth	Salt and freshly ground black pepper to taste

1. Preheat the oven to 400 degrees.
2. Rub each roast with 3 tablespoons of the Worcestershire sauce.
3. Put the roasts into one large or two medium-sized roasting pans, bone side down. Roast for 1 hour and 45 minutes for rare. (Cook 10 to 15 minutes longer for medium-rare.) Allow the roasts to rest 30 minutes before carving.
4. To make the gravy, discard all but 4 tablespoons of the fat in the roasting pan. Stir the flour into the fat until the roux is smooth. Stir in the stock and sherry. Whisk constantly over high heat until the gravy thickens. Season with salt and pepper and serve with the carved roasts.

FRICASSEE OF VEAL WITH MORELS

SERVES 12

5 pounds boneless veal, cut into 1½-inch cubes Salt and freshly ground black pepper All-purpose flour	1 teaspoon dried thyme 1 bay leaf 6 ounces dried morels, soaked in 1 cup of water for 30 minutes, drained and then chopped (Reserve the strained soaking liquid.)
2 cups dry white wine	
4 tablespoons butter	
2 tablespoons vegetable oil	
48 whole shallots, peeled	2 tablespoons Dijon mustard
3 cups homemade chicken stock or canned broth	3 cups heavy cream

1. Season the veal pieces with salt and pepper and dust them lightly with flour.

2. Heat the butter and oil in a large frying pan and brown the pieces of veal in batches. Transfer the veal cubes to a bowl as they cook.

3. Pour the wine into the pan and cook over high heat for 1 minute, scraping up any browned-on bits in the pan.

4. Pour this mixture into an 8-quart pot. Add the veal, shallots, chicken stock, thyme, bay leaf, chopped morels, and morel soaking liquid. Bring to a boil and simmer for 1 hour and 30 minutes, stirring occasionally.

5. Combine the mustard and cream and stir the mixture into the fricassee. Cook for 10 minutes; then taste for seasoning.

HOT AND SPICY BEEF STROGANOFF

SERVES 16

¾ cup (1½ sticks) butter, or as needed
1 large onion, halved and cut into thin slivers
1¾ pounds mushrooms, thinly sliced
  Vegetable oil
5 pounds sirloin or tenderloin of beef, cut into strips 2 inches long and ¼ inch wide
2 cups dry red wine

3 cups canned beef broth
1 6-ounce can tomato paste
2 tablespoons Dijon mustard
1 tablespoon paprika
½ cup all-purpose flour
3 cups heavy cream
  Salt and freshly ground black pepper to taste
3 pounds medium egg noodles

1. Melt 4 tablespoons of the butter in a 6-quart pot and cook the onion over medium heat for about 8 minutes, stirring often. Do not brown. Add 3 more tablespoons of the butter and the mushrooms. Cook for about 8 minutes, stirring often.

2. Transfer the mixture to a large bowl using a slotted spoon. Pour the juices in the pot into another bowl.

3. Heat 2 tablespoons of the butter and 2 tablespoons of vegetable oil in a large frying pan. Brown the beef strips over high heat, about a

sixth of the total amount at a time, turning the strips often. As the beef is browned, transfer it to the bowl with the onion and mushrooms. Add small equal amounts of butter and oil as needed.

4. When all the beef has been browned, pour the wine into the frying pan and reduce it by half.

5. Pour the reduced wine into a clean 6-quart pot. Add the reserved mushroom liquid, 2¼ cups of the broth, tomato paste, mustard, and paprika. Stir to mix well and bring to a boil.

6. Combine the flour and the remaining ¾ cup of broth into a paste and whisk it into the liquid. Stir and cook over high heat until the sauce thickens. Cook for 3 minutes.

7. Stir in the heavy cream and season with salt and pepper. Cook over high heat for about 3 minutes, or until the sauce thickens.

8. Add the beef, mushrooms, and onions and heat through. Serve with hot buttered noodles.

ROAST BEEF TENDERLOINS EN CROÛTE WITH SPINACH AND STILTON CHEESE SAUCE

SERVES 16

2 4-pound ready-to-cook beef tenderloins
4 pounds fresh spinach, washed and stemmed
Salt
Freshly ground black pepper

Freshly ground nutmeg
2 sheets (1 pound total weight) homemade or thawed frozen puff pastry
1 large egg, beaten

STILTON CHEESE SAUCE
⅓ cup chopped shallots
1 cup dry white wine
2½ cups heavy cream
4 ounces Stilton cheese, crumbled

½ cup (1 stick) butter
Salt and freshly ground black pepper to taste

1. Roast the tenderloins following the directions in the recipe on page 136, but for only 10 minutes. Cool completely.

2. Stir the spinach into 1½ quarts of lightly salted boiling water in a pot and cook over medium heat for 5 minutes. Drain the spinach and chop it finely. Squeeze out any excess water. Season with salt, pepper, and a few gratings of nutmeg.

3. Preheat the oven to 425 degrees.

4. Pat the roasts dry with paper towels and season them. Press half of the spinach over the top of each roast.

5. Roll each of the sheets of puff pastry into rectangles ⅛ inch thick and about 3 inches longer than each roast. Cover each roast with a sheet of the pastry; then fold the pastry underneath and seal the bottom and ends. Cut a small circle in the top of each.

6. Put the roasts on a large ungreased baking sheet, and brush the pastry with the beaten egg.

7. Roast for about 18 minutes, or until the pastry has puffed and is golden brown. Let rest 10 minutes before slicing.

8. Meanwhile, prepare the sauce: Cook the shallots and wine in a large non-metallic heavy saucepan over high heat until reduced by half. Stir in the cream and boil until thickened, whisking constantly. Stir in the Stilton and whisk until melted. Beat in the butter a tablespoon at a time. Season with salt and pepper. Serve the sauce with the sliced roasts.

JACK YOGMAN'S TAMALE JIVE

SERVES 24

3 tablespoons olive oil	2 teaspoons salt
3 pounds ground beef	Freshly ground black pepper
2 large onions, chopped	to taste
2 large sweet green pepper, seeded and chopped	3 tablespoons chili powder
	1 teaspoon dried oregano
6 cups chopped peeled canned tomatoes	4 cups (1 quart) water
	3 cups yellow cornmeal
2 20-ounce packages frozen corn kernels, cooked and drained	4 dozen pitted black olives
	Paprika

1. Heat the oil in an 8-quart heavy pot. Cook the beef, onions, and peppers, stirring often, until the meat loses its pink color. Add the tomatoes, corn, salt, pepper, chili powder, and oregano. Combine well and simmer for 20 minutes.

2. Preheat the oven to 325 degrees.

3. Bring the water to a boil in a large saucepan and stir in the cornmeal. Add it to the meat mixture and combine thoroughly.

4. Turn the mixture into two 5-quart casseroles, or one 8-quart casserole. Press the olives into the mixture, making sure that the mixture covers them. Sprinkle with paprika.

5. Cover the casserole and bake for 1 hour.

MATRAMBE

◇ ══════════════ ◇

SERVES 24

4 2-pound flank steaks (Butterfly each steak by cutting through the center of each steak horizonally lengthwise to about ¾ inch from the opposite side.)

2 tablespoons chili powder
Salt and freshly ground black pepper

4 large garlic cloves, minced

2 teaspoons dried oregano

8 large (the longest possible) carrots, scraped and quartered lengthwise

1 large onion, cut into ¼-inch-thick slivers

1 cup chopped fresh parsley leaves

1 pound whole string beans with ends trimmed

4 cups (1 quart) homemade beef stock or canned broth

1 cup red wine vinegar

1. Open up each steak and sprinkle the insides with chili powder, salt, pepper, garlic, and oregano.

2. Place 8 carrot sticks across each roast, opposite the grain of the meat. In the same direction, put equal amounts of the onion, parsley, and string beans.

3. Preheat the oven to 400 degrees.

4. Roll up each steak from the end opposite to where the cut was made and tie up the steak with string.

5. Put each steak in the center of an 18-inch-long sheet of heavy duty

aluminum foil and lift all sides up. Pour 1 cup of the stock and ¼ cup of the wine vinegar over each steak. Gather and close the foil securely over the top of the steaks.

6. Put the foil-wrapped steaks on a large baking sheet and bake for 1 hour. Let rest for 15 minutes before opening the packages. Drain the liquid in the packages into a pan. Let the steaks rest for an additional 10 minutes before slicing. Serve the heated liquid with the steak slices.

COLD ROAST FILLET OF BEEF WITH GREEN PEPPERCORN AND MUSTARD SAUCE

SERVES 36

4 4½-pound ready-to-cook beef tenderloins
4 tablespoons butter

1 cup coarsely chopped shallots
Salt and freshly ground black pepper

GREEN PEPPERCORN AND MUSTARD SAUCE

1 cup Dijon mustard
3 cups mayonnaise
3 cups sour cream
4 tablespoons drained green peppercorns (Use peppercorns from Madagascar, if possible.)

½ cup chopped fresh parsley leaves

1. Preheat the oven to 425 degrees.
2. Sear each roast in a large frying pan with 1 tablespoon of the butter until it is browned all over.
3. Put the roasts in two large roasting pans. Add ½ cup of the shallots to each pan. Season the roasts with salt and pepper.
4. Roast for 20 minutes for rare. Remove two roasts and return the remaining two tenderloins to the oven for 5 minutes longer for medium-rare. This will give your guests a choice of doneness.
5. Cool the roasts. Cover them and chill thoroughly.
6. Combine the sauce ingredients, cover, and chill.
7. Carve the roasts into very thin slices and serve with the sauce.

BEEF CURRY WITH CARROTS

SERVES 36

14 pounds lean cross-rib roast, cut into ¼-inch-thick slices about 2 inches long and 1 inch wide
2 tablespoons salt
6 tablespoons curry powder
Freshly ground black pepper
10 tablespoons all-purpose flour
3 large onions, chopped

4 large garlic cloves, minced
4 pounds carrots, scraped and diced
4 cups (1 quart) homemade or canned tomato sauce
4 cups (1 quart) dry red wine
4 cups (1 quart) homemade beef stock or canned broth
4 cups diced peeled potatoes

1. Preheat the oven to 425 degrees.
2. Put the meat into a 12-quart casserole or baking dish and sprinkle with the salt, curry powder, and pepper. Toss well and bake, uncovered, for 30 minutes. Sprinkle with the flour and toss. Bake for 5 minutes.
3. Remove the casserole from the oven and lower the oven temperature to 300 degrees.
4. Add the remaining ingredients, except the potatoes. Combine, cover, and bake for 1 hour and 15 minutes.
5. Add the potatoes and gently combine with the other ingredients. Cover and bake for 1 hour. Season with additional salt and pepper, if necessary.

WILLIAM E. BURROWS' KOREAN BEEF

William E. Burrows is the director of New York University's new graduate program in science and environmental reporting. Recently he told me, "This zesty recipe debuted at our home when we had the first annual barbecue for the new program for one hundred guests. The idea was to offer a meat course that was simple to prepare and cook, but which was far more exotic than the usual frank and hamburger combination. We bought and prepared sixty pounds of flank steak, which was about twelve pounds too much. (More about the solution to that later.) The beef was cooked over charcoal on a large stone barbecue, and was turned repeatedly about ten minutes per batch. Platters of the steaming beef were sent to join salad primavera, capponata, and assorted cheeses, and they disappeared as fast as they were sent to the table.

"We divided the twelve pounds of uncooked beef that survived into meal-sized portions, and wrapped and stored them in the freezer. On a hunch, I took out one of the packages during the football season and, after it thawed, pan-fried the beef and spread it on split hero rolls, which were then doused with barbecue sauce and sprinkled with shredded mozzarella. Then I broiled the sandwiches until the cheese began to brown and bubble. The sandwiches were served with cold beer. They disappeared rapidly, accompanied by a chorus of contented, and very audible, sighs."

SERVES 50

12 2-pound flank steaks, cut into ¼-inch-thick slices
1½ cups sugar
24 scallions, cut into 2-inch lengths and shredded
½ cup minced garlic
1½ cups light soy sauce
2 teaspoons freshly ground black pepper
1 cup sesame seeds, toasted
1 cup Oriental sesame oil
1 cup peanut oil

1. Combine the beef and sugar in a very large bowl and let stand at room temperature for 1 hour.

2. Combine the remaining ingredients and pour the mixture over the beef. Turn the beef pieces to coat them evenly. Marinate for 30 minutes, or up to 1 hour.

3. Grill as many strips of beef as will fit comfortably onto the grill at a time, about 5 inches from the heat source. Take care not to let the strips slip off the grill into the coals. Serve as cooked.

CHILI

◇ ══════ ◇

I can think of no other dish that creates such passionate disagreement as chili. The many annual chili cook-offs only seem to increase opposing views on the best formulas or secret ingredients: which meat is better—brisket or chuck, beans or no beans, masa harina or none, tomatoes or no tomatoes, beer or water, a square of Mexican chocolate, oregano, or tequila.

The rules of the Annie Oakley Cook-Off several years ago were: 1. Re-

strain from snuff dipping while leaning over chili pots; 2. Avoid playing tricks on other contestants, and absolutely no rubber snakes or plastic spiders in the cooking area; and 3. When the winners are announced, there will be no pinching, biting, or jostling.

Here are two chili offerings that will allow you to continue the debate right in your own home. Every guest can sample some of each.

SERVES 50

TEXAS WATERLESS CHILI

9 pounds chuck roast, cut into 1½-inch cubes
3 pounds pork roast, cut into 1½-inch cubes
½ cup bacon drippings
2 large onions, coarsely chopped
8 large garlic cloves, minced

8 tablespoons chili powder
4 tablespoons cumin seeds
2 tablespoons paprika
Beer
1 tablespoon salt, or to taste
2 tablespoons masa harina
Finely chopped jalapeño peppers to taste

1. In a large heavy kettle, sear the meat on all sides, in the bacon drippings, a few cups at a time.
2. Return the meat to the kettle and sprinkle with the onions, garlic, chili, cumin, and paprika. Combine well. Add enough beer to cover the meat by 1 inch. Bring to a boil; then immediately lower the heat and simmer the chili for 3 hours, stirring occasionally.
3. Remove the meat and shred it with two forks.
4. Return the meat to the pot and season the chili with salt. Add more beer, if necessary; the meat should be just covered. Simmer for 2 hours longer, stirring often.
5. Just before serving stir in the masa harina and the peppers.

GRINGO CHILI

6 tablespoons olive oil
2 large onions, finely chopped
4 large garlic cloves, minced
5 large sweet green peppers,
  seeded and chopped
10 pounds ground beef
3 16-ounce cans tomato purée
2 28-ounce cans imported
  Italian whole tomatoes with
  liquid, chopped
4 cups (1 quart) water, or as
  needed

1 cup tomato paste
8 tablespoons chili powder
4 tablespoons ground cumin
2 teaspoons ground coriander
¼ teaspoon cayenne pepper
1 tablespoon dried oregano
  Salt to taste
6 cups (1½ quarts) canned chili
  beans, rinsed and drained
1 cup finely chopped mild
  green chilies

1. Heat the oil in a large heavy kettle. Cook the onion, garlic, and green pepper for about 5 minutes, stirring often.

2. Add the meat and cook until it has lost its pink color.

3. Add the remaining ingredients, except the beans and green chilies. Simmer over low heat for 2 hours, stirring often. Add water when necessary.

4. Stir in the beans and green chilies and taste for seasoning. Simmer for 30 minutes.

BROILED BONELESS LOIN LAMB CHOPS WITH FRIED ROSEMARY

SERVES 8

16 1½-inch-thick loin lamb
   chops
1 tablespoon fresh rosemary,
   or 1 teaspoon dried rosemary
5 tablespoons butter, melted

Salt and freshly ground black
pepper
Peanut oil
16 sprigs fresh rosemary

1. Bone the lamb chops; then wrap each into a circle and tie them with kitchen string.

2. Put the chops into one or two large broiler pans and brush them with the combined rosemary and butter. Sprinkle with salt and pepper.

3. Cook the lamb chops under the broiler for about 6 minutes per side, brushing with the rosemary butter after turning them, until they are golden brown on the outside and pink on the inside. Cook 2 minutes longer for well-done.

4. Meanwhile, heat 1 inch of peanut oil in a heavy saucepan and fry the rosemary sprigs, four or five at a time, until they are crisp; this will only take a few seconds. Drain on paper towels. Garnish each chop with a sprig of fried rosemary.

FRENCH ROAST LEG OF LAMB

Over the years, many families joyfully establish special traditional meals for particular holidays. A classic French menu, which might start an Easter tradition in your home, begins with fresh asparagus with hollandaise sauce, followed with a Roast Leg of Lamb, Gratin Dauphinois, a mixed green salad, and a cheese tray. For dessert, an Apple Tart with Crème Fraîche. There is nothing innovative about this menu, but it is, in my opinion, an elegant, perfectly balanced, and satisfying meal for any occasion. The recipes for Gratin Dauphinois and Apple Tart are listed in the index.

SERVES 8

1 7½-pound leg of lamb
2 large garlic cloves, cut into 4 slivers each
2 tablespoons butter, melted
½ teaspoon dried rosemary

½ teaspoon dried thyme
Salt and freshly ground black pepper
4 medium-sized onions, quartered

NATURAL GRAVY
2 cups homemade beef stock or canned broth

½ cup red Bordeaux wine

1. Preheat the oven to 450 degrees.

2. Make eight shallow slits in the lamb in various areas and insert one garlic sliver in each.

3. Brush the lamb with the melted butter, sprinkle with the herbs, and season lightly with salt and pepper. Insert a meat thermometer into the thickest part of the lamb, not touching the bone, and put the lamb in a shallow roasting pan. Roast for 15 minutes.

4. Lower the oven temperature to 350 degrees and surround the roast with the onions. Return to the oven for about 1½ hours for pink or medium-rare. The thermometer should register 145 degrees.

5. Transfer the roast to a carving platter and let rest for 20 minutes.

6. Spoon the fat out of the roasting pan. Add the beef stock and the wine. Bring to a boil and stir, scraping up the browned-on bits in the bottom of the pan. Add the juices that have accumulated in the platter with the roast. Season with salt and pepper to taste and cook over high heat for about 3 minutes.

7. Strain the gravy and serve it in a sauceboat with the carved lamb.

More Servings
Roast two legs of lamb and double the gravy ingredients to serve 16.

BUTTERFLIED HERB-MARINATED GRILLED LEG OF LAMB

◇ ═══════════════════════════════════════ ◇

SERVES 12

1 cup vegetable oil
1 cup olive oil
½ cup red wine vinegar
½ cup fresh lemon juice
1 cup finely chopped onion
4 large garlic cloves, minced
1 tablespoon dried rosemary
2 teaspoons dried oregano
2 teaspoons dried mint

½ cup chopped fresh parsley
  leaves
¼ teaspoon Tabasco sauce
1 teaspoon salt
  Freshly ground black pepper
  to taste
2 6½-pound legs of lamb,
  boned and butterflied with
  fat cut off

1. In a large bowl, put the oils, vinegar, lemon juice, onion, garlic, rosemary, oregano, mint, parsley, Tabasco sauce, salt, and pepper. Combine with a wire whisk.

2. Put the legs of lamb, opened with the boned side up, in one or two large glass or ceramic rectangular-shaped dish or dishes. Pour equal amounts of the marinade over each leg of lamb. Cover them tightly and refrigerate overnight. Turn the lamb every few hours.

3. Wipe off any onion, garlic, or herbs from the legs of lamb. Strain the marinade and reserve it.

4. Cook the legs of lamb on a large grill, or two regular-sized grills, or cook one at a time for 15 minutes. Turn the lamb and baste it with the marinade. Grill for about 12 minutes on the other side for pink on the inside, or 4 or 5 minutes longer for medium-well done.

5. Remove the lamb to a cutting board and let it rest for 10 minutes before carving it into thin slices.

6. In a small saucepan, heat the remaining marinade and brush it over the lamb slices before serving them.

MOROCCAN LAMB TAGINE

SERVES 12

3 tablespoons butter

3 tablespoons Oriental sesame oil

2 teaspoons ground turmeric

1½ teaspoons ground coriander

1 tablespoon ground ginger

1½ teaspoons ground cumin

½ teaspoon powdered saffron

2 cinnamon sticks

7 pounds boneless lamb shoulder, cut into ½-inch pieces

4 cups (1 quart) homemade chicken stock or canned broth

1 large onion, chopped

½ cup honey

1 12-ounce package pitted prunes

3 tablespoons toasted sesame seeds (Toast under the broiler on a baking sheet for 3 minutes, stirring often.)

1 12-ounce package dried apricots

1. Heat the butter and oil in a heavy 6-quart pot. Add the spices and stir. Add the lamb and turn to coat the pieces evenly. Simmer for 10 minutes.

2. Add the stock and bring to a boil slowly. Cover and cook for 1 hour, stirring occasionally.

3. Add the onion and honey, stir well, and simmer, uncovered, for about 45 minutes, or until the lamb is tender.

4. Stir in the prunes and sesame seeds and simmer for 5 minutes.

5. Add the apricots, stir, and simmer for 5 minutes.

More Servings
Double the recipe to serve 24, using 12 pounds of lamb. Cook in a 10- to 12-quart pot.

MOUSSAKA
◇ ══════════ ◇

SERVES 16

4 medium-sized eggplants, cut lengthwise into ¼-inch-thick slices
Salt
Olive oil
2½ pounds ground lamb
2 cups chopped onion
3 large garlic cloves, minced
½ cup chopped fresh parsley leaves
½ teaspoon dried thyme
1 teaspoon dried oregano

1 teaspoon ground cinnamon
Few gratings of fresh nutmeg
1 35-ounce can imported Italian whole tomatoes, chopped (Reserve 1¼ cups of the liquid in the can.)
3 tablespoons tomato paste
2 large eggs, lightly beaten
½ cup plain dry bread crumbs
½ cup freshly grated Parmesan cheese

SAUCE
6 tablespoons all-purpose flour
6 tablespoons butter
3 cups milk
½ teaspoon salt

4 large egg yolks
2 tablespoons freshly grated Parmesan cheese

1. Sprinkle the eggplant slices with a little salt and cook in batches in a large frying pan with a little oil until lightly browned on each side. Set aside.

2. In a large pot, combine the meat with the onion and garlic and cook until the the lamb has lost its pink color. Drain off the fat.

3. Stir in 1 teaspoon salt, the herbs, spices, tomatoes with the 1¼ cups liquid, and tomato paste. Simmer for 20 minutes; then cool slightly and stir in the beaten eggs.

4. To make the sauce, melt the butter in a saucepan; then add the flour and cook for 1 minute, whisking constantly. Stir in the milk and salt and bring to boil. Cook until thickened and smooth, whisking constantly. Remove from the heat and cool for 5 minutes. Beat in the egg yolks and simmer for a few minutes over very low heat.

5. Preheat the oven to 350 degrees.

6. Grease two 9- by 13- by 3-inch baking pans with olive oil. Sprinkle ¼ cup of the bread crumbs over the bottom of each pan. Cover the bread crumbs with a layer of eggplant slices; then make a layer of half of the meat mixture in each pan. Top with another layer of the eggplant slices and the rest of the meat mixture. Pour equal amounts of the sauce over each pan and sprinkle each with ¼ cup of Parmesan cheese. Bake for 1 hour. Let stand for 10 minutes before serving.

MARINATED GREEK LAMB KEBABS

SERVES 24

9½ pounds lean boneless lamb (leg or shoulder), cut into 1½-inch cubes
2 cups olive oil
½ cup fresh lemon juice
½ cup dry white wine
2 teaspoons minced garlic

1 tablespoon dried rosemary
1 teaspoon freshly ground black pepper
2 tablespoons salt
2 large onions, cut into 1½-inch pieces

1. Put the meat in a large dish or bowl.

2. Combine the next 7 ingredients (through the salt) and pour the

mixture over the lamb. Turn the pieces to coat them evenly, cover, and refrigerate for 3 or 4 hours or overnight.

3. On each of 24 8- to 9-inch metal or dampened wooden skewers, center alternating pieces of lamb and onion, about 4 or 5 pieces of meat per skewer. (Save the marinade.)

4. Cook the kebabs, as many as will fit comfortably on your grill at a time, about 5 inches over the heat source, for 8 minutes on each side. After turning the kebabs, brush them with the marinade. Serve as cooked.

More Servings
Double the recipe to serve 48 or to make 48 kebabs.

IRISH STEW

SERVES 36

9 pounds boneless lean lamb shoulder, cut into 1½-inch cubes
4 large onions, chopped
10 pounds boiling potatoes, peeled and cubed
3 pounds carrots, scraped and diced
6 celery stalks, sliced

1 bay leaf
2 teaspoons dried thyme
20 cups (5 quarts) homemade chicken stock or canned broth
Salt and freshly ground black pepper
½ cup chopped fresh parsley leaves

1. In a 12-quart pot, make layers of the lamb cubes, onions, potatoes, carrots, and celery. Add the bay leaf and sprinkle with thyme. Pour the stock over the top and season with salt and pepper.

2. Bring to a boil, cover, and simmer for about 2 hours and 30 minutes. Stir gently twice during the cooking time. Taste for seasoning and add the parsley.

CHRIS PAPPAS' SPIT-ROASTED LAMB

◊ ══════════════════════════════════ ◊

Chris Pappas, born in Greece, has roasted many lambs for block parties, christenings, and other celebrations. He originally gave me this recipe for a previous cookbook, Fearless Cooking for Men. *I have to agree with him that spit-roasting a lamb is a rather Herculean task, but one that always brings with it a festive feeling, great satisfaction, and delicious lamb.*

I have spiced up the seasoning in this recipe, but the clear instructions remain Chris'.

SERVES 50

1 30- to 35-pound whole lamb, cleaned, washed, and dried
1 cup salt
½ cup dried oregano
½ cup dried rosemary
10 garlic cloves, crushed and peeled
2 tablespoons sweet paprika
1 tablespoon freshly ground black pepper

Combine the seasonings and set aside.

EQUIPMENT

1 large spit: approximately 6 feet long, pointed iron or wooden rod for holding meat over the fire. The diameter can range from ½ inch to 1½ inches. It should have a turning handle at one end.
2 stakes: Y-shaped to hold the spit.
Butcher cord: To tie lamb to spit.
Needle and heavy thread: For sewing up cavity.
Sharp pointed knife and butcher's cleaver.
Meat holders: Metal prongs to secure lamb to spit (optional)
Several 20-pound bags coal, depending on size of lamb and weather.
(A large outdoor grill or rotisserie with electric spit attachments can be rented, too.)

PREPARATION OF PIT

Prepare a barbecue pit slightly larger than the length of the lamb. Line the bottom of the pit with flat stones, a sheet of metal, or heavy duty foil. Drive the stakes into the ground at each end of the pit, slightly off center. Prepare a good hot charcoal fire.

PREPARATION OF LAMB

Insert the spit through the lamb. Secure the centered lamb onto the spit by making holes on both sides of the spine in three places: before kidney chops or hind legs, at middle of rib cage, and at the end of the shoulder blades. Put string through holes and tie tightly to prevent slipping during cooking. Flatten front legs to neck and tie securely. Spread and extend hind legs before tying.

Season the shoulder blades by making two slashes the width of a knife and putting some of the seasoning inside the slashes. Repeat for hindquarters. Season the inside of the lamb with the remaining seasoning, rubbing some into the outer skin surface. Using a large needle and heavy thread sew up the entire belly and rib cage of lamb.

Place the spit onto Y-shaped stakes about 1 to 1½ feet from the coals. During the first hour, the coals are spread evenly the full length of the lamb. Turn the lamb continuously about 40 rpm. Have everyone take turns. As the lamb cooks, rake the coals away from the center of the lamb and concentrate the heat on the shoulder and rump sections. Depending on weather conditions, heat reflectors may be used to concentrate the heat on critical areas. Turning may be slowed as cooking continues. Cooking varies due to conditions. A 30-pound lamb will cook in about 4 hours. Check for doneness when meat starts separating from the shoulder blades and legs. The lamb is cooked if the hip bones expose themselves and are cool to the touch. Remove the cooked lamb from the fire but still on the spit and lean against a wall for 15 minutes to cool.

Carve the lamb with a meat cleaver and sharp knife.

INDONESIAN PORK AND PINEAPPLE RAGOUT WITH PEANUT SAUCE

◇ ══════════════════════════════════════ ◇

Serve this dish with sautéed green bananas and hot cooked rice.

SERVES 8

⅓ cup peanut oil
3½ pounds boneless lean pork loin, cut into ¾-inch cubes
⅓ cup finely chopped shallots
Canned ground black pepper
3 16-ounce cans pineapple chunks including liquid
2 tablespoons curry powder

2 large sweet green peppers, chopped
3 tablespoons chopped fresh parsley leaves
⅛ teaspoon Tabasco sauce
Salt to taste
¾ cup chunky peanut butter

1. Heat the oil in a 6-quart heavy-bottomed pot. Add the pork cubes and shallots. Sprinkle liberally with the pepper and cook over medium-high heat for 15 minutes, stirring often.

2. Add the pineapple and liquid and curry powder. Stir, cover, and simmer for 20 minutes.

3. Add the green peppers, parsley, Tabasco sauce, and salt. Simmer, uncovered, for 20 minutes.

4. Stir in the peanut butter and cook for a few minutes, or until it is throughly heated and the sauce has thickened.

PORK CHOPS NORMANDY

SERVES 8

8 1½-inch-thick large loin pork chops
Salt and freshly ground black pepper
All-purpose flour
4 tablespoons butter
1 tablespoon vegetable oil
1 cup chopped onion
1 large garlic clove, minced
1½ cups apple juice
1 pound fresh mushrooms, quartered
3 Red Delicious apples, cored, peeled, and cut into ¼-inch-thick slices
⅓ cup Calvados
1 tablespoon arrowroot or cornstarch
1½ cups heavy cream

1. Season the chops with salt and pepper. Then dust them with flour. Heat the butter and oil in one or two large frying pans and brown the chops on each side.

2. Add the onion, garlic, and apple juice. Cover and simmer for 25 minutes. Turn the chops. (If using two pans, divide the onion, garlic, and apple juice between the two pans.)

3. Add the mushrooms, apples, and Calvados. Cover and simmer for 15 minutes, or until the chops are completely cooked.

4. Transfer the chops to a heated serving dish. Spoon the onions, mushrooms, and apples on top of the chops using a large slotted spoon, letting as much liquid as possible drain out of each spoonful back into the pan.

5. Dissolve the arrowroot in a little cold water and stir into the liquid in the pan. Season with salt and pepper to taste. Add the cream and bring to a boil. Cook over high heat for about 5 minutes, whisking often, until the sauce has thickened. Spoon the sauce over the chops and vegetables. Serve immediately.

PORK MÉDAILLONS WITH MUSTARD AND CORNICHON SAUCE

SERVES 8

1 6½-pound boned, rolled, and
tied pork loin roast

Salt and freshly ground black
pepper

MUSTARD AND CORNICHON SAUCE

1 cup dry white wine
¼ cup finely chopped shallots
3 cups heavy cream
2 tablespoons Dijon mustard,
or to taste

¾ cup thinly sliced cornichon
pickles
Salt and freshly ground black
pepper to taste

1. Preheat the oven to 350 degrees.

2. Season the roast with salt and pepper and put it in a roasting pan. Roast for about 1 hour and 30 minutes, or until thoroughly cooked but not dry. Let rest for 15 minutes.

3. Meanwhile, make the sauce by combining the wine and shallots in a small heavy saucepan. Reduce the wine to ¼ cup over high heat.

4. Boil the cream in a non-metallic saucepan until it has thickened, about 5 to 8 minutes. Whisk in the shallots, wine, mustard, and cornichons. Season with salt and pepper.

5. Discard the string and carve the pork into thin slices. Serve with the sauce.

More Servings
Prepare two roasts and double the sauce recipe to serve 16.

BARBECUED SPARERIBS

SERVES 12

4 sides of spareribs, about 3½
  to 4 pounds each
¾ cups (1½ sticks) butter
1 large onion, finely chopped
2 large garlic cloves, minced
3 cups ketchup

⅓ cup red wine vinegar
⅓ cup dark soy sauce
3 tablespoons Worcestershire
  sauce
3 tablespoons chili powder
¼ cup honey

1. Preheat the oven to 375 degrees.

2. Put the spareribs in two large roasting pans, two sides per pan. Bake for 30 minutes. Turn the ribs in each pan.

3. Meanwhile, melt the butter in a large saucepan. Add the onion and garlic and cook for 5 minutes. Add the remaining ingredients and simmer over very low heat for 20 minutes.

4. Transfer the ribs from the pans to a large platter. Pour off the fat from the pans. Cut the sides into individual ribs.

6. Return the ribs to the pans and brush them with the sauce. Bake for 15 minutes. Turn the ribs and baste and cook for 15 minutes longer. Pass under the broiler to crisp them. Serve immediately.

More Servings
Double the recipe to serve 24 and cook in two batches. Reheat the first batch on the middle shelf of the oven during the last 10 minutes of cooking time for the second batch.

SPICY BONELESS PORK ROAST
WITH LIME AND RUM SAUCE

SERVES 12

2 5½-pound boneless pork roasts, with no more than ½ inch of fat, rolled and tied
2 large garlic cloves, minced
2 teaspoons ground ginger
2 teaspoons ground cumin
½ teaspoon ground nutmeg
1 teaspoon ground coriander
1 cup packed dark brown sugar
½ cup dark rum
2 cups homemade chicken stock or canned broth
½ cup fresh lime juice
2 tablespoons light soy sauce
1 tablespoon cornstarch
Salt and freshly ground black pepper to taste

1. Preheat the oven to 350 degrees.

2. Put the roasts in a large roasting pan and roast, fat side up, for 1 hour.

3. Remove the roasts from the oven and pour off any fat. Combine the garlic, spices, brown sugar, and rum and spread equal amounts over each roast. Combine the stock, lime juice, and soy sauce and pour the mixture into the pan.

4. Return to the oven and roast for 1 hour, basting the roasts with the liquid in the pan every 15 minutes.

5. Transfer the roasts to a cutting board and let them rest for 10 minutes.

6. Meanwhile, bring the liquid in the pan to a boil. Dissolve the cornstarch in a little cold water and whisk it into the pan. Stir until the sauce thickens slightly. Season with salt and pepper.

7. Carve the roasts into thin slices and spoon the sauce over the slices.

BÄCKEOFE

◊ ══════════ ◊

Alsatian Baker's Casserole

SERVES 16

(PREPARATION BEGINS THE NIGHT BEFORE)

3 pounds boneless cross-rib roast, cut into 1½-inch cubes

3 pounds boneless lean pork loin, cut into 1½-inch cubes

3 pounds boneless lean leg or shoulder of lamb, cut into 1½-inch cubes

2 large onions, chopped

4 leeks (white parts only), washed and cut into ½-inch lengths

4 large garlic cloves, minced

3 bay leaves

4 cups Riesling (The same wine should be served with the dish.)

¼ cup gin

1 teaspoon dried thyme
  Salt and freshly ground black pepper

4 pounds small boiling potatoes, peeled and cut into ⅓-inch-thick slices

¼ cup chopped fresh parsley leaves

1½ cups homemade beef stock or canned broth

1. Combine the cubed meat, half of the onions, the leeks, garlic, and bay leaves in a very large bowl. Pour 2 cups of the wine and the gin over the meat and mix well. Cover and refrigerate overnight.

2. Preheat the oven to 375 degrees.

3. Arrange alternating layers of the combined potatoes and remaining cup of chopped onion and the meat in a 10-quart *earthenware* casserole, if possible, seasoning the layers with salt and pepper, and ending with a layer of potatoes and onions.

4. Stir the parsley into the marinade and combine with the remaining 2 cups of wine and the beef stock in a saucepan. Bring to a boil. Pour the hot stock over the top of the casserole. Cover tightly and bake for 3 hours, or until the meat is fork-tender.

FRESH ROAST HAM

◇════════════════◇

SERVES 16

6 medium-sized onions,
   chopped
6 large garlic cloves, chopped
6 carrots, scraped and chopped
6 celery stalks, chopped

2 parsnips, peeled and chopped
1 14-pound fresh ham
2 bottles dry white wine
   Salt and freshly ground black
   pepper

1. Preheat the oven to 400 degrees.
2. Put the vegetables into a large roasting pan.
3. Put the ham, fat side up, over the vegetables and pour in the wine. Season the ham with salt and pepper.
4. Lower the oven temperature to 325 degrees and bake for about 7 hours, basting occasionally, or until the ham is thoroughly cooked or a meat thermometer registers 185 degrees. Let the ham rest for 30 minutes before carving.
5. Strain the liquid in the pan, discarding the vegetables, and spoon off as much fat as possible. Serve the pan gravy with the roast.

SWEET AND HOT ITALIAN SAUSAGE CACCIATORE

◇════════════════◇

SERVES 24

24 Italian sweet sausages
24 Italian hot sausages
½ cup olive oil
 2 large onions, halved
   lengthwise and cut into thin
   slices
 4 large garlic cloves, minced
 4 large sweet red peppers,
   seeded and cut into thin
   strips

4 large sweet green peppers,
  seeded and cut into thin
  strips
2 28-ounce cans imported
  Italian whole tomatoes with
  liquid, coarsely chopped
1 cup dry white wine
8 cups (2 quarts) homemade
  chicken stock or canned
  broth

1 teaspoon dried oregano
1 teaspoon dried basil
1 teaspoon dried thyme
3 tablespoons chopped fresh
  parsley leaves

1 bay leaf
  Salt and freshly ground black
  pepper to taste
½ cup (1 stick) butter, softened
6 tablespoons all-purpose flour

1. Preheat the oven to 325 degrees.

2. Prick each sausage in several places with the point of a small sharp knife. Put in 1 or 2 large roasting pans and bake for 30 minutes. Turn the sausages halfway through the cooking time.

3. Drain the sausages.

4. Meanwhile, in an 8-quart heavy pot, heat the oil. Cook the onions, garlic, and peppers over low heat for 10 minutes. Add the next 8 ingredients (through the bay leaf) and combine.

5. Cut the sausages into ¼-inch-thick slices and stir them into the mixture. Season with salt and pepper and slowly bring to a boil. Simmer for 30 minutes.

6. Mash the butter and flour together with a fork and stir the paste into the pot bit by bit. Bring to a boil, stirring, and cook for about 5 minutes. Serve with hot cooked buttered spaghetti or other pasta, if desired.

HUNGARIAN PORK GOULASH

SERVES 36

1 cup vegetable oil
9 pounds boneless pork loin,
  cut into 1½-inch cubes
4 large onions, cut into thin
  slivers
5 large garlic cloves, minced
3 tablespoons mild paprika
1 tablespoons dried savory
2 teaspoons dried marjoram
2 tablespoons caraway seeds

2 35-ounce cans imported
  Italian whole tomatoes with
  liquid, chopped
6 cups (1½ quarts) homemade
  beef stock or canned broth
1 cup dry white wine
1 tablespoon salt
  Freshly ground black pepper
  to taste
6 large sweet red peppers,
  seeded and thinly sliced

1. Heat the oil in a 12-quart pot and toss with the meat while heating. Add the next 9 ingredients (through the wine) and combine. Season with salt and pepper. Bring to a boil; then immediately lower the heat and simmer, covered, for 1 hour.

2. Stir in the red peppers and simmer, covered, for another hour. Taste for seasoning. Serve with hot buttered noodles.

Vegetable
and Fruit Dishes

◇════════════════════════◇

Vegetables and fruits are good reasons to rejoice, whether you're cooking for one or fifty. There has never been a more bountiful variety available to us.

A healthy change in our eating habits had resulted in an enormous demand for fresh vegetables and fruit, which is being met by America's own farms, from many countries around the world, and our own backyards and terrace gardens.

Thomas Jefferson said, "There is no other occupation as rewarding as the culture of the earth." This year, I ate my first grown-from-seed papaya, and served it with a wedge of a lime from the tree in the front yard of my home in St. Thomas. I never enjoyed fruit more. In New York City, fat basil leaves from a windowsill herb garden for a fresh tomato salad, and world-class zucchini and tomatoes from my miniscule garden in Long Island have brought incredible satisfaction. Thomas Jefferson was right.

The recipes included here offer different vegetables and fruits in many combinations—fried, broiled, baked, braised, steamed, and stewed. They include: Batter-Fried Zucchini Rings, Broiled Apple Slices, Corn Pudding with Pimientos and Cumin, Braised Cabbage and Carrots in Riesling, Chinese Mixed Vegetables, and Sweet-and-Sour Fruit Ratatouille.

Extra care should be taken not to overcook vegetables or fruits, and to buy them seasonally, when they are plentiful, delicious, and inexpensive.

Remember that vegetables and fruits should be cooked just before serving, unless they are to be served cold.

165

BATTER-FRIED ZUCCHINI RINGS

SERVES 8

4 medium-to-large zucchini (each about 2 inches in diameter)

Salt
Peanut or vegetable oil

BEER BATTER

1½ cups all-purpose flour
1½ cups beer at room temperature
1 large egg, lightly beaten

1½ teaspoons salt
Freshly ground black pepper to taste

1. Cut the zucchini into ⅓-inch-thick slices. Cut out the center of each slice of zucchini using a 1¼-inch-round pastry or cookie cutter. (This can be done by hand with a small pointed knife, but it will take much longer.) Sprinkle the zucchini slices with salt.

2. Combine the Beer Batter ingredients in a large bowl and beat with a wire whisk.

3. Heat 1½ inches of oil in a deep-fat fryer or deep heavy frying pan. Pat the zucchini rings dry and dip them in the batter, letting any extra batter drip off. Fry the rings in the oil, several at a time, until they are golden brown on each side. Drain on paper towels; then sprinkle the rings with additional salt and serve immediately.

SAUTÉED ASPARAGUS WITH ENDIVE

SERVES 8

2½ pounds fresh asparagus with stalk ends removed, cut on the diagonal into 1-inch lengths
4 tablespoons butter
3 tablespoons olive oil

4 large Belgian endives, cut on the diagonal into ½-inch slices and separated
Salt and freshly ground black pepper to taste
3 tablespoons chopped fresh parsley leaves

1. Bring 3 quarts of water to a rolling boil. Add the asparagus and cook at a medium boil for exactly 5 minutes. Drain immediately.

2. Heat the butter and oil in a large pot, such as a Dutch oven, and add the endives. Stir-fry over medium-high heat for 1 minute; add the asparagus. Season with salt and pepper and sprinkle with the parsley. Toss and cook for 1 minute. Serve at once.

More Servings
Double the recipe to serve 16 and cook in two batches.

CARROTS, APRICOTS, AND TOASTED ALMONDS

SERVES 8

6 tablespoons butter
¾ cup blanched slivered almonds
2 pounds carrots, scraped and cut into julienne strips

16 dried apricots, cut into thin strips
½ cup canned chicken broth
2 tablespoons apricot liqueur

1. Melt 3 tablespoons of the butter in a large frying pan and toast the almonds, stirring often, until they are golden brown. This will take only 2 or 3 minutes. Drain.

2. Bring 2 quarts of water to a boil. Add the carrots and apricots and cook over high heat for exactly 4 minutes. Drain immediately and transfer to a large bowl.

3. Heat the broth with the remaining 3 tablespoons of butter and the liqueur. Pour this mixture over the carrots and apricots and add the almonds. Toss gently and serve at once.

More Servings
Double the recipe to serve 16.

COLD MARINATED BROCCOLI WITH SESAME OIL

SERVES 8

8 medium-sized fresh broccoli
   stalks, stems peeled and cut
   into 1½-inch lengths and
   flowerets
½ cup Oriental sesame oil

3 tablespoons fresh lemon juice
3 tablespoons light soy sauce
3 tablespoons sesame seeds,
   toasted

1. Steam the broccoli in 1½ inches of water for 12 minutes in a covered 5-quart pot. Drain well and place in a gratin dish.

2. Whisk together the remaining ingredients and pour over the broccoli. Turn gently and cool. Cover and refrigerate for several hours. Toss again before serving.

More Servings
Double the recipe to serve 16, cooking the broccoli for 15 minutes and turning halfway through the cooking time.

BROILED APPLE SLICES

SERVES 8

4 large Red Delicious apples,
   cored, peeled, and halved
6 tablespoons warm melted
   butter

2 tablespoons honey
3 tablespoons fine 1-inch
   julienne strips orange rind

1. Carefully slice each apple half into thin slices. Arrange the slices in overlapping rows, close together, in a jelly roll pan or on baking sheets with ½-inch sides.

2. Combine the butter, honey, and rind and spoon evenly over the apple slices.

3. Cook under a hot broiler for about 5 minutes, or until golden brown. Serve at once.

More Servings
Double the recipe to serve 16 and cook in two pans in two batches. Keep the first batch warm on the lower shelf of the oven while the second is cooking.

SIR CHARLES BATCHELDER'S TOMATOES À LA CRÈME

Sir Charles Batchelder is the president of the Orchid Society in St. Thomas. On the grounds of his exquisite home, the historic Louisenhoj Castle, he raises many vegetables. He recently shared his favorite tomato recipe with me, which he cooks only when the tomatoes in his garden are ripe.

SERVES 12

10 large ripe tomatoes, peeled and cut into 1/4-inch-thick slices	2 1/2 cups fresh bread crumbs
	4 medium-sized onions, cut into 1/4-inch-thick slices
Salt and freshly ground black pepper	2 1/2 cups sour cream
Sugar	4 tablespoons butter, melted

1. Preheat the oven to 350 degrees.
2. In a large baking or gratin dish, make a layer of half of the tomato slices. Sprinkle lightly with salt, pepper, sugar, and 3/4 cup of the bread crumbs.
3. Add a layer of all the onion slices. Top with the remaining tomato slices and 3/4 cup of the bread crumbs, and sprinkle lightly with salt, pepper, and sugar. Spoon the sour cream over the top.
4. Toss the remaining 1 cup of bread crumbs with the butter and sprinkle over the sour cream. Cover tightly and bake for 30 minutes.

5. Uncover and bake for about 10 minutes longer, or until the top is golden brown.

More Servings
Double the recipe to serve 24 and bake in two large baking dishes or one large roasting pan.

CORN PUDDING
WITH PIMIENTOS AND CUMIN

SERVES 12

3 tablespoons butter
½ cup finely chopped onion
4 large eggs, lightly beaten
1 cup heavy cream
¾ cup evaporated milk
¾ cup water
¼ cup all-purpose flour
1 teaspoon ground cumin

1 teaspoon salt
Freshly ground black pepper
  to taste
4 10-ounce packages frozen
  corn kernels
1 4-ounce jar pimientos,
  drained and chopped

1. Preheat the oven to 350 degrees.
2. Melt the butter in a small saucepan and cook the onion over medium-low heat for 5 minutes, stirring often.
3. Put the onion and butter in a large bowl with all the remaining ingredients, except the corn and pimientos, and beat together with a wire whisk. Add the corn and pimientos and combine well.
4. Pour the pudding into a non-stick or lightly buttered 9- by 13- by 3-inch baking pan and bake for 40 to 45 minutes, or until set. Let the pudding stand for 10 minutes before cutting into equal-sized serving pieces.

More Servings:
Make in two batches and bake in two pans to serve 24.

BAKED ACORN SQUASH WITH RED AND YELLOW PEPPERS AND BACON STUFFING

SERVES 12

6 acorn squash, halved
   lengthwise and seeded
6 tablespoons butter
3 large sweet yellow peppers,
   seeded and diced

3 large sweet red peppers,
   seeded and diced
1 cup chopped onion
12 strips bacon, cooked crisp
   and chopped

1. Preheat the oven to 400 degrees.
2. Put the squash halves, cut side down, in two large baking pans. Add 1 cup of water to each pan and bake for 20 minutes.
3. Meanwhile, melt the butter in a large frying pan and cook the peppers and onion over low heat for 5 minutes. Remove from the heat and stir in the bacon.
4. Turn the squash halves over and spoon the pepper mixture in equal amounts into the hollow of each. Lower the oven temperature to 350 degrees and bake for about 15 minutes longer, or until the squash is tender.

CUBAN TWICE-FRIED PLANTAINS

Plantains are long, large, banana-shaped fruit which are grown in tropical regions all over the world. They are a highly regarded member of the banana family.

Plantains, thinly sliced, deep-fried, and lightly sprinkled with salt and pepper, make the world's best chips. Boiled and mashed, they make delectable fritters, but twice-frying them brings out their best qualities—the unique flavor and unusual potato-like texture.

SERVES 12

5 green plantains
   Peanut or vegetable oil

Salt and freshly ground black
pepper

1. Peel each plantain with a small sharp knife. Trim off the ends and cut each plantain into 1½-inch lengths.

2. Heat ½ inch of oil in a large frying pan. Stand the pieces of plantain on end in the hot oil, as many pieces as will fit comfortably into the pan, and cook until they are lightly browned. Turn and brown on the opposite ends.

3. Transfer to paper towels to drain and cool. Meanwhile, cook the remaining plantain lengths in the same manner, adding enough oil to keep the ½-inch depth in the pan.

3. Now comes a rather unusual procedure: Gently smash or flatten each plantain piece. This is easily accomplished by placing a small sheet of heavy duty aluminum foil in the center of a dish towel. Put a plantain piece in the center of the piece of foil, fold it and the towel over, and, with the palm of your hand, push down as evenly as possible to flatten the plantain to about a ⅓-inch thickness. Transfer the plantain to a dish and flatten the remaining pieces.

4. Preheat the oven to 300 degrees. Heat ½ inch of oil in a frying pan and cook several pieces of plantain at a time until they are golden brown on each side. Drain on paper towels. As the plantain pieces are cooked and drained, put them on a baking sheet. Reheat in the oven for 10 minutes, sprinkle with salt and pepper, and serve at once.

More Servings
Double the recipe to serve 24.

RATATOUILLE WITH POTATOES

SERVES 12

½ cup olive oil
1 large onion, cut into thin slivers
2 large garlic cloves, minced
2 medium-sized eggplants, cubed

3 large sweet green peppers, seeded and cut into ¼-inch-thick strips
3 medium-sized zucchini with ends trimmed, cut in half lengthwise and cut into ¼-inch-thick slices

¼ cup chopped fresh parsley
  leaves
  Salt and freshly ground black
  pepper to taste

½ cup canned chicken broth
10 new potatoes, boiled, peeled,
  and cubed

1. Heat the oil in a 6-quart pot. Add the onion and garlic and cook for 5 minutes, stirring often.

2. Add the remaining ingredients, except the potatoes, and combine gently. Cover and simmer for 30 minutes.

3. Add the potatoes, combine, and cook, uncovered, for about 15 minutes. Taste for seasoning.

More Servings
Double the recipe to serve 24 and cook in a 12-quart pot, but use only ¾ cup of olive oil.

ZUCCHINI, TOMATO, YELLOW SQUASH, AND ONION TIAN

A tian is a dish of layered sliced vegetables with olive oil and herbs, which is baked in the oven in a shallow dish. It is popular in Provence.

The dish makes a beautiful presentation, because all of the vegetables are arranged in neat colorful even-sized rows. Therefore, it is important that all the vegetables selected for the dish are almost the same diameter.

SERVES 16

4 medium-sized zucchini,
  thinly sliced
8 medium-sized tomatoes,
  thinly sliced
4 medium-sized yellow squash,
  thinly sliced
8 medium-sized onions, thinly
  sliced
¾ cup olive oil

2 large garlic cloves, minced
1 teaspoon dried thyme
3 tablespoons white wine
  vinegar
  Salt and freshly ground black
  pepper to taste
½ cup fresh bread crumbs
½ cup freshly grated Parmesan
  cheese

1. Preheat the oven to 350 degrees.

2. Arrange the zucchini, tomatoes, yellow squash, and onions in alternating slices in layered rows in a large rectangular or gratin baking dish.

3. Combine the oil, garlic, thyme, and vinegar and season with salt and pepper. Pour the mixture over the vegetables. Sprinkle with the combined bread crumbs and Parmesan cheese. Bake for 30 minutes, or until the top is golden brown.

More Servings
Double the recipe and bake the *tian* in two dishes to serve 32.

SAUTÉED MUSHROOMS WITH HERBS

SERVES 16

½ cup (1 stick) butter
3 pounds medium-sized mushrooms, wiped clean and stem ends trimmed
½ cup chopped fresh parsley leaves

1 teaspoon dried thyme
1 teaspoon dried tarragon
Salt and freshly ground black pepper to taste

1. Melt 4 tablespoons of the butter in a large frying pan or seasoned paella pan. Cook half of the mushrooms and herbs over high heat for 5 minutes, tossing often. Season with salt and pepper and transfer to a large bowl. Cover and keep warm.

2. Clean the pan and melt the remaining 4 tablespoons of butter. Cook the remaining half of the mushrooms and herbs over high heat for 5 minutes, tossing often. Season with salt and pepper. Transfer to the bowl with the other mushrooms and toss. Serve at once.

More Servings
Double the recipe and cook in four batches to serve 32, always cleaning the pan after each batch.

CAULIFLOWER RANCHEROS

SERVES 16

4 tablespoons olive oil
1 cup chopped onion
1 large garlic clove, minced
2 large sweet green peppers, seeded and thinly sliced
1 large sweet red pepper, seeded and thinly sliced

3 cups peeled and chopped ripe tomatoes
1 cup canned chicken broth
3 medium-sized heads cauliflower, cored and separated into small flowerets
Salt and freshly ground black pepper to taste

1. Heat the olive oil in a large frying pan. Add the onion, garlic, and green and red peppers. Combine and cook over medium heat for 5 minutes, stirring often. Add the tomatoes and chicken broth and simmer for 8 minutes.

2. Meanwhile, cook the cauliflower for 8 minutes in 3 inches of lightly salted boiling water in a large pot.

3. Drain the cauliflower and transfer it to a serving dish.

4. Season the tomato mixture with salt and pepper and spoon it over the cauliflower.

More Servings
Double the recipe to serve 32 and cook the tomato mixture in a Dutch oven.

POACHED PEARS
WITH MANGO AND DATE CHUTNEY

Serving poached pears and chutney together make a delicious marriage. The combination complements roast Cornish game hens, roast duck, baked fresh ham, or broiled fish.

The chutney recipe below yields about 5 cups and, as only about 2 cups are required for this dish, there is plenty of chutney left over to savor later. If desired, double the chutney recipe and store it in sterilized jars in the refrigerator.

SERVES 16

MANGO AND DATE CHUTNEY

1½ cups packed dark brown sugar

1 cup granulated sugar

1½ cups apple cider vinegar

8 ounces pitted dates, chopped

3 large ripe mangoes, peeled and coarsely chopped

1 cup dark raisins

1 fresh lime, diced (including the rind)

1 large onion, chopped

3 large garlic cloves, minced

1 tablespoon grated fresh gingerroot

1 teaspoon ground cinnamon

2 teaspoons light mustard seeds

¼ teaspoon freshly grated nutmeg

½ teaspoon ground turmeric

1 teaspoon ground coriander

1 teaspoon ground allspice

1 teaspoon chili powder

½ teaspoon hot red pepper flakes

1 teaspoon pure vanilla extract

1 cup dry white wine

2 cups water

1½ cups granulated sugar

8 large firm ripe pears, peeled, halved, and cored

1 3-inch-long cinnamon stick

1. Put all the ingredients for the chutney in a 6- to 8-quart heavy pot. Stir the mixture and bring to a boil. Lower the heat and simmer for 30 minutes, stirring often.

2. Cool and transfer to a jar with a tight-fitting lid. Refrigerate for several hours before serving.

3. To cook the pears, bring the wine, water, and sugar to a boil in a 5-quart heavy pot. Add the pears and cinnamon stick and simmer, covered, for 12 minutes. Remove the pears with a slotted spoon and drain, cut side down.

4. Put the pears on a serving platter or dish and spoon about 2 tablespoons of the chutney into the center of each pear. Serve at room temperature or well chilled.

More Servings

To serve 32, double the pear recipe and cook them in a 9-quart pot. There will be enough chutney.

CARROTS LYONNAISE WITH CREAM

SERVES 16

½ cup (1 stick) butter
2 cups onion slivers
4 pounds carrots, scraped and cut on the diagonal into ¼-inch-thick slices
2 tablespoons fresh lemon juice

1½ cups heavy cream
Salt and freshly ground black pepper to taste
½ teaspoon dried thyme
3 tablespoons chopped fresh parsley leaves

1. Melt the butter in a large heavy pot. Add the onion and cook over low heat, stirring often, for 15 minutes.

2. Put the carrots in a large saucepan or pot and cover them with boiling water. Cook for exactly 6 minutes. Drain well.

3. Meanwhile, in a large non-metallic saucepan, reduce the lemon juice over high heat to 1 tablespoon. Immediately add the heavy cream and cook over high heat, whisking often, until the cream has thickened enough to coat a spoon. Season with salt and pepper and add the thyme.

4. Add the carrots and the cream to the onion and combine gently. Cook for 1 minute, sprinkle with the parsley, and serve.

More Servings
Double the recipe to serve 32, using a 6- to 8-quart Dutch oven in step 3.

BRAISED CABBAGE
AND CARROTS IN RIESLING

SERVES 24

2 cups Riesling
1 cup homemade chicken stock
   or canned broth
6 tablespoons butter
2 large heads cabbage, about 3
   pounds each
1 large onion, cut into thin
   slivers

2 pounds carrots, scraped and
   cut into thin slices
   Salt and freshly ground black
   pepper to taste
3 tablespoons chopped fresh
   parsley leaves

1. In an 8- to 9-quart pot, bring the Riesling and stock to a boil with the butter. Add the cabbage and onion. Stir, cover, and simmer for 15 minutes.

2. Add the carrots and mix well. Cover and cook for about 10 minutes, or until the cabbage and carrots are tender but still crisp. Season with salt and pepper. Transfer to a large serving dish using a slotted spoon and sprinkle with the parsley before serving.

More Servings
Double the recipe to serve 48 and cook in a 12-quart pot.

BRUSSELS SPROUTS
WITH RED PEPPER BUTTER

SERVES 24

5 pints Brussels sprouts
1 cup (2 sticks) butter
2 large sweet red peppers,
   seeded and coarsely chopped

1 large garlic clove, coarsely
   chopped
2 tablespoons fresh lemon juice
   Salt and freshly ground black
   pepper to taste

1. Cook the Brussels sprouts in lightly salted simmering water in a large pot for about 8 minutes, or just until they are tender.

2. Meanwhile, put the butter in a large saucepan and add the red peppers, garlic, and lemon juice. Stir and cook over medium heat for 5 minutes.

3. Purée the butter and pepper mixture in a food processor until it is very smooth. Season with salt and pepper.

4. Drain the Brussels sprouts and transfer them to a serving dish. Pour the red pepper butter over the Brussels sprouts and serve immediately.

More Servings
To serve 48, double the recipe and cook the Brussels sprouts in a 10- to 12-quart pot.

CREAMED SPINACH AND WATERCRESS

SERVES 24

6 tablespoons butter
½ cup finely chopped shallots
2 bunches watercress with stems trimmed, washed and finely chopped
6 10-ounce packages frozen chopped spinach, cooked and well drained

2½ cups sour cream
Salt and freshly ground black pepper to taste
Freshly grated nutmeg

1. Melt the butter in a 9-quart Dutch oven or pot. Add the shallots and cook for 5 minutes, stirring occasionally. Add the watercress, combine, cover, and simmer for 5 minutes.

2. Add the spinach and sour cream. Combine well and season with salt and pepper and a few gratings of nutmeg. Heat thoroughly but do not boil.

More Servings
Double the recipe to serve 48.

STRING BEANS WITH DILL VINAIGRETTE

SERVES 24

5 pounds fresh string beans
with ends trimmed

DILL VINAIGRETTE

½ cup white wine vinegar
2 tablespoons Dijon mustard
1 large garlic clove, crushed
and peeled
2 cups olive oil

⅓ cup chopped fresh dill, or 1½
tablespoons dried dill
Salt and freshly ground black
pepper to taste

1. Bring 3½ quarts of water to a boil in a 7- to 8-quart pot. Add the string beans and cook for exactly 6 minutes. Drain immediately and place in a large shallow dish.

2. Whisk the vinegar, mustard, and garlic together. Then, drop by drop, whisk in the olive oil. Add the dill and season with salt and pepper.

3. Pour the viniagrette over the beans and toss to coat them evenly. Serve warm, or cover and chill for a few hours or overnight. Toss again before serving.

More Servings
Double the recipe to serve 48 and cook the beans in a 10- to 12-quart pot.

FRESH CRANBERRY SAUCE

MAKES ABOUT 3 QUARTS

1½ pounds sugar
2 large navel oranges (including
rinds), well washed and diced
2 teaspoons grated fresh
gingerroot

2 cups dark raisins
1 teaspoon ground cinnamon
4 pounds fresh cranberries
1 teaspoon pure vanilla extract

1. In a large heavy pot, cook the sugar over high heat until it melts and turns medium brown and caramelizes.

2. Stir in the oranges, ginger, raisins, and cinnamon. Cook, stirring often, over high heat for 5 minutes. Add the cranberries and vanilla and combine well. Simmer for 15 minutes, stirring often.

3. Cool completely and put into jars with tight-fitting lids. Refrigerate. Use immediately, or store for up to 3 weeks.

More Servings
Double the recipe to make 6 quarts.

ASPARAGUS WITH ROASTED WALNUTS

SERVES 36

6 pounds asparagus, stalk ends cut off on the diagonal and asparagus cut on the diagonal into 1-inch lengths
Salt
¼ cup fresh lemon juice
1 cup walnut oil

1 cup vegetable oil
Freshly ground black pepper
2 cups chopped roasted walnuts (Roast in a preheated 400-degree oven on a baking sheet for 10 minutes, stirring during roasting.)

1. Bring 5 quarts of water to a rolling boil in an 8-quart pot. Add 2 tablespoons of salt, stir, and add the asparagus. Cook for exactly 5 minutes. Drain.

2. Meanwhile, combine the lemon juice and oils in a blender and season with salt and pepper to taste.

3. Put the asparagus and walnuts into a large bowl, and pour the walnut oil mixture over the top. Toss gently. Taste for seasoning. Serve warm or chilled.

BABY LIMA BEANS
WITH LEEKS AND BACON

◊ ════════════════════ ◊

SERVES 36

1½ cups (3 sticks) butter
 6 large leeks (white parts only), washed and thinly sliced
 5 20-ounce packages frozen baby lima beans

20 strips (about ¾ pound) bacon, cooked crisp and crumbled
Salt and freshly ground black pepper to taste

1. Melt the butter in a large frying pan and cook the leeks over medium heat for 6 minutes, stirring often. Set aside.

2. Cook the lima beans in a Dutch oven covered with lightly salted boiling water for 6 minutes. Drain well. Transfer to a large bowl and add the leeks and butter and the bacon. Toss gently and season with salt and pepper.

More Servings
Double the recipe to serve 72.

GREEN BEANS ALLA POSITANO

◊ ════════════════════ ◊

SERVES 36

7 pounds string beans with ends trimmed, cut into 1-inch lengths
  Salt
½ cup (1 stick) butter
½ cup olive oil
 2 teaspoons minced garlic

1 cup chopped sun-dried tomatoes
⅓ cup fresh lemon juice
¼ cup chopped fresh parsley leaves
  Freshly ground black pepper

1. Cook the beans in a 10-quart pot in salted boiling water (about 5 quarts) that covers them by 1 inch for exactly 6 minutes. Drain well and transfer to a large bowl.

2. Meanwhile, heat the butter and olive oil in a frying pan and cook the garlic for 5 minutes, stirring often; do not allow it to brown. Remove from the heat and stir in the sun-dried tomatoes, lemon juice, parsley, and salt and pepper to taste.

3. Pour the mixture over the beans and toss gently. Serve immediately.

SWEET AND SOUR FRUIT RATATOUILLE

SERVES 36

½ cup olive oil
1 large onion, chopped
2 large garlic cloves, minced
2 large sweet green peppers, seeded and cut into thin strips
3 cups sugar
½ cup white wine vinegar
2 cups dark raisins
2 pounds cranberries
2 pounds Red Delicious apples, cored, peeled, and cut into cubes

2 12-ounce packages prunes, cut into cubes
2 16-ounce cans pineapple chunks, drained
1 large cantaloupe, seeded, peeled, and cut into bite-sized cubes
3 cups grapefruit sections
2 cups seedless green grapes

1. Heat the oil in a large frying pan and cook the onion, garlic, and green peppers over medium heat for 8 minutes, stirring often.

2. Dissolve the sugar in the vinegar in a heavy 12-quart pot. Add the fruits and onion mixture. Combine gently, cover, and simmer over low heat for 15 minutes. Mix well, and cook, uncovered, for 5 minutes longer. Chill thoroughly before serving.

GREEN PEAS AND CORN ALLA ROMANA

SERVES 50

1 cup (2 sticks) butter
1 cup minced onion
1 tablespoon dried sage
1 tablespoon dried rosemary
2 teaspoons dried oregano
4 20-ounce bags frozen green
peas

3 20-ounce bags frozen corn
kernels
2 cups canned chicken broth
8 large romaine lettuce leaves,
cut into thin strips
Salt and freshly ground black
pepper to taste

1. Bring 7 quarts of water to a rolling boil in an 18- to 20-quart pot.

2. Meanwhile, melt the butter in a heavy saucepan. Add the onion and herbs and simmer for 10 minutes.

3. Cook the vegetables in the water over high heat until the water returns to a boil, stirring often. When the water is boiling, cook at a medium boil for 5 minutes. Drain well and transfer to a large bowl.

4. Add the broth and romaine leaves to the onion mixture and bring to a boil. Season well with salt and pepper. Pour over the vegetables and combine gently.

Fewer Servings
Cut the recipe in half to serve 25. Use only half of one 20-ounce bag of corn kernels or a 10-ounce package.

CHINESE MIXED VEGETABLES

SERVES 50

3 pounds carrots, scraped, cut into julienne strips, parboiled for 4 minutes, and drained

1½ pounds fresh snow pea pods with strings removed, blanched in boiling water for 30 seconds and drained

2 pounds sugar snap beans with ends trimmed, blanched in boiling water for 1 minute and drained

10 stalks broccoli, cut into bite-sized pieces, blanched in boiling water for 4 minutes, and drained

1 large cauliflower, cut into bite-sized pieces, blanched for 3 minutes, and drained

2 cups sliced water chestnuts

12 celery stalks, very thinly sliced on the diagonal

¾ cup thinly sliced scallions

⅓ cup Oriental sesame oil, or as needed

2 cups peanut oil

6 tablespoons fresh lemon juice

¼ cup soy sauce
Salt and freshly ground black pepper to taste

1. Combine the prepared vegetables in a very large bowl (about 20-quart size).

2. Combine the remaining ingredients in a bowl using a wire whisk. Pour the mixture over the vegetables in a drizzle. Then toss. The vegetables should be just lightly coated with the sauce.

CARROTS VICHY WITH HONEY AND GRAND MARNIER

Here's one of the easiest vegetable dishes imaginable for a large crowd. Carrots are inexpensive, available all year, and their vibrant color brightens any meal. Adding a small amount of honey and Grand Marnier brings new life to an already classic dish.

SERVES 50

12 pounds carrots, scraped and thinly sliced (The carrots can be scraped and sliced, put in plastic bags, and refrigerated for several hours before cooking them.)

1 pound (4 sticks) butter

1 cup honey

1 cup Grand Marnier

1½ cups chopped fresh parsley leaves

Salt and freshly ground black pepper to taste

1. Bring 6 quarts of water to a rolling boil in an 18- to 20-quart pot. Cook the carrots in the water at a medium boil for exactly 6 minutes, stirring often.

2. Meanwhile, in a saucepan over medium-low heat, heat the butter, honey, and Grand Marnier until the butter has melted.

3. Drain the carrots well and return them to the pot in which they cooked. Pour the butter mixture over them and add the parsley. Season with salt and pepper and toss gently.

Fewer Servings
Cut the recipe in half to serve 25.

Side-Dish
and Main-Course Salads

◇ ══════════════════════════════ ◇

A glance at the produce section of your local market will tell you that salads are more popular than ever. In preparing salads for crowds, whether as a side dish or the main cours,, the greens and other vegetables being used must be fresh and crisp.

Although French restaurants insist on serving a green salad only after the entrée, a salad can be served as a first course or a side dish before, during, or after the main course, and as a substantial main course itself.

The composition of a salad can be left up to your imagination—crisp greens, meat, poultry, seafood, vegetables, or fruit can all be used. On the following pages you will find such delightful combinations as Chicory, Bacon, and Crouton Salad with Warm Vinaigrette, Raw Cauliflower and Danish Blue Cheese Salad with Vinaigrette Dressing, Cantaloupe, Cucumber, Cherry Tomato, and Cucumber Salad with Mint Dressing, and Endive and Diced Radish Salad with Creamy Vinaigrette.

Exquisite greens can be selected from arugula, Bibb lettuce, Belgian endive, Boston lettuce, chicory, Chinese lettuce, escarole, iceberg and oak leaf lettuce, radicchio, romaine lettuce, spinach, and watercress, to name just some of the varieties available.

Salad greens need to be washed under a cold gentle spray of water. Lettuce should be dried in paper or dish towels or spun dry. Dry spinning isn't recommended for the more fragile varieties, such as oak leaf lettuce, which should be hand dried and then put in a plastic bag and refrigerated until used. This method produces cool crisp leaves. It is imperative that lettuce leaves be dry, so that the dressing will cling to them. If they are not thoroughly dry, the salad will be soggy.

When making a salad dressing, consider the many kinds of aromatic vinegars and oils available: red and white wine vinegars, sherry wine vinegar, herb-flavored vinegars, rice, malt, and cider vinegars, balsamic vinegar (which is always used sparingly), and the fruit-flavored vinegars, such as raspberry and lemon.

Different oils bring a variety of tastes to salad dressings. Fragrant olive oils, virgin or extra virgin, vegetable, corn, peanut, soy, and safflower oils, and those with more pronounced flavors, such as Oriental sesame, hazelnut, and walnut, make distinctive dressings.

Whichever vinegar and oil combination you select, choose those that complement each other and the herbs, spices, and salad ingredients they are served with. The formula for dressings is usually three parts oil to one part vinegar, plus additions of mustard, egg yolks, herbs, spices, or cream, if desired.

Sometimes simplicity is the best strategy, so never discount the idea of a simple crisp green salad with a delicious vinaigrette dressing when cooking for crowds.

CHICORY, BACON, AND CROUTON SALAD WITH WARM VINAIGRETTE

SERVES 8

Olive oil

2 cups ½-inch cubes day old French bread

2 heads chicory, washed, dried, and torn into 2-inch pieces

½ pound bacon, cooked crisp and crumbled

Freshly ground black pepper

WARM VINAIGRETTE

¼ cup white wine vinegar

⅓ cup minced shallots

1¼ cups olive oil

3 tablespoons Dijon mustard

Salt and freshly ground black pepper to taste

1. Heat ¼ inch of olive oil in a large frying pan. Add the bread cubes and cook them over medium-high heat, turning them with a slotted spoon, until they are golden brown. This will take a minute or so. Drain the croutons on paper towels.

2. To make the vinaigrette, put the vinegar, shallots, and olive oil in a medium-sized saucepan and bring to a boil. Immediately remove the pan from the heat and whisk in the mustard. (The vinaigrette for this salad should be quite tart.) Season with salt and pepper.

3. Put the lettuce in a large salad bowl with the bacon and croutons. Pour the sauce over the salad and toss it well. Serve immediately and pass the peppermill at the table.

More Servings
Double the recipe to serve 16, and use a large saucepan to make the dressing.

ENDIVE AND DICED RADISH SALAD WITH CREAMY VINAIGRETTE DRESSING

SERVES 8

6 large Belgian endives with stems removed, cut crosswise into ½-inch lengths

12 large red radishes, cut into ¼-inch cubes

CREAMY VINAIGRETTE DRESSING

1 large egg yolk at room temperature

1 tablespoon Dijon mustard at room temperature

3 tablespoons fresh lemon juice

¾ cup olive oil

¼ cup heavy cream

Salt and freshly ground black pepper to taste

1. Put the endives and radishes into a salad bowl. (The mixture can be wrapped in a plastic bag and refrigerated for a few hours.)

2. In a medium-sized bowl, whisk together the egg yolk, mustard,

and lemon juice. Drop by drop, whisk in the olive oil. Beat in the cream and season with salt and pepper.

3. Pour the dressing over the salad and toss.

More Servings
Double the recipe to serve 16.

MARINATED THREE-PEPPER SALAD

This lovely cold salad should be made in the morning and served at dinner on the same day for the best flavor and texture.

SERVES 8

3 large sweet red peppers
3 large sweet green peppers
3 large sweet yellow peppers
¾ cup olive oil
2 large garlic cloves, minced

¼ cup minced shallots
8 anchovy fillets (optional)
3 tablespoons fresh lemon juice
Salt and freshly ground black pepper to taste

1. Pare away the skin of each pepper with a vegetable peeler as you would a potato. Then cut the peppers into ¼-inch-thick strips.

2. Heat the olive oil with the garlic and shallots in a large frying pan over low heat for 5 minutes.

3. Add the peppers and cook over medium heat for 5 minutes, stirring often.

4. Add the anchovies, lemon juice, and salt and pepper. Toss and cook for 2 minutes.

5. Transfer the mixture to a ceramic bowl, cover, and refrigerate for several hours.

More Servings
Double the recipe to serve 16 and cook in a 4- to 5-quart heavy pot.

CHERRY TOMATO SALAD WITH HERB VINAIGRETTE AND SCALLION DRESSING

SERVES 8

2 pints cherry tomatoes, stemmed and halved lengthwise

4 scallions, white parts only, thinly sliced
4 large Belgian endives

DRESSING
1 large egg yolk
1 tablespoon fresh lemon juice
1 tablespoon Dijon mustard
1 tablespoon finely chopped shallots
1 tablespoon chopped fresh basil leaves, or 1 teaspoon dried basil

1 tablespoon chopped fresh parsley leaves
½ cup olive oil
½ cup vegetable oil
1½ tablespoons red wine vinegar
Salt and freshly ground black pepper to taste

1. Put the tomatoes and scallions into a bowl.
2. To mix the dressing, beat the egg yolk, lemon juice, mustard, shallots, and herbs in a bowl for 15 seconds, using a wire whisk. Drop by drop whisk in the olive oil and the vegetable oil. Add the vinegar and salt and pepper to taste and combine well.
3. Pour the dressing over the tomatoes and scallions and toss gently.
4. Cut the ends off of the endives and separate them into individual leaves.
5. Arrange the endive leaves, inner parts of leaves facing up, around the edge of a large shallow salad bowl and spoon the salad mixture into the center.

More Servings
The salad is easily doubled to serve 16. Use 6 endives for the salad.

CELERY ROOT ROMAINE, AND ENDIVE SALAD WITH WALNUT OIL DRESSING

◇══════════════════════════════◇

SERVES 12

1 large celery root, peeled and cut into julienne strips, or 1 14-ounce jar celery root, rinsed, well drained, patted dry, and thinly sliced
1 tablespoon fresh lemon juice

2 large heads romaine lettuce, cut on the diagonal into ½-inch-thick slices
6 large Belgian endives with ends trimmed, cut on the diagonal into ½-inch lengths

WALNUT OIL DRESSING
1 tablespoon Dijon mustard at room temperature
5 tablespoons white wine vinegar

¾ cup walnut oil
1 cup vegetable oil
Salt and freshly ground black pepper to taste

1. Bring 1 quart of water to a boil. Add the celery root and lemon juice and cook over medium-high heat for 6 minutes. Drain and cool complete. Pat dry with paper towels. If using jarred celery root, do not heat or use the lemon juice.

2. Put the romaine, endive, and celery root into a large salad bowl.

3. In a medium-sized bowl, whisk together the mustard and vinegar. Drop by drop, whisk in the walnut and vegetable oils. Season with salt and pepper.

4. Pour the dressing over the salad and toss. Serve at once.

More Servings
Double the recipe to serve 24.

RAW CAULIFLOWER AND DANISH BLUE CHEESE SALAD WITH VINAIGRETTE DRESSING

◇ ══════════════════════════════════════ ◇

This nearly instant salad has become a great favorite of mine. The crunchy cauliflower, Danish blue cheese, and vinaigrette dressing make a faultless marriage. It is requested often, which is always a good gauge in determining the success of a recipe.

SERVES 12
(CAN BE PREPARED THE NIGHT BEFORE)

2 medium-sized heads cauliflower

½ pound Danish blue cheese, crumbled

½ cup chopped fresh parsley leaves

12 Boston lettuce leaves

VINAIGRETTE DRESSING

2 heaping tablespoons Dijon mustard

Scant ½ cup white wine vinegar

1¾ cups olive oil

Salt and freshly ground black pepper to taste

1. Cut away the core of the cauliflower heads. Break each apart into individual flowerets. Holding a floweret with the stem pointing up, thinly slice each. Some of the cauliflower flowerets will crumble, others will become beautiful exotic-shaped fans.

2. Put the cauliflower into a large bowl and sprinkle it with the cheese and parsley.

3. Whisk together the mustard and vinegar in a medium-sized bowl. Drop by drop, whisk in the olive oil. Season with salt and pepper. The dressing should taste strongly of the vinegar, which the cauliflower needs. (The strength will diminish during marinating.) Cover and chill for 1 hour before serving.

More Servings
Double the recipe to serve 24.

SHREDDED CAESAR SALAD
ON FRIED CROUTONS

◇ ═══════════════════════════════ ◇

*Here is a slightly new twist on a classic salad. In this Caesar Salad, the ro-
maine lettuce, which has been shredded, delicately tops a fried crouton and
is crowned with a crisscross of anchovies. This salad makes an excellent first
course at a sit-down dinner. If the dinner is to be served buffet style, the
salad can be assembled and placed on a platter. Each guest can then put the
salad and meat or fish and vegetable course right on their dinner plate.*

SERVES 12

12 slices firm white bread with
crusts trimmed
Vegetable oil

1 large, or 2 medium-sized,
heads romaine lettuce,
washed, dried, and cut into
¼-inch-thick shreds
¾ cup freshly grated Parmesan
cheese

CAESAR SALAD DRESSING
20 anchovy fillets (about two
2-ounce cans), well drained
2 large garlic cloves, minced
2 tablespoons Dijon mustard
¼ cup fresh lemon juice

2 teaspoons Worcestershire
sauce
1 large egg yolk
1½ cups olive oil, or as needed

1. Fry the slices of bread in ¼ inch of vegetable oil in a large frying
pan, a few slices at a time, until they are golden brown on each side. Drain
on paper towels.

2. Put the romaine lettuce shreds in a large bowl.

3. Prepare the dressing by mixing 8 chopped anchovy fillets, the garlic, mustard, lemon juice, and Worcestershire sauce together in a shallow
bowl with the back of a fork. Beat in the egg yolk with a wire whisk.
Drop by drop, beat in the oil.

4. Pour the dressing over the lettuce and toss. Add the cheese and
toss again.

5. Serve the salad in equal amounts on top of the croutons. Top each
salad with a crisscross of 1 halved (lengthwise) anchovy fillet.

More Servings
Double the recipe to serve 24.

MIXED GREENS WITH SUN-DRIED TOMATOES AND SHERRY WINE VINEGAR DRESSING

SERVES 12

2 bunches arugula, washed and dried

3 large heads Boston lettuce, washed, dried, and torn into bite-sized pieces

1 bunch watercress with stems removed and leaves washed and dried

1 cup sun-dried tomatoes cut into thin strips

SHERRY WINE VINEGAR DRESSING

2 tablespoons Dijon mustard

4 tablespoons sherry wine vinegar

1 large garlic clove, minced

1½ cups olive oil

Salt and freshly ground black pepper to taste

1. Put the arugula, lettuce, and watercress into a salad bowl and top with the sun-dried tomatoes.

2. In a medium-sized bowl, whisk together the mustard and vinegar. Add the garlic. Drop by drop, whisk in the olive oil. Season with salt and pepper. Strain.

3. Pour the dressing over the salad and toss.

More Servings
Double the recipe to serve 24.

COMPOSED GREEK SALAD

◇ ══════════════════ ◇

SERVES 12

2 large heads romaine lettuce,
  washed, dried, and cut into
  1/3-inch-thick shreds
2 pounds feta cheese, drained
  and cubed
24 black Greek olives
3 medium-sized cucumbers,
  peeled and cut into 1/4-inch-
  thick slices
6 hard-boiled eggs, shelled and
  quartered lengthwise

3 medium-sized red onions,
  thinly sliced and separated
  into rings
2 pints cherry tomatoes
  Olive oil
  Red wine vinegar
  Salt and freshly ground black
  pepper to taste
  Dried oregano
  Chopped fresh parsley leaves

1. Cover a large serving dish with the lettuce. If the dish is round, work in a circle. If the dish is oval, square, or rectangular in shape, work in rows placing the feta cheese first in the middle, surrounded by the black olives. Next make rows of the cucumbers and then the egg quarters, onion rings, and cherry tomatoes.

2. Put cruets of olive oil and vinegar, a salt shaker and peppermill, and small bowls of oregano and parsley next to the salad. Serve buffet style. If individual salads are preferred, arrange equal amounts of the ingredients in the same manner on each of twelve individual salad plates, with cruets of oil and vinegar, salt shakers and peppermills, and bowls of the oregano and parsley on the table or tables.

More Servings
The recipe can be doubled to serve 24, but it will have to be assembled on two large serving dishes or 24 individual salad plates.

FENNEL, CELERY, MUSHROOM, AND GRUYÈRE SALAD WITH MUSTARD-VINAIGRETTE DRESSING

SERVES 16

3 cups thinly sliced fennel
stalks (about 2 whole fennel
bulbs)
4 cups thinly sliced celery
(about 1 large whole celery)
1½ pounds small mushrooms,
thinly sliced

3½ cups shredded Gruyère
cheese
1 cup chopped fresh parsley
leaves

MUSTARD-VINAIGRETTE DRESSING

4 tablespoons Dijon mustard
6 tablespoons white wine
vinegar, or to taste
1 cup olive oil

2 cups vegetable oil
Salt and freshly ground black
pepper to taste

1. Put the vegetables, cheese, and parsley into a large bowl. (The vegetables can be cut, the cheese shredded, and the parsley chopped, and wrapped individually in plastic bags and refrigerated several hours before serving.)

2. Whisk together the mustard and vinegar in a large shallow bowl. Drop by drop, whisk in the olive and vegetable oils. Season with salt and pepper.

3. Pour the dressing over the salad and toss gently.

SLICED TOMATO AND CUCUMBER SALAD WITH ITALIAN DRESSING

◊ ═══ ◊

SERVES 16

10 medium-sized ripe firm tomatoes, cored and thinly sliced

6 medium-sized cucumbers, peeled and thinly sliced

ITALIAN DRESSING
1/3 cup red wine vinegar
3 tablespoons balsamic vinegar
16 fresh basil leaves, coarsely chopped, or 1 1/2 tablespoons dried basil
1 1/2 teaspoons dried rosemary

1/3 cup chopped fresh parsley leaves
3 large garlic cloves, minced
1 1/2 cups olive oil
Salt and freshly ground black pepper to taste

1. Arrange the tomatoes and cucumbers in alternating slices in rows on a large serving dish with at least 1 inch sides.

2. Combine all the dressing ingredients in a blender and purée.

3. Spoon the dressing over the tomatoes and cucumbers and serve within the hour.

More Servings
Double the recipe to serve 32. Prepare the dressing in the blender using only 1 cup of the oil. Pour the mixture into a bowl and whisk in the remaining 2 cups of oil. At least two large serving dishes will be necessary to serve the salad.

ELLIE ASHWORTH'S ARTICHOKE AND HEARTS OF PALM SALAD WITH BLUE CHEESE DRESSING

SERVES 16

(PREPARATION BEGINS THE NIGHT BEFORE)

24 strips bacon, cooked crisp and crumbled

3 14-ounce cans hearts of palm, drained and thinly sliced

3 14-ounce cans artichoke hearts, drained and coarsely chopped

1/2 cup thinly sliced scallions

2 large garlic cloves, minced

3 large heads romaine lettuce, washed, dried, and torn into bite-sized pieces

BLUE CHEESE DRESSING

1 tablespoon Dijon mustard

6 tablespoons fresh lemon juice

2 1/2 cups olive oil

Freshly ground black pepper

1 3/4 cups crumbled blue cheese

1. Put the bacon, hearts of palm, artichokes, scallions, and garlic in a large bowl.

2. In another bowl, whisk together the mustard and lemon juice. Drop by drop, whisk in the oil. Season with pepper and stir in the cheese. Pour the dressing over the hearts of palm mixture, cover, and refrigerate overnight.

3. Just before serving, place the lettuce in a large salad bowl and top with the marinated mixture. Toss gently and serve at once.

More Servings
Double the recipe to serve 32. More oil may be needed.

POTATO SALAD
WITH FRESH PESTO DRESSING
◇ ═══════════════════════════════════ ◇

SERVES 16

10 pounds large boiling
   potatoes, peeled, quartered,
   and cut into ¼-inch-thick
   slices

3 tablespoons salt
1 large red onion, diced

FRESH PESTO DRESSING
2 cups packed coarsely
   chopped fresh basil leaves
   (Do not use dried basil for
   this salad.)
½ cup chopped fresh parsley
   leaves
3 large cloves garlic, coarsely
   chopped

1 3-ounce package cream
   cheese, softened
¾ cup white wine vinegar
1 cup olive oil
1½ cups vegetable oil, or as
   needed
   Salt and freshly ground black
   pepper to taste

1. Boil the potatoes in boiling salted water to cover for about 8 minutes, or just until they are tender, stirring occasionally. Drain well and put into a large bowl with the red onion.

2. Meanwhile, purée the basil, parsley, garlic, cream cheese, white wine vinegar, and olive oil in a blender. Pour the mixture into a bowl and whisk in the vegetable oil. Season well with salt and pepper.

3. Pour the dressing over the hot potatoes and toss gently. Taste for seasoning. Add a little more oil, if necessary. Cool, cover, and chill for several hours. The salad is excellent the second day.

More Servings
Double the recipe to serve 32. The amounts of vinegar and oil will have to be watched carefully. The salad should be moist but not wet.

CORNUCOPIA VEGETABLE SALAD

SERVES 24

3 pounds carrots, scraped and cut into thin julienne strips

3 pounds medium-sized zucchini, washed, dried, and cut into thin julienne strips

2 pounds medium-sized fresh mushrooms, wiped clean and thinly sliced

4 large sweet red peppers, seeded and cut into thin strips

5 medium-sized cucumbers, peeled, halved lengthwise, seeds scooped out, and thinly sliced

4 pints cherry tomatoes (the smallest possible)

1 large head cauliflower, cored, separated into flowerets, and thinly sliced

24 red radishes, thinly sliced

4 bunches watercress with ends trimmed, washed and dried

HAZELNUT DRESSING

3 tablespoons Dijon mustard

1/2 cup white wine vinegar

3/4 cup hazelnut oil

1 cup olive oil

3/4 cup vegetable oil

Salt and freshly ground black pepper to taste

1. Combine the prepared vegetables, except the watercress, in a large bowl.

2. Beat the mustard and vinegar together with a wire whisk. Drop by drop, add the oils. Season with salt and pepper.

3. Pour the dressing over the vegetables and toss.

4. Make a border of the watercress on a large platter. Spoon the vegetables into the center of the platter. Serve at once.

BEAUJOLAIS SALAD

SERVES 24

2 large heads chicory, washed, dried, and torn into bite-sized pieces

1 large head romaine lettuce, washed, dried, and torn into bite-sized pieces

1 large head Boston lettuce, washed, dried, and torn into bite-sized pieces

1 pound string beans with ends trimmed, boiled for 5 minutes and drained

1 pound new potatoes, boiled and thinly sliced

4 cooked beets, peeled and thinly sliced

3 tablespoons Dijon mustard

1 large garlic clove, chopped

⅔ cup red wine vinegar

3 cups olive oil, or as needed

Salt and freshly ground black pepper to taste

1. Put the lettuce into a large bowl and toss with the vegetables.

2. Combine the mustard, garlic, and vinegar in a blender or food processor. In a slow steady stream, add the olive oil through the hole in the cover. Season with salt and pepper.

3. Pour the dressing over the salad and toss gently. Add a little more oil, if necessary.

COLD GREEN PEA SALAD WITH HERBS

Here's a wonderfully unique and delicious salad for a large gathering. My friend, Nancy Dussault, makes an excellent cold green pea and cheese salad with herbs, which inspired this recipe.

SERVES 24

6 10-ounce packages frozen green peas, partially thawed
Salt
½ cup thinly sliced scallions
1 cup diced well-drained pimientos
½ cup chopped fresh parsley leaves
¼ cup chopped fresh basil leaves, or 1 tablespoon dried basil

2 teaspoons chopped fresh thyme leaves, or 1 teaspoon dried thyme
1 cup mayonnaise
2 cups sour cream
Freshly ground black pepper to taste
10 large Boston lettuce leaves
2 pints cherry tomatoes

1. Bring 2 quarts of water to a rolling boil in a Dutch oven or similar-sized pot. Add 1 tablespoon of salt, stir, and add the peas. Cover and cook over high heat until the water returns to a boil. Remove the cover, stir, and cook for 2 or 3 minutes, or until the peas are thoroughly heated. Drain well and set aside.

2. Combine the remaining ingredients, except the lettuce and cherry tomatoes, in a large bowl. Season with salt to taste. When the peas have cooled, gently fold the peas into the mixture. Cover and chill until ready to serve. (The salad can be made several hours in advance.) At serving time, turn the salad onto a large serving dish or platter lined with the lettuce leaves, and make a border with the cherry tomatoes.

More Servings
Double the recipe to serve 48.

Variations
Substitute the same amount of cooked baby lima beans or Italian green beans for the peas.

SALADE VERTE
WITH HERB VINAIGRETTE

◇ ══════════════════════════ ◇

SERVES 36

3 bunches arugula with ends trimmed, washed, dried, and torn into bite-sized pieces

3 large heads Boston lettuce, washed, dried, and torn into bite-sized pieces

2 large heads romaine lettuce, washed, dried, and torn into bite-sized pieces

3 large heads red-tipped lettuce, washed, dried, and torn into bite-sized pieces

HERB VINAIGRETTE

2 tablespoons dried dill
2 tablespoons dried basil
1 tablespoon dried tarragon
2 teaspoons dried oregano
1/2 cup chopped fresh parsley leaves

1/2 cup Dijon mustard
1 1/4 cups red wine vinegar
3 1/2 cups olive oil
2 1/2 cups vegetable oil
Salt and freshly ground black pepper to taste

1. Prepare the lettuce first. This can be done several hours before serving. There will be about 2 1/2 gallons of mixed greens, so storage can cause a problem. It is easiest to store the prepared greens in one or two small garbage bags in the refrigerator. Be sure to allot space in the refrigerator by cleaning out the most spacious shelf in advance.

2. To make the dressing, combine the herbs with 1/4 cup of the mustard and 1/2 cup of the vinegar with 2 cups of the olive oil in a blender. Pour the mixture into a large bowl, and beat in the remaining mustard, vinegar, olive oil, and vegetable oil with a wire whisk. Season with salt and pepper. Store in a large tightly sealed jar in the refrigerator.

3. Put the combined salad greens into one very large or two large bowls and pour on three quarters of the dressing. Toss and add the remaining dressing as needed. Serve immediately.

CANTALOUPE, CHERRY TOMATO, AND CUCUMBER SALAD WITH MINT DRESSING

SERVES 36

5 large cantaloupes, halved, peeled, seeded, and cut into 1-inch cubes

6 large seedless cucumbers, peeled and thinly sliced

5 pints cherry tomatoes, stemmed and halved

MINT DRESSING

1 cup fresh lemon juice

1 quart vegetable oil

Salt and freshly ground black pepper to taste

⅔ cup chopped fresh mint leaves, or ¼ cup dried mint

½ cup chopped fresh parsley leaves

1. Put the cantaloupe, cucumbers, and tomatoes into a very large salad bowl.

2. Make the dressing in a blender, half of the amount of the ingredients given in the recipe at a time, by puréeing for 15 seconds.

3. Pour the dressing over the salad and toss gently. Serve immediately, or cover and chill until ready to be served. Toss again before serving.

More Servings
Double the recipe to serve 72 and make the dressing in four batches.

Fewer Servings
Cut the recipe in half to serve 18.

COLESLAW AND POTATO SALAD WITH PINEAPPLE AND KIDNEY BEANS

SERVES 50

15 pounds new potatoes
2 heads green cabbage, cored and finely shredded
2 16-ounce cans pineapple chunks, well drained
3 cups canned red kidney beans, rinsed and drained

1 cup thinly sliced scallions
8 cups (2 quarts) mayonnaise
¾ cup sugar, or to taste
3 tablespoons celery seeds
Salt and freshly ground black pepper to taste

1. Cook the potatoes in a large stock pot in boiling water until they are just tender.

2. Meanwhile, put the cabbage, pineapple, kidney beans, and scallions into a very large salad bowl. Combine.

3. Combine the remaining ingredients in a large bowl with a large wire whisk. Taste for seasoning.

4. Drain the potatoes but do not peel them. Cut them into bite-sized pieces. Add to the salad bowl with the cabbage mixture.

5. Pour the dressing over the salad and combine gently. Taste for seasoning. Sprinkle with parsley, if desired. Chill thoroughly before serving.

CUCUMBER AND YOGURT SALAD
WITH FRESH HERBS

◊ ════════════════════════ ◊

SERVES 50

12 medium-sized cucumbers
   Salt
 6 cups (1½ quarts) plain yogurt
 ½ cup white wine vinegar
 1 cup chopped fresh parsley
   leaves
 ⅓ cup chopped fresh dill, or 1½
   tablespoons dried dill
 ¼ cup chopped fresh tarragon
   leaves, or 1 tablespoon dried
   tarragon

 ¼ cup chopped fresh mint
   leaves, or 1½ tablespoons
   dried mint
   Freshly ground black pepper
 6 small white onions, thinly
   sliced and separated into
   rings
 2 heads radicchio, cored and
   separated into individual
   leaves, washed, dried,
   wrapped, and refrigerated

1. Peel the cucumbers. Cut each in half lengthwise. Scoop out the seeds and thinly slice the cucumbers. Sprinkle with salt and put into a large colander to drain for 30 minutes.

2. Meanwhile, in a large bowl combine the yogurt, vinegar, and herbs, and season with salt and pepper to taste.

3. Combine the cucumbers and onions in a large bowl. Pour the dressing over the salad and toss gently. Cover and refrigerate for several hours. Toss again before serving. Arrange the radicchio leaves around the edge of a large shallow bowl or platter. Spoon the salad into the center of the dish.

MAIN-COURSE SALADS

MIXED SEAFOOD SALAD

SERVES 8

1 pound large shrimp, boiled, shelled, deveined, and chopped

½ pound cooked crab meat, chopped

1 pound bay or sea scallops, cooked in 3 tablespoons of butter in a frying pan for 5 minutes and then drained (If using sea scallops, quarter them before cooking.)

½ pound cooked lobster meat, chopped

1 cup diced peeled and seeded firm ripe tomatoes

6 tablespoons fresh lemon juice

1½ cups olive oil, or as needed

⅓ cup thinly sliced scallions

¼ cup chopped fresh parsley leaves

Salt and freshly ground black pepper to taste

1. Combine the seafood in a large bowl with the tomatoes.

2. Combine the remaining ingredients in a separate bowl; then pour the mixture over the seafood and toss. Serve well chilled. The salad should just be coated with the dressing, but add a little more oil, if necessary.

More Servings
Double the recipe to serve 16.

Smoked Chicken Salad with Cucumbers and Sun-Dried Tomatoes

SERVES 8

2 pounds smoked chicken, cut into bite-sized cubes
1 large seedless cucumber, peeled, halved lengthwise, and thinly sliced
¾ cup chopped sun-dried tomatoes

¼ cup fresh lemon juice
1 tablespoon Dijon mustard
1 teaspoon dried tarragon
1½ cups olive oil
Salt and freshly ground black pepper to taste

1. Combine the chicken, cucumbers, and sun-dried tomatoes in a large bowl.
2. Whisk the lemon juice, mustard, and tarragon together in a medium-sized bowl. Drop by drop, whisk in the olive oil. Season with salt and pepper.
3. Pour over the salad and toss.

More Servings
Double the recipe to serve 16, adding a little more olive oil, if necessary.

Chinese Beef and Broccoli Salad

SERVES 12

2 2½- to 3-pound flank steaks
½ cup soy sauce
¼ cup dry sherry
1 cup peanut oil
2 large garlic cloves, crushed
10 fresh broccoli stalks, stalks peeled and cut into bite-sized pieces with flowerets
1½ cups safflower oil
¼ cup Oriental sesame oil

½ cup oyster sauce (available in Oriental markets)
3 tablespoons fresh lemon juice
1 teaspoon five-spice powder (available in Oriental markets)
Freshly ground black pepper to taste
½ cup thinly sliced scallions

1. Cut each steak lengthwise into three equal-sized pieces. Put the pieces into a large bowl.

2. Combine ¼ cup of the soy sauce, the sherry, peanut oil, and garlic and pour over the beef. Turn to coat evenly and let stand at room temperature until ready to cook.

3. Steam the broccoli in a large pot for about 8 minutes, or until it is crisp-tender. Cool.

4. Combine the remaining ingredients, except the scallions.

5. Cook the beef strips in a large pan under a hot broiler for about 10 minutes per side. Cool.

6. Thinly slice the beef and put it into a large bowl with the broccoli and scallions. Pour the sauce over the salad and toss.

More Servings
Double the recipe to serve 24, cooking the beef in two batches.

KEVIN WHITE'S
CHICKEN AND GREEN PEA SALAD

SERVES 16

5½ pounds skinned and boned chicken breasts, poached, cooled, and cut into bite-sized pieces

3½ cups mayonnaise

3 tablespoons fresh lemon juice

½ cup chopped fresh parsley leaves

Salt and freshly ground black pepper to taste

1 20-ounce package frozen green peas, cooked, drained, and cooled

1. Put the chicken into a large bowl.

2. In a medium-sized bowl, combine the mayonnaise, lemon juice, parsley, and salt and pepper.

3. Add the mixture to the chicken and combine well. Add the green peas and toss gently. Season with additional salt and pepper.

More Servings
The recipe can be doubled easily to serve 32.

CURRIED TUNA AND CHUTNEY SALAD

SERVES 16

4 12½-ounce cans white meat tuna, drained and flaked
2 cups thinly sliced celery
2 cups diced peeled seedless cucumber
1½ cups diced sweet green pepper
1 cup toasted shredded coconut
1½ cups golden raisins
3½ cups mayonnaise, or as needed

1½ cups chopped Mango and Date Chutney (recipe page 175)
4 tablespoons fresh lemon juice
3 tablespoons grated orange rind
Salt and freshly ground black pepper to taste
2 navel oranges, halved crosswise and thinly sliced
1½ cups toasted almond slivers

1. Put the tuna in a large bowl with the celery, cucumber, green pepper, coconut, and raisins. Combine gently.

2. In another large bowl, combine the remaining ingredients, except the oranges and almond slices. Combine well.

3. Pour the dressing over the tuna mixture and combine gently but thoroughly.

4. Spoon the salad onto a large serving platter. Decorate the edge of the platter with the orange slices and sprinkle the almonds over the salad.

More Servings
The recipe doubles easily to serve 32; however, more mayonnaise may be needed.

GREEK TUNA SALAD

SERVES 24

12 large ripe tomatoes, cored and cut into wedges

2 large red onions, cut into thin slivers

2½ pounds feta cheese, crumbled

96 Greek olives

4 12½-ounce cans solid white meat tuna, separated into bite-sized pieces

2 cups drained canned chick-peas

⅓ cup chopped fresh parsley leaves

1½ teaspoons dried oregano
Salt and freshly ground black pepper
Extra virgin olive oil
Red wine vinegar

1. Gently combine the first 8 ingredients (through the oregano) in a large bowl.

2. Season lightly with salt and pepper. Drizzle 1 cup of the olive oil and ½ cup of the vinegar over the salad and toss gently. The ingredients should only be coated lightly with the oil and vinegar. Add a little more of each and gently toss again. Serve with crisp lettuce greens, if desired.

More Servings
Double the recipe to serve 48.

CHICKEN AND NEW POTATO SALAD WITH CELERY LEAVES AND PARSLEY AND MUSTARD SAUCE

SERVES 24

6 large chicken breasts, skinned, boned, and cut into bite-sized pieces

5 pounds new potatoes, boiled with skins just until tender

1 cup coarsely chopped celery leaves

½ cup chopped fresh parsley leaves

6 scallions, thinly sliced

MUSTARD SAUCE

3 tablespoons Dijon mustard

1½ cups mayonnaise

¾ cup white wine vinegar

Salt and freshly ground black pepper to taste

1½ cups olive oil

1. Poach the chicken pieces in a 4-quart pot in simmering water to cover for 12 minutes. Cool in the water and drain well.

2. Cut the potatoes into bite-sized cubes and put them into a large bowl with the chicken, celery leaves, parsley, and scallions.

3. In a blender, combine the mustard and mayonnaise. Through the hole in the cover, slowly add the vinegar and oil.

4. Pour the sauce over the chicken mixture and combine gently. Chill until ready to serve.

More Servings

Double the recipe to serve 48 and mix the sauce in two batches.

CURRIED TUNA AND FRUIT SALAD

SERVES 36

6 12½-ounce cans solid white meat tuna, drained and flaked

¾ cup thinly sliced scallions

2 large Red or Golden Delicious apples, cored and cubed

1½ cups currants

1 15-ounce package dried apricots, coarsely chopped

3 cups seedless green grapes

3½ cups mayonnaise, or as needed

3 tablespoons curry powder

3 tablespoons fresh lime juice

Salt and freshly ground black pepper to taste

3 large cantaloupes, cut into small balls

4 cups (1 quart) small seeded watermelon balls

1. Combine the tuna, scallions, apples, currants, apricots, and grapes in a large bowl.

2. Whisk together the mayonnaise, curry powder, and lime juice in another bowl. Season with salt and pepper. Pour the mayonnaise mix-

ture over the tuna and combine well, adding a little more mayonnaise, if necessary.

3. Spoon the salad into the center of a large serving dish and surround it with the combined cantaloupe and watermelon balls.

TABBOULEH-SHRIMP SALAD

SERVES 36

7 cups bulgar wheat	2 pounds shrimp, boiled, shelled, deveined, and chopped
7 cups chopped fresh parsley leaves	
1½ cups chopped fresh mint leaves	3 cups olive oil
	2 cups fresh lemon juice
3 cups peeled and seeded diced cucumber	¼ cup white wine vinegar Salt and freshly ground black pepper to taste
1 cup thinly sliced scallions	
2 cups diced sweet green pepper	36 large pimiento-stuffed green olives
3 cups diced tomatoes	

1. Pour 7 cups of water over the bulgar in a large bowl, toss, and let stand for 1 hour and 30 minutes, stirring occasionally. Drain.

2. In a very large bowl, toss the bulgar with the next 7 ingredients (through the shrimp).

3. Combine the oil, lemon juice, vinegar, and salt and pepper.

4. Pour the dressing over the salad and toss well. Make a border of the olives around the Tabbouleh.

CHICKEN SALAD WITH DILL

SERVES 50

1 bottle dry white wine
8 cups (2 quarts) homemade chicken stock or canned broth
2 bay leaves
16 cups (4 quarts) water
20 large chicken breasts, halved
4 cups (1 quart) mayonnaise
3 cups sour cream, or as needed
¼ cup fresh lemon juice
4 cups thinly sliced celery
1 cup thinly sliced scallions
¾ cup chopped fresh dill, or to taste
½ cup chopped fresh parsley leaves
Salt and freshly ground black pepper to taste

1. Bring the wine, chicken broth, bay leaves, and water to a boil in a 12-quart pot. Lower the heat to a simmer and add the chicken breasts. If necessary, add boiling water to cover the chicken. Simmer for 30 minutes, stirring occasionally.

2. Drain the chicken breasts well. When cool enough to handle, skin the breasts and remove the meat. Shred the meat into bite-sized pieces and put them into a large bowl.

3. Combine the mayonnaise, sour cream, and lemon juice in a separate large bowl. Add the remaining ingredients and mix throughly. Pour the mixture over the chicken and combine. Taste for seasoning. Chill well. Serve on a large platter. If desired, surround the salad with fresh dill sprigs and cherry tomatoes.

Bean and Lentil Dishes

◇ ════════════════════════ ◇

In cooking for crowds, small quantities of beans (dried or canned), or lentils can be used in limitless savory casseroles, stews, salads, and side dishes. Beans and lentils are not only versatile, delicious, and nutritious, but they are incredibly inexpensive. In the winter, they are especially welcome as a warming and substantial food.

All of the many different varieties of dried beans require soaking in water overnight; and they do take a few hours to cook.

Lentils, on the other hand, need no soaking, and less than half the cooking time of beans. Both have superb flavors of their own, and can easily take on the flavors of added ingredients. After cooking, storing beans or lentils overnight, covered, in the refrigerator allows flavors to develop further.

Advance preparation of beans and lentils saves last-minute preparation time while enhancing flavor as well.

GREAT NORTHERN BEANS AND CABBAGE WITH WHITE WINE

SERVES 8

¼ cup olive oil
1 large onion, coarsely chopped
2 large garlic cloves, minced
2 pounds dried Great Northern beans, sorted, washed, and soaked in cold water to cover overnight
1 small head green cabbage, shredded

½ cup chopped fresh parsley leaves
1 teaspoon dried thyme
1 smoked ham hock
12 cups (3 quarts) homemade chicken stock or canned broth
1 bottle dry white wine
Salt and freshly ground black pepper to taste

1. Heat the oil in a 6 quart-pot. Cook the onion and garlic for 5 minutes, stirring.

2. Stir in the beans, cabbage, parsley, and thyme. Add the ham hock, stock, and wine and bring to a boil.

3. Simmer, partially covered, for about 3 hours, or until the beans are tender. Add water to keep the beans moist, if necessary, and stir often. Season with salt and pepper.

SAM GALLU'S LIMA BEANS WITH SHORT RIBS AND SAUSAGE

Serve this with black bread, butter, and red wine.

SERVES 12

2 pounds small dried lima beans, sorted and rinsed
4 carrots, scraped and chopped
4 celery stalks, sliced
1 large onion, chopped
2 large garlic cloves, minced
2 bay leaves
1 large smoked ham hock
1 tablespoon salt
Freshly ground black pepper to taste

12 cups (3 quarts) homemade chicken stock or canned broth
4 pounds smoked sausage, cut into 2-inch lengths
4 pounds smoked spareribs, cut into 3-inch pieces, ribs separated
2 tablespoons Worcestershire sauce

1. Soak the lima beans overnight in cold water to cover.

2. Drain and put the beans in a heavy 10-quart pot with the carrots, celery, onion, garlic, bay leaves, ham hock, salt, pepper, stock, and enough water to cover all. Slowly bring to a boil. Immediately lower the heat and simmer, partially covered, for 1 hour and 30 minutes.

3. Add the sausages, ribs, and Worcestershire sauce. Mix well and cook for 1 hour and 30 minutes to 2 hours, or until the beans are tender and the meat is just about falling from the bones. Taste for seasoning.

LENTILS PROVENÇALE

SERVES 16

5 tablespoons olive oil
1 large onion, chopped
2 large garlic cloves, minced
2 pounds dried lentils, sorted
   and washed
1 teaspoon dried thyme
½ cup chopped fresh parsley
   leaves

1 teaspoon salt
1 28-ounce can imported
   Italian tomatoes with liquid
   Boiling water
   Freshly ground black pepper
   to taste

1. Heat the oil in a 4- to 5-quart pot and cook the onion and garlic for 5 minutes, stirring often.

2. Add the *drained* lentils, parsley, salt, and tomatoes. Pour in enough boiling water to cover the lentils and mix well. Cover and simmer for about 1 hour and 15 minutes. Stir once halfway through the cooking time, adding a little water, if necessary. Taste for seasoning, adding salt and pepper, if necessary.

More Servings
Double the recipe to serve 32 and cook in an 8-quart pot.

MARTHA ROSE SHULMAN'S
BLACK BEAN CHALUPAS

Martha Rose Shulman, the cookbook author and food writer, lives in Paris. Her Black Bean Chalupas are irresistible. Martha says, "This is one of those fabulous party dishes that is assembled at the buffet, and whose chief component can be prepared way ahead of time. Your table will be very colorful, with all the delightful ingredients in their bowls, waiting to be layered onto the tortilla rounds. Guests can assemble their own, or the chalupas can be assembled by somebody at the buffet and either passed or picked up. They are versatile enough to be the main attraction for anything from a sit-down party to an informal buffet on a boat, and you won't be able to beat the cost."

SERVES 24

BLACK BEANS

2 tablespoons safflower oil, or as needed
4 medium-sized onions, chopped
8 garlic cloves, minced
4 pounds dried black beans, sorted, washed, and soaked overnight in 6 quarts of cold water (Reserve the soaking water.)

Salt
1 bunch fresh coriander (cilantro)
4 tablespoons ground cumin
4 tablespoons mild chili powder

SALSA

15 firm ripe tomatoes, chopped
1 large onion, minced
4 fresh serrano or jalapeño peppers, minced, or to taste

1/2 cup chopped fresh coriander leaves
1/4 cup red wine vinegar
Salt

GUACAMOLE

10 Hass avocadoes (the dark, gnarly-skinned variety)
5 ripe tomatoes, chopped
1 small onion, finely chopped
4 garlic cloves, minced

Juice of 3 lemons, or to taste
Cumin and chili powder to taste
Salt

100 or more tortilla rounds (Chalupa crisps)
2 pounds mild white Cheddar cheese, shredded

1 large head romaine lettuce, finely shredded
2 cups finely chopped toasted almonds
3 cups plain yogurt

1. To prepare the beans after soaking them, heat the safflower oil in a large heavy bottomed stock pot and add the onions and half of the garlic. Cook, stirring, for about 5 minutes. Add the soaked beans and their soaking water. Bring to a boil and skim off any foam that rises to the top. Lower the heat, cover, and simmer for 1 hour.

2. Stir in the remaining garlic, fresh coriander, and salt to taste. Sim-

mer for about 1 hour and 30 minutes, or until the beans are soft and the broth thick and savory. Add more garlic and/or salt, if desired.

3. Cool the beans. Drain off half the liquid from the beans and reserve it.

4. Purée three fourths of the beans in batches in a food processor or blender, using some of the liquid in the pot to moisten the beans. Add the cumin and chili powder. The beans should *not* be a smooth purée but textured. This can be achieved by using the pulse action on the food processor or blender.

5. Mix the purée with the whole beans and moisten with some of the broth. The mixture shouldn't be soupy, but should have the familiar consistency of Mexican refried beans.

6. Heat a tablespoon or two of the oil in a wide heavy bottomed frying pan, and add the beans in batches. Cook, mashing with the back of a wooden spoon, and stirring until a crust begins to form. Add some broth if the mixture becomes too dry. Continue until all the beans have been refried, about 10 minutes per batch, adding more oil as needed. At this point the beans can be cooled and refrigerated for 2 days, or frozen. Save at least 2 cups of the leftover broth to moisten the beans before you reheat them. The broth can be frozen, too, of course.

7. Prepare the Salsa several hours in advance. Mix together the tomatoes, onion, minced chili peppers, coriander, vinegar, and salt to taste in a large bowl. Correct the seasonings, cover, and refrigerate until ready to serve.

8. Close to serving time, prepare the Guacamole. Mash together the avocadoes and tomatoes, and add the onion, garlic, lemon juice, cumin, chili, and salt to taste.

9. Transfer to a bowl and press plastic wrap directly onto the surface of the Guacamole. This will help prevent it from darkening.

10. Preheat the oven to 325 degrees and thoroughly reheat the beans, mixing in a little broth so that they won't dry out. Cover with aluminum foil.

11. Meanwhile, place all the ingredients in attractive serving dishes, using a basket for the tortilla chips. Arrange the dishes on the buffet with spoons or tongs next to each dish in the following order: tortilla chips, Black Beans, Guacamole, yogurt, grated cheese, lettuce, Salsa, and chopped almonds. For each chalupa, spread a generous layer of the beans on a chip, top with a layer of Guacamole, then a spoonful of yogurt, a sprinkling of grated cheese, then the lettuce, and top with Salsa and chopped almonds.

More Servings
Double the recipe to serve 48.

Menu Suggestion
Martha suggests serving seviche, Spanish rice, fruit, and a choice of margaritas, beer, or Côtes du Rhone.

RED BEANS AND RICE

SERVES 36

6 pounds dried kidney beans, sorted, rinsed, and soaked overnight in cold water to cover
40 cups (10 quarts) water, or as needed
½ pound bacon, cooked crisp and chopped
4 large onions, chopped

6 celery stalks, thinly sliced
1 pound carrots, scraped and diced
6 tablespoons ground chili powder, or to taste
2 tablespoons cumin seeds
Salt and freshly ground black pepper to taste

1. Bring all the ingredients, except the salt and pepper, to a boil in a 14-quart pot.

2. Lower the heat and simmer for 1 hour and 30 minutes. Add the salt and pepper and continue simmering for 1 hour, or until the beans are tender.

3. Purée 4 cups of the beans in a food processor or blender and return the purée to the pot. Check the seasoning. Serve with hot cooked rice (see chart for cooking rice on page 259). If desired, serve with 36 grilled smoked sausages.

STEWED PINTO BEANS
WITH GROUND BEEF AND MUSHROOMS

SERVES 36

4 pounds dried pinto beans, sorted and rinsed
36 cups (6 quarts) homemade beef stock or canned broth
1 bottle dry white wine
½ cup vegetable oil
4 cups chopped onion
1 tablespoon minced garlic
5 pounds ground beef
4 cups chopped canned whole tomatoes

1 6-ounce can tomato paste
1 teaspoon dried thyme
1 teaspoon dried rosemary
2 bay leaves
Salt and freshly ground black pepper to taste
½ cup (1 stick) butter
3 pounds mushrooms, wiped clean and thinly sliced

1. Soak the beans in cold water to cover overnight.

2. Drain the beans well. Put them into an 14- to 16-quart heavy pot with the stock and wine and bring to a boil. Immediately lower the heat to a simmer and cook for 1 hour and 30 minutes.

3. Meanwhile, heat the oil in a large frying pan and cook the onion and garlic for 10 minutes over low heat, stirring often.

4. Transfer the mixture to a large bowl and cook one third of the beef in the pan until it is no longer pink, stirring often. When one batch has cooked, add it to the bowl with the onion and continue cooking the beef in the same manner in two more batches.

5. Add the tomatoes, tomato paste, herbs, and salt and pepper to the mixture and combine well.

6. Add the mixture to the beans after 1 hour and 30 minutes, stir, cover, and simmer for 1 hour. It will be necessary to stir often to prevent the meat and beans from sticking to the bottom of the pot. Add water, if needed; the mixture should just be wet.

7. Thirty minutes before the end of the cooking time, cook the mushrooms. Divide the butter into three equal portions. Melt one portion of the butter in a large frying pan or paella pan or wok and stir-fry one third of the sliced mushrooms for 3 or 4 minutes. Cook the two remaining portions in batches in the same way.

8. After the beans have cooked for 1 hour, add the mushrooms, stir,

and season with salt and pepper. Simmer, uncovered, for 15 minutes, or until the beans are tender, stirring often.

NOTE: The dish is excellent the next day, if covered and refrigerated overnight. It can also be frozen.

SEVEN-BEAN SALAD

As good as the standard three-bean salad can be, today it's considered run-of-the-mill. Being a long-time fan of the cold marinated bean mixture, I did some experimenting, using freshly cooked string beans and frozen baby lima beans mixed with a variety of good-quality canned beans. Red onions, celery, and parsley were added for crunch and extra flavor, and all were incorporated into a potent mustard dressing to produce this easy-to-make winner. I know it is a winner, because it was recently served to a crowd as part of a cold buffet, and it was devoured down to the last bean.

SERVES 50

2 15-ounce cans chick-peas
3 16-ounce cans black beans
2 15-ounce cans flageolets
2 16-ounce cans canneloni beans
2 16-ounce cans red kidney beans
3 pounds fresh string beans with ends trimmed, cut into 1-inch lengths, boiled for 4 minutes, drained, and cooled

1 20-ounce bag frozen baby lima beans, cooked, drained, and cooled
3 cups diced red onion
3 cups diced celery
1½ cups chopped fresh parsley leaves

DRESSING
½ cup Dijon mustard
1 tablespoon light mustard seeds
1 cup white wine vinegar

1 tablespoon sugar
2 cups olive oil
2 cups vegetable oil

1. Rinse the canned beans under cold running water in a large colander and drain them well.

2. Gently combine all the beans (including the string beans and lima beans) with the onion, celery, and parsley.

3. Combine the dressing ingredients well and pour over the salad. Toss gently. Taste for seasoning.

4. Cover the salad and chill for at least 6 hours or overnight. Toss again before serving.

Pasta and Noodle Dishes

◇ ════════════════════════ ◇

The mere suggestion of pasta and noodles dishes evokes hunger: Tagliatelle with Radicchio and Prosciutto in Basil Cream Sauce, Sesame Noodles, Fusilli with Green Primavera Vegetables and Italian Parsley Sauce, Bombay Curried Noodles, or Linguine with Walnut Sauce. We have become a nation of pasta and noodle lovers, and cooking them for crowds provides us with inexpensive and quick and easy fare.

Amazingly, different-shaped pasta and noodles made of the same ingredients, acquire a different taste when eaten with the same sauce.

When cooking for crowds, remember that bite-sized pasta or noodles are more manageable fork food, particularly rigatoni, ziti, penne, elbow macaroni, ditali, rotelle, shells, and fine egg noodles, or square noodles.

It is really impractical to make fresh pasta and noodles when cooking for crowds unless time and space permits it. Excellent dried imported and domestic brands are available and they are superb when properly prepared. Instructions for cooking pasta and noodles in large quantities follow.

Special Instructions for Cooking Pasta and Noodles in Large Quantities

Cooking over 2 pounds of pasta or noodles requires special cooking instructions and suggestions.

The most important factors in cooking pasta and noodles are to use rapidly boiling salted water, stir frequently, cook it *al dente* (or just until tender) by tasting, drain well, and add the sauce or moistening and flavoring ingredients immediately.

A pound of pasta or noodles requires 3½ quarts of water and 1 tablespoon of salt; 2 pounds call for 6½ quarts of water and 2 tablespoons of salt. For quantities of more than 2 pounds, see the chart below.

If you don't have a 16- to 24-quart pot for cooking large quantities of pasta, use two 8- to 12-quart pots, or cook the pasta or noodles in batches, draining and adding some of the sauce.

There are pros and cons over the use of oil in cooking pasta and noodles. Some believe that it helps keep the pasta and noodles separate. Stirring often is far more effective in accomplishing separation. Oil does, however, seem to help eliminate the problem of the water boiling over. Although I don't use oil, a tablespoon or two can be added for every 3½ quarts of water used, if desired.

Draining large amounts of pasta is difficult, because of the weight of the water. The pasta can be collected from the pot by using a hand strainer. To stop the pasta from further cooking during this process, add 1 quart of cold water to the water in the pot.

Pasta	Water	Salt	Pot Size
3 pounds	7½ quarts	3 tbls.	12 to 14 quart
4 pounds	8½ quarts	3½ tbls.	14 to 16 quart
5 pounds	10 quarts	4½ tbls.	18 to 20 quart
6 to 8 pounds	12 quarts	5 tbls.	20 to 24 quart

HOMEMADE TOMATO SAUCE

MAKES ABOUT 1 GALLON (16 CUPS)

4 35-ounce cans imported Italian whole plum tomatoes with liquid	2 bay leaves
	¼ cup finely chopped fresh basil leaves, or 1 tablespoon dried basil
1 6-ounce can tomato paste	
½ cup olive oil	½ cup chopped fresh parsley leaves
4 tablespoons butter	
2 cups finely chopped onion	1 tablespoon sugar
2 teaspoons finely chopped garlic (optional)	Salt and freshly ground black pepper to taste

1. Drain the liquid from the tomatoes and put it in a large pot.

2. Purée the tomatoes, a few cups at a time, in a blender. Add the purée to the liquid in the pot.

3. Heat the olive oil with the butter in a large frying pan and cook the onion and garlic for 5 minutes, stirring often.

4. Add the mixture to the pot with the tomatoes. Add the bay leaves, basil, parsley, sugar, and salt and pepper.

5. Simmer the sauce for 30 minutes, stirring often.

6. Strain the sauce and use immediately or store in containers and freeze until needed.

TAGLIATELLE WITH RADICCHIO AND PROSCIUTTO IN BASIL-CREAM SAUCE

If I were making restaurant suggestions for friends visiting Venice, I would begin this way: The minute you have checked into your hotel call Trattoria "da Arturo," and make a reservation for lunch or dinner toward the end of your stay in Venice. Ernesto Ballarin's "da Arturo" is one of the rare restaurants in Venice that serves no seafood. After a few days of sampling extraordinary treasures from the lagoon and the Adriatic, you might welcome some of "da Arturo's" superb veal, pork, or beef dishes. And, best of all, the restaurant's pasta dishes are inventive and perfectly cooked and sauced.

Each visit I make to Venice includes at least one meal at "da Arturo." A few years ago, while marveling over Ernesto Ballarin's pasta with radicchio, I asked him why the radicchio that I cook is always bitter. He told me the secret is to cook it in a little olive oil and garlic over very low heat for two hours . . . no less, or it will be bitter.

The following recipe is my adaptation of the wonderful dish served in "da Arturo."

SERVES 8

1¾ pounds radicchio
½ cup olive oil
 1 teaspoon minced garlic
12 chopped fresh basil leaves, or
 2 teaspoons dried basil

2 pounds tagliatelle or linguine
½ cup dry white wine
3 cups heavy cream
½ pound prosciutto, thinly
 sliced and cut into thin strips

1. Quarter each head of radicchio lengthwise through the root end and cut off the stems. Slice the lettuce into ¼-inch-thick strips.

2. Heat the olive oil in a large nonstick pan and add the radicchio and garlic. Stir and turn the heat to very low. Partially cover and simmer for 1 hour, stirring occasionally. Add the basil and sprinkle lightly with salt, stir, and continue to simmer, uncovered, for 1 hour.

3. Bring 6½ quarts of water to a rolling boil in a large pot. Add 2 tablespoons of salt, stir, and add the pasta. Stir and cook that pasta until it is *al dente,* or just until tender. Stir the pasta often to prevent it from sticking together.

4. Meanwhile, add the wine and cream to the radicchio mixture. Bring to a boil and cook over high heat for about 5 minutes, stirring constantly, or until the sauce thickens slightly. Add the prosciutto and mix well.

5. Drain the pasta and put it into a large bowl. Immediately pour the sauce over the pasta and toss it well. Serve at once and pass the *pepe,* as Ernesto always says.

PENNE WITH SHRIMP AND
CURRIED CREAM AND SCALLION SAUCE

◇ ══ ◇

Curry and pasta? An emphatic, yes! I first experienced this celestial com-
bination in Venice, Italy, at Trattoria "da Arturo," the same venerable
establishment written about in the preceding recipe. Ernesto Ballarin's soo-
thing version of curried cream sauce clung to giant cheese-filled ravioli.

I have seen curried pasta dishes on menus in several New York and Los
Angeles restaurants, and there is now a new focus in East Indian cuisine in
general.

SERVES 8

½ cup minced onion
3 tablespoons fresh lemon juice
¼ cup dry white wine
3½ cups heavy cream, or as needed
2 tablespoons curry powder, or
  to taste
1½ pounds raw shrimp, shelled
  and deveined, and each
  shrimp cut lengthwise into 4
  pieces

6 scallions, thinly sliced
  Salt and freshly ground black
  pepper to taste
2 pounds penne (ziti can be
  substituted)
  Chopped fresh parsley leaves

1. Put the onion, lemon juice, and white wine into a large heavy saucepan and cook over high heat for about 3 minutes, stirring often, to reduce slightly.

2. Add the heavy cream and bring the mixture to a boil, whisking often. The cream will rise up in the pan, so it will be necessary to whisk constantly and occasionally remove the pan from the heat. When this happens, stir it down and replace the pan over the high heat. Cook for about 5 minutes, or until the mixture thickens slightly.

3. Add the curry powder, shrimp, and scallions and simmer for 5 minutes, stirring often. The sauce should coat a spoon but not be too thick; add a little more cream, if necessary. Season with salt and pepper.

4. Meanwhile, bring 6½ quarts of water to a rolling boil in a large pot. Stir in 2 tablespoons of salt, stir, and add the pasta. Stir and cook the pasta until it is *al dente,* or just until tender. Drain the pasta and transfer it to a large bowl. Pour the hot curry sauce over the pasta and toss. Garnish with the parsley. Serve at once.

LINGUINE WITH WALNUT SAUCE

SERVES 8

1½ cups chopped walnuts
½ cup toasted pine nuts
1 cup ricotta
1 3-ounce package cream
  cheese, softened
Salt

2 pounds linguine
¾ cup olive oil
½ cup water
3 tablespoons butter
Freshly ground black pepper

1. Bring 6½ quarts of water to a rolling boil in a large pot.

2. Meanwhile, grind the walnuts and pine nuts in a food processor. Add the ricotta and cream cheese and combine well.

3. Add 2 tablespoons of salt to the boiling water, stir, and add the pasta. Cook the pasta until it is *al dente,* or just until tender, stirring often.

4. Meanwhile, put the walnut mixture into a saucepan and stir in the olive oil, water, and butter. Simmer for 5 minutes, or until thoroughly heated. Season with salt and pepper to taste.

5. Drain the pasta and toss with the sauce. Serve at once.

More Servings
Double the sauce recipe to serve 16 and combine in two batches. Cook 4 pounds of pasta following the directions on page 227 for cooking large quantities of pasta.

ZITI WITH PESTO SAUCE AND TOASTED PINE NUTS

◊ ════════════════════════════ ◊

SERVES 8

Olive oil

6 ounces pine nuts

1 cup packed fresh basil leaves

1 large garlic clove, chopped

1 8-ounce package cream cheese, softened

Salt

1½ pounds ziti

⅓ cup butter, melted

1 cup freshly grated Parmesan cheese

1½ cups heavy cream, heated

Freshly ground black pepper to taste

1. Melt 3 tablespoons of olive oil in a large frying pan. Add the pine nuts and cook over medium heat until the nuts are golden brown, stirring often. Drain.

2. Put the basil leaves, garlic, cream cheese, half of the toasted pine nuts, and ½ cup of olive oil in a food processor and purée. (The pesto can be jarred and frozen at this point.)

3. Bring 6½ quarts of water to a rolling boil in a large pot. Stir in 1½ tablespoons of salt and add the ziti. Stir and cook the pasta until it is *al dente*, or just until tender.

4. Drain the pasta and transfer it to a large bowl. Add the butter and toss. Add the pesto and Parmesan cheese and toss well. Pour in the heavy cream, add the remaining pine nuts, and toss. Season with salt and pepper to taste. Serve hot or at room temperature.

More Servings
Double the recipe and follow the directions on page 227 for cooking large quantities of pasta.

Rigatoni Hans Lollick

◇ ══════════════════════════ ◇

Hans Lollick is a small island in the Caribbean a short motor boat ride northeast of St. Thomas. In May of 1984, a group of friends planned a last-minute picnic there, and I was to bring the main course. With departure imminent, whatever I prepared had to be made from ingredients that were on hand; this recipe was the happy result.

SERVES 12

2　pounds rigatoni	1　cup dark raisins
Salt	6　scallions, thinly sliced
½　cup olive oil	6　celery stalks, sliced
2　cups mayonnaise	2　large sweet green peppers,
3　tablespoons fresh lemon juice	seeded and chopped
⅓　cup chopped fresh parsley	1　cup chopped sun-dried
leaves	tomatoes
4　6½-ounce cans solid white	Freshly ground black pepper
meat tuna, drained and flaked	to taste

1. Bring 6½ quarts of water to a rolling boil in a large pot. Add 2 tablespoons of salt, stir, and add the pasta. Cook the pasta until it is *al dente,* or just until tender, stirring often.

2. Meanwhile, in a medium-sized bowl, combine the oil, mayonnaise, lemon juice, and parsley with a wire whisk.

3. Drain the cooked pasta well and put it in a large bowl. Add the mayonnaise mixture and toss. Add the remaining ingredients and combine gently. Season with salt and pepper to taste. The mixture should be moist but not wet. If necessary, add a little extra olive oil. The dish is excellent served hot or cold.

More Servings
The recipe doubles beautifully to serve 24. For cooking 4 pounds of pasta, see page 227 for the instructions for cooking large quantities of pasta.

ROTELLE WITH VEGETABLES AND TOMATO AND BUTTER SAUCE

SERVES 12

10 tablespoons butter
4 tablespoons olive oil
1¼ cups diced celery
1¼ cups diced carrots
1¼ cups finely chopped onion
1¼ cups diced sweet green
   pepper
   Salt
3 pounds rotelle
1 teaspoon dried oregano
1 teaspoon dried basil
⅓ cup chopped fresh parsley
   leaves

6 cups (1½ quarts) freshly
   made or imported Italian
   tomato sauce
4 tablespoons tomato paste
¾ cup dry white wine
¾ cup homemade chicken stock
   or canned broth
   Freshly ground black pepper
   Freshly grated Parmesan
   cheese

1. Heat 4 tablespoons of the butter and the olive oil in a large heavy pot. Add the vegetables, stir, cover, and simmer for 10 minutes.

2. Meanwhile, bring 7½ quarts of water to a rolling boil in a large pot. Add 3 tablespoons of salt, stir, and immediately add the pasta. Stir and cook over high heat until the pasta is *al dente,* or just until tender. Stir the pasta often to prevent it from sticking.

3. To the vegetables, add the herbs, tomato sauce, tomato paste, wine, and chicken stock and bring to a boil, stirring. Lower the heat and simmer for 5 minutes. Stir in the remaining 6 tablespoons of butter and season with salt and pepper to taste.

4. Drain the pasta and put it into a large bowl. Immediately add the vegetable sauce and toss. Pass the Parmesan cheese at the table.

BAKED ZITI AND SAUSAGE CASSEROLE

SERVES 12

2 pounds Italian sweet sausages
½ cup olive oil
2 large sweet green peppers, seeded and diced
1 cup chopped onion
2 pounds ziti
1 tablespoon salt
1½ pounds ricotta
½ cup heavy cream
2 large eggs
½ teaspoon fennel seeds
2 teaspoons dried basil
1 teaspoon dried oregano
½ cup chopped fresh parsley leaves
Freshly ground black pepper to taste
7 cups homemade or canned tomato sauce
½ cup (1 stick) butter, melted
1½ cups freshly grated Parmesan cheese
2 pounds mozzarella, thinly sliced

1. Remove the sausage meat from the casings and crumble it. Cook the sausage in a large frying pan until it is lightly browned, stirring often. Transfer it to a colander to drain.

2. Add the olive oil to the pan and cook the peppers and onions over medium heat for about 5 minutes.

3. Meanwhile, bring 6½ quarts of water to a boil in a large pot.

4. Preheat the oven to 350 degrees.

5. Combine the peppers and onion with the sausage.

6. In another bowl, combine the ricotta, heavy cream, eggs, fennel seeds, and herbs and season well with salt and pepper.

7. Add 1 tablespoon of salt to the boiling water in the pot. Stir and add the ziti. Cook the pasta until it is *al dente*, or just until tender, stirring often.

8. Meanwhile, spread 2 cups of the tomato sauce over the bottom of a large 9- to 10-quart shallow casserole or large roasting pan.

9. Drain the pasta well and toss with the butter. Put half of the pasta over the sauce in the pan. Add half of the ricotta mixture, half of the sausage mixture, and half of the remaining tomato sauce. Top with half of the mozzarella and sprinkle with half of the Parmesan cheese. Repeat all the layers again in the same order.

10. Bake the casserole for about 45 minutes, or until the top is golden brown and the casserole bubbles.

More Servings
Double the recipe to serve 24 and cook in two large casseroles or roasting pans.

Freeze the cooled casserole, covered tightly. To reheat it, bake in a preheated 325-degree oven for about 1 hour.

JULIENNE OF CARROTS AND PEAS WITH FINE EGG NOODLES

SERVES 12

½ cup (1 stick) butter
¼ cup finely chopped shallots
1 pound carrots, scraped and cut into thin julienne strips
2 10-ounce packages frozen green peas

1 pound fine egg noodles
2 tablespoons chopped fresh parsley leaves
Salt and freshly ground black pepper to taste

1. Melt the butter in a saucepan and cook the shallots over medium heat for 5 minutes, stirring often.

2. Bring 3½ quarts of water to a boil in a pot.

3. Meanwhile, cook the carrots and peas in 1½ quarts of boiling water for 5 minutes. Drain.

4. Add 1 tablespoon of salt to the water, stir, and cook the egg noodles in the 3½ quarts boiling water just until tender, about 5 minutes. Drain and toss in a large bowl with the butter and shallots, carrots, peas, and parsley. Season with salt and pepper.

More Servings
Double the recipe to serve 24. Cook the noodles in 5½ quarts of boiling water with 2 tablespoons of salt.

MUSHROOM AND SPINACH LASAGNE WITH TOMATO-CREAM SAUCE

◇ ═══════════════════════════════════ ◇

The Tomato-Cream Sauce in this recipe is also excellent with 3 pounds of cheese or meat tortellini, penne, ziti, or rigatoni, to serve 16.

SERVES 16

TOMATO-CREAM SAUCE

2 28-ounce cans Italian imported whole tomatoes with liquid, chopped

3/4 cup (1½ sticks) butter

1/2 cup olive oil

3 medium-sized onions, chopped

2 large garlic cloves, minced

1 teaspoon dried thyme

1 teaspoon dried oregano

12 fresh basil leaves, finely chopped, or 1½ teaspoons dried basil

1/3 cup chopped fresh parsley leaves

1 6-ounce can tomato paste

1/2 cup dry white wine

2 cups heavy cream

Salt and freshly ground black pepper

4 10-ounce packages frozen chopped spinach, cooked and well drained

2 pounds fresh mushrooms, thinly sliced

2 15-ounce containers ricotta

3 large eggs

Freshly grated nutmeg

Salt and freshly ground black pepper to taste

2 pounds lasagne

2 pounds mozzarella

1 cup freshly grated Parmesan cheese

1. Prepare the sauce first. In a 5-quart pot, heat ½ cup of the butter with the oil. Add the onions and garlic and cook over medium heat for 5 minutes, stirring often.

2. Add the herbs and stir. Add the remaining sauce ingredients, stir, and bring to a boil. Immediately lower the heat and simmer for 15 minutes.

3. Meanwhile, melt the remaining 4 tablespoons of butter in a large deep pot. Add the mushrooms and cook for about 10 minutes, stirring often.

4. Bring a large pot of water, about 6½ quarts, to a rolling boil. Add 3 tablespoons of salt, stir, and add the lasagne. Cook for 10 minutes.

5. Meanwhile, transfer the mushrooms to a large bowl. Stir in the

spinach and ricotta and mix well. Stir in the eggs and several gratings of fresh nutmeg. Season with salt and pepper. Set aside.

6. Purée the sauce, a few cups at a time, in a blender or food processor.

7. Preheat the oven to 375 degrees.

8. Drain the pasta well.

9. To assemble the lasagne, spoon a thin layer of the sauce over the bottom of two 9- by 14- by 3-inch baking dishes or pans. Add a layer of pasta in three rows in each pan, lengthwise. The lasagne noodles will not be long enough to fit the entire length of the pans, so add extra lengths to fit the pans perfectly.

10. Spoon a little sauce over the lasagne and spread evenly. Top with half of the mushroom-spinach mixture, using one fourth of the mixture for each pan. Press down slightly. Sprinkle the top with one third of the mozzarella and Parmesan cheese. Top with another layer of lasagne and repeat the layering of the sauce, mushroom and spinach mixture, and mozzarella and Parmesan cheese. Top with another layer of lasagne and sprinkle with the remaining mozzarella. Spoon the remaining sauce over the top of the lasagne in each pan in equal amounts. Sprinkle with the remaining Parmesan cheese.

11. Bake for about 45 minutes, or until the lasagne bubbles and is golden brown on top. Let stand for 10 minutes before serving. The lasagne can be cooled, tightly covered, and frozen. To reheat it, bake in a preheated 350-degree oven for about 45 minutes, or until thoroughly heated.

More Servings
Double the recipe to serve 32 and cook in two batches.

ROTELLE WITH CHERRY TOMATOES, MUSSELS, AND BASIL SAUCE

SERVES 16

1 bottle dry white wine
9 dozen mussels, well scrubbed and beards removed
3 pounds rotelle
3 pints cherry tomatoes
1 cup packed fresh basil leaves (do not use dried basil)

1 teaspoon chopped garlic
3½ cups olive oil
½ cup fresh lemon juice
¼ cup white wine vinegar
Salt and freshly ground black pepper to taste
½ cup thinly sliced scallions

1. In a large pot, bring the wine and 1½ quarts of water to a rolling boil. Add the mussels, stir, cover, and cook over high heat for 8 minutes. Drain the mussels and remove from the shells. Set aside.

2. Cook the pasta following the directions given on page 227 for cooking large quantities of pasta.

3. While bringing the water to a boil, cut the cherry tomatoes in half. Set aside.

4. In a blender or food processor, purée the basil, garlic, 2 cups of the olive oil, and the lemon juice.

5. Transfer the mixture to a large bowl and whisk in the remaining 1½ cups of olive oil and the vinegar. Season well with salt and pepper.

6. Drain the pasta and put it into a very large bowl. Top with the mussels, tomatoes, and scallions and pour the basil sauce over all. Toss and taste for seasoning. Serve warm or cold, tossing again before serving.

FUSILLI WITH ARTICHOKE HEARTS AND BEL PAESE MORNAY SAUCE

SERVES 16

3 pounds fusilli
3 10-ounce packages frozen artichoke hearts, cooked, drained, and cooled
6 tablespoons butter
6 tablespoons all-purpose flour
2½ cups milk

1½ cups heavy cream
6 ounces Bel Paese cheese
¾ cup freshly grated Parmesan cheese
Salt and freshly ground black pepper to taste

1. Cook the pasta following the directions given on page 227 for cooking large quantities of pasta.
2. Meanwhile, coarsely chop the artichoke hearts and set them aside.
3. In a large heavy saucepan, melt the butter and whisk in the flour. Add the milk and heavy cream and bring to a boil, whisking constantly.
4. Stir in the Bel Paese and Parmesan cheeses and continue stirring until the sauce is creamy and smooth. Add the artichokes and combine. Season well with salt and pepper.
5. Toss the fusilli and sauce in a large bowl and serve immediately.

More Servings
Double the recipe to serve 32.

ZITI CARBONARA

SERVES 24

2 pounds slab bacon, cut into ½-inch cubes, cooked crisp and drained
3 pounds ziti
Salt
2½ cups heavy cream
6 large eggs, beaten

½ cup (1 stick) butter, melted
1 cup freshly grated Parmesan cheese, or to taste
Salt and freshly ground black pepper

1. Cook the pasta following the directions given on page 227 for cooking large quantities of pasta.

2. Meanwhile, bring the heavy cream to a boil and simmer over very low heat for 5 minutes.

3. Drain the pasta well. Turn into a large bowl and immediately toss with the eggs and butter. Add the cream and Parmesan cheese and combine thoroughly. Taste for seasoning. Serve at once.

SESAME NOODLES

This dish is very rich. Three pounds of noodles are sufficient.

SERVES 24

1 cup crunchy peanut butter
½ cup Oriental sesame oil, or as needed
½ cup tahini (sesame seed paste)
2 cups peanut oil
3 tablespoons light soy sauce
2 tablespoons rice wine vinegar
1 tablespoon grated fresh gingerroot

Salt
3 pounds Chinese egg noodles, spaghetti, or linguine
1 large sweet red pepper, seeded and thinly sliced
6 scallions, thinly sliced
Freshly ground black pepper

1. Bring 7 quarts of water to a rolling boil in a large pot.

2. Meanwhile, combine the peanut butter, sesame oil, tahini, peanut oil, soy sauce, vinegar, and ginger in a large saucepan. Heat but do not boil. Immediately remove from the heat and set aside.

3. Stir 3 tablespoons of salt into the boiling water, stir, and cook the noodles until done, about 5 minutes. (If using spaghetti or linguine, cook until the pasta is al *dente*.) Drain well.

4. In a large bowl, combine the sauce, noodles, red pepper, and scallions. Season with salt and pepper to taste. Cover and chill thoroughly. Toss before serving.

RIGATONI WITH RAGU SAUCE

Ragu is Bologna's famous meat sauce: Bolognese. Spaghetti Bolognese is probably on more menus in Italian restaurants in America than any other, and the supermarkets are inundated with various brands of Bolognese sauce. None of the bottled blends approach homemade ragu. The real thing is quickly assembled, but it must be simmered for at least 2 hours. The sauce freezes well, so it can be made in advance, thawed, and reheated for about 20 minutes.

The popularity of Ragu sauce is threefold: It is simple to prepare; it's relatively inexpensive for serving so many; and it is delicious. It remains a great dish for a casual gathering.

To the classic recipe I've added onions, sweet red peppers, and dried hot pepper flakes. For me, these additions enhance the dish, but they can be eliminated for a purer version.

As with so many pasta meals, all that is required for a satisfying menu is a tossed green salad, toasted Italian plain or garlic bread, and red wine. Gorgonzola and fresh pears provide a simple and delectable dessert.

SERVES 24

RAGU SAUCE

- 3 pounds ground beef
- 1/2 cup olive oil
- 1/2 cup (1 stick) butter
- 2 cups chopped onion
- 3 large garlic cloves, minced
- 3 large sweet red peppers, chopped
- 2 28-ounce cans imported Italian tomatoes with liquid, chopped
- 2 cups homemade beef stock or canned broth
- 1 cup dry white wine
- 16 fresh basil leaves, finely chopped, or 1 tablespoon dried basil

- 1 tablespoon chopped fresh oregano, or 1 teaspoon dried oregano
- 1/2 teaspoon dried red pepper flakes
- 1/2 cup chopped fresh parsley leaves
- 1 tablespoon salt (optional) Freshly ground black pepper to taste
- 3 cups freshly grated Parmesan cheese

- 5 pounds rigatoni

1. Put the meat into a large heavy pot and cook it over medium heat, stirring often, until it loses all its pink color. Add the remaining ingredients, except the Parmesan cheese. Stir and bring slowly to a boil. Immediately lower the heat, partially cover, and simmer the sauce for 2 hours.

2. When the sauce has cooked, bring 15 quarts of water to a rolling boil. Add 5 tablespoons of salt, stir, and add the rigatoni. Stir frequently, and cook until the pasta is *al dente,* or just until tender, about 12 minutes.

3. Drain the pasta (see instructions page 228).

4. Put the pasta into a very large bowl and spoon the sauce over it. Toss well and serve at once. Serve the Parmesan cheese in a bowl on the side.

More Servings
The recipe can be doubled to serve 48.

NOODLES WITH CHEDDAR CHEESE-CREAM SAUCE

SERVES 24

4 pounds medium-wide egg noodles
Salt
1 cup milk
3 cups heavy cream

1 pound sharp Cheddar cheese, shredded
Freshly ground black pepper
3 tablespoons chopped fresh parsley leaves
1/2 cup (1 stick) butter, melted

1. Cook the noodles in 8 quarts of rapidly boiling water with 4 tablespoons of salt until done, about 8 minutes, stirring often.

2. Meanwhile, bring the milk and cream to a boil in a large nonmetallic saucepan. Stir in the cheese and cook over medium heat, stirring constantly, until the cheese has melted. Season with salt and pepper to taste.

3. Drain the noodles. Toss in a large bowl with the butter. Pour the cheese sauce over the noodles and combine well. Sprinkle with the parsley and serve at once.

FUSILLI WITH GREEN PRIMAVERA VEGETABLES AND ITALIAN PARSLEY SAUCE

SERVES 36

3 tablespoons vegetable oil
1 cup pine nuts
2 pounds fresh asparagus with stalk ends trimmed, cut into 1-inch lengths
2 pounds fresh string beans with ends trimmed, cut into 1-inch lengths
1 pound fresh snow pea pods, strings removed

8 broccoli stalks with stems peeled, cut into bite-sized pieces (including flowerets)
3 medium-sized zucchini, halved lengthwise, and cut into ¼-inch-thick slices
5 pounds fusilli

ITALIAN PARSLEY SAUCE

½ cup fresh lemon juice
½ cup white wine vinegar
1 tablespoon crushed garlic (about 3 large cloves)
2 tablespoons dried basil

1 cup chopped fresh parsley leaves
3 cups olive oil, or as needed
Salt and freshly ground black pepper to taste

1. Heat the 3 tablespoons of oil in a large frying pan and toast the pine nuts, stirring often for a few minutes. Drain and set aside.

2. At this point bring the water for the pasta to a boil following the directions on page 227 for cooking large quantities of pasta.

3. Meanwhile, cook the asparagus and string beans in lightly salted water to cover for 5 minutes. Remove the vegetables to a large bowl using a slotted spoon or large Chinese strainer.

4. Cook the snow pea pods in the same boiling water for 30 seconds. Remove, drain, and add to the bowl with the asparagus.

5. Cook the broccoli and zucchini in the boiling water for 5 minutes. Remove, drain, and put in the bowl with the other vegetables.

6. To make the sauce, put the lemon juice, vinegar, garlic, basil, parsley, and 1 cup of the olive oil in a blender or food processor. Blend very well. Pour into a bowl and whisk in the remaining oil. Season well with salt and pepper.

7. Drain the cooked pasta and add it to the bowl with the vegetables. Pour the sauce over and toss gently, combining the pasta, vegetables, and dressing. Taste for seasoning, adding a little more oil or lemon juice, if necessary. Serve warm or cold. If serving cold, toss again before serving.

BOMBAY CURRIED NOODLES

SERVES 36

7 pounds wide egg noodles	2½ cups currants
Salt	1 cup thinly sliced scallions
2½ cups (5 sticks) butter	Salt and freshly ground black
6 tablespoons curry powder	pepper to taste

1. Bring 10 quarts of water to a boil in a large pot. Add 3 tablespoons of salt, stir, and cook the noodles until tender, about 8 minutes, stirring often.

2. Meanwhile, melt the butter in a saucepan. Stir in the curry powder and cook over low heat for 3 minutes. Set aside.

3. Drain the noodles and turn into a very large bowl. Pour the curry butter over the noodles and toss gently.

4. Add the currants and scallions and combine well. Season with salt and pepper.

Variation
In place of the scallions, 10 very thinly sliced small yellow onions can be deep-fried, drained, and then added to the noodles with the currants.

ANTIPASTO PASTA

◇ ══════════════════ ◇

Although there are many ingredients in this dish, it is still relatively simple to prepare, considering that you are cooking for fifty people. And, because of the volume of the ingredients in the recipe, only five pounds of pasta are required.

SERVES 50

4 tablespoons butter
6 tablespoons olive oil
2 cups chopped onion
6 large celery stalks, thinly sliced
1 pound mushrooms, thinly sliced
4 large sweet green peppers, seeded and thinly sliced
1 tablespoon dried oregano
2 tablespoons dried basil
1 cup chopped fresh parsley leaves
2 16-ounce cans large pitted black olives, drained and halved lengthwise
2 cups pimiento-stuffed green olives, drained and halved crosswise

3 12½-ounce cans solid white meat tuna, drained and flaked
1 2-ounce can anchovy fillets, drained and coarsely chopped
1½ cups jarred roasted red peppers, drained and chopped
3 14-ounce cans artichoke hearts, drained and halved
1½ pounds Provolone, cut into ½-inch cubes
1½ pounds mortadella, thinly sliced and cut into thin strips
1½ pounds Genoa salami, cut into ½-inch cubes
5 pounds ziti
Salt and freshly ground black pepper

DRESSING

4 tablespoons Dijon mustard
¾ cup white wine vinegar, or as needed

4 cups olive oil, or as needed
Salt and freshly ground black pepper to taste

1. Heat the butter and oil in a large heavy pot. Add the onion, celery, mushrooms, and green peppers. Stir and simmer, covered, for 10 minutes. Add the herbs and combine. Cook, uncovered, over low heat for 10 minutes, stirring often.

2. Transfer the mixture to a very large bowl. (A large plastic salad

bowl is excellent.) Of course, two large bowls can also be used, if you divide all the ingredients evenly.

3. Cook the pasta following the directions on page 227 for cooking large quantities of pasta.

4. Meanwhile, put all the remaining ingredients, except the dressing, in the large bowl with the vegetables, or divide them between the two bowls. Combine gently.

5. Make the dressing in a blender, half of the amount given in the recipe at a time, by combining the mustard and vinegar. With the blender turned on, add the oil in a slow steady stream through the opening in the lid. Season well with salt and pepper.

6. Drain the pasta well, and add it to the bowl with the other ingredients, or divide it evenly between the two bowls. Pour the dressing over the pasta and toss gently. If necessary, add a little extra vinegar and/or olive oil. The pasta should be moist but no liquid should remain in the bottom of the bowl. Taste for seasoning. Serve at room temperature or cold. Toss before serving.

More Servings

Double the ingredients to serve 100 and make in two or more batches. The dressing will have to be made in four batches.

Fewer Servings

Cut the recipe in half to serve 25.

Potato and Rice Dishes

$\diamond \equiv\equiv\equiv\equiv\equiv\equiv\equiv \diamond$

POTATO DISHES

The virtues of potatoes, the champion of vegetables, are many. Potatoes, nutritious, versatile, and inexpensive, are always available in several varieties and are great crowd-pleasers.

Potatoes are fat-free, low in calories, easily stored, and relatively quick-cooking.

Potatoes lend themselves to most cooking methods beautifully; they have a natural affinity for butter, cream, milk, and cheese, and, happily, for many other foods, as well.

Today, aside from the ubiquitious French fries, the multitude of stuffed baked potato possibilities, old-fashioned mashed potatoes, potato salads, and boiled new potatoes, there is an endless array of excellent classical potato dishes. My favorite recently discovered potato dishes are Belgian Scalloped Potatoes with Leeks and Caraway Seeds, Caribbean Sautéed Potatoes, and Steven Gregor's Roquefort Potatoes au Gratin, which are all included in this chapter.

BELGIAN SCALLOPED POTATOES WITH LEEKS AND CARAWAY SEEDS

SERVES 8

8 medium-sized Idaho potatoes, peeled and thinly sliced
4 leeks (white parts only), well washed and thinly sliced
1 teaspoon caraway seeds

Salt and freshly ground black pepper to taste
6 tablespoons butter, cut into thin slices
1 cup heavy cream
1 cup milk

1. Preheat the oven to 425 degrees.
2. In the bottom of a large gratin dish or roasting pan, arrange half of the potato slices in layers. Top with the leeks and sprinkle with the caraway seeds and salt and pepper. Add half of the sliced butter. Top with the remaining potatoes and butter and sprinkle with salt and pepper.
3. Combine the heavy cream and milk and pour the mixture over the top. Bake for 30 minutes, or until the top is golden brown.

More Servings
To serve 16, double the recipe and bake in an extra-large roasting pan or make two batches in two dishes or pans.

SWEET POTATO TIMBALES WITH PINEAPPLE

SERVES 8

5 sweet potatoes (about 3 pounds), well washed and dried
3 tablespoons butter, plus extra for greasing the molds
1/3 cup heavy cream

1 8-ounce can crushed pineapple, very well drained and squeezed dry
Salt and freshly ground black pepper to taste

1. Preheat the oven to 400 degrees.

2. Put the sweet potatoes on a baking sheet and bake until they are tender, about 45 minutes.

3. When cool enough to handle, cut the potatoes in half, scoop out the pulp, and put it into a large bowl.

4. Mash the potatoes with a hand masher. Stir in the butter, cream, and pineapple and combine well. Season with salt and pepper.

5. Spoon the mixture into 8 well-greased ½-cup timbale molds, small soufflé dishes, or custard cups.

6. Set the timbales in a pan with ½ inch of boiling water and return to the 400 degree oven for 10 minutes.

7. Using hot pads, invert the molds onto a platter or individual dinner plates. Serve at once.

More Servings
Double the recipe to serve 16.

TURBAN OF POTATO AND EGG SALAD WITH DILL

SERVES 12

5 pounds Idaho potatoes	3 tablespoons Dijon mustard
Salt	½ cup chopped fresh dill, or 3
¾ cup minced onion	tablespoons dried dill, plus 8
¾ cup white wine vinegar, or as	full sprigs of dillweed
needed	Freshly ground black pepper
2 cups vegetable oil	6 hard-boiled eggs, chopped

1. Bring 5½ quarts of water to a boil in a large pot.

2. Meanwhile, peel the potatoes and quarter them. Cut each potato piece into ½-inch cubes.

3. Add 2 tablespoons of salt to the boiling water and stir. Add the potatoes and cook for about 6 minutes, or just until they are tender, stirring often.

4. Meanwhile, put the onion, vinegar, and oil into a medium-sized

saucepan and bring the mixture to a boil. Immediately lower the heat to a simmer and cook for 5 minutes.

5. Remove the saucepan from the heat and whisk in the mustard and dill. Season with salt and pepper to taste and set aside.

6. Drain the potatoes well and put them into a large bowl with the eggs. Pour the sauce over the top and combine gently. Taste for seasoning.

7. Lightly grease a 12-cup ring mold. Spoon the potato salad into the mold and pat the top down gently. Refrigerate for several hours.

8. Put a large plate over the mold and invert it. Holding firmly onto both, give a good shake; the molded salad should release onto the plate. Decorate the perimeter of the salad with the dill sprigs.

More Servings
Double the recipe to serve 24 and use two 12-cup ring molds.

DIANA BACHUS'
BAKED HASH BROWN POTATOES WITH
SOUR CREAM AND CHEDDAR CHEESE

◇══════════════════════════════◇

SERVES 12

2 pounds frozen hash brown potatoes, thawed for 30 minutes (Discard any potato pieces containing potato skin.)
1 cup diced onion
12 ounces sharp Cheddar cheese, grated (about 2 cups)

½ cup (1 stick) butter, melted
2 cups sour cream
1 cup heavy cream
1 large egg, lightly beaten
Salt and freshly ground black pepper to taste
Chopped fresh parsley leaves

1. Preheat the oven to 375 degrees.

2. Combine the potatoes, onions, and 1 cup of the grated cheese in a large bowl.

3. In another bowl, mix together the butter, sour cream, heavy

cream, and egg. Season well with salt and pepper. Pour the sauce over the potato mixture and combine gently.

4. Turn the potatoes into a 9- by 13- by 3-inch baking dish and smooth the surface evenly. Bake for 30 minutes. Sprinkle the remaining cheese evenly over the top and continue baking for 30 minutes. If desired, pass the potatoes under the broiler for further browning for a minute or two. Sprinkle with parsley. Let the potatoes stand 5 minutes before cutting them into 12 equal-sized square portions.

More Servings
Double the recipe to serve 24 by making two batches and bake in two 9- by 13- by 3-inch baking pans.

Variations
For Rosemary Potatoes, add 1 teaspoon dried rosemary to the cream sauce before mixing it with the potatoes. Other herbs that can be added in the same amount are thyme, tarragon, or dill.

For a one-dish meal add 1½ cups chopped shrimp, flaked canned tuna, or chopped cooked chicken or turkey to the potato mixture. Add ¼ cup more of heavy cream to the sauce mixture. One cup cooked crumbled sausage or ground meat can also be added with ½ cup of diced sweet green pepper. Add the extra ¼ cup of heavy cream to the sauce. Serve with a mixed salad and French bread. This one-dish meal will serve 6 to 8.

CARIBBEAN SAUTÉED POTATOES

◇ ══════════════════════════════════════ ◇

It will be necessary to cook the potatoes in two large frying pans or in two batches because of the volume. Transfer the first batch to a warmed covered serving dish while cooking the second batch.

SERVES 16

6 pounds Idaho potatoes, unpeeled, quartered, and cut into ¼-inch-thick slices
Butter
Vegetable oil

1 large onion, coarsely chopped
2 large garlic cloves, minced
2 large sweet green peppers, seeded and diced

2 tablespoons curry powder
½ teaspoon hot red pepper
flakes
Salt and freshly ground black
pepper to taste

¼ cup chopped fresh parsley
leaves

1. Boil the potatoes in water to cover for 6 minutes. Drain immediately.

2. Meanwhile, heat 3 tablespoons each of butter and oil in a large frying pan. Add the onion, garlic, and green pepper. Cook over medium heat, stirring often, for about 8 minutes. Add the curry and hot pepper flakes and mix in well.

3. Transfer half of the mixture to a second frying pan and heat.

4. Add half of the potatoes to each pan. Add a little butter and oil to each pan, cover, and cook both over medium heat for 5 minutes.

5. Turn the potatoes and cook until golden brown and tender. Season well with salt and pepper and sprinkle with the parsley. Serve at once.

MASHED SWEET POTATOES IN CRÊPES

◇ ═══════════════════════════════════ ◇

To save last-minute time for other dishes on the menu, I suggest making the crêpes first. They can be covered and refrigerated for two days, if desired.

SERVES 16

CRÊPES

1½ cups water
1⅓ cups milk
1⅓ cups all-purpose flour
6 large eggs

4 tablespoons melted butter,
plus extra for cooking the
crêpes
1 teaspoon salt

8 large sweet potatoes, washed
and dried
4 tablespoons butter, plus 4
tablespoons melted butter for
the topping
⅓ cup heavy cream
½ teaspoon ground cinnamon

Freshly grated nutmeg to
taste
3 tablespoons dark rum
Salt and freshly ground black
pepper to taste
Sugar

1. Combine the crêpe ingredients in a large bowl using a wire whisk.

2. Melt 1 teaspoon of butter in a non-stick 10-inch frying pan with curved sides. Pour about ⅓ cup of the batter into the pan. Immediately tilt the pan in a circle to distribute the batter evenly. When the crêpe turns light brown around the edges, turn with a cake spatula and cook for a few seconds, or until it is lightly browned on the other side. Transfer the crêpe to a plate. Add 1 teaspoon of butter to the pan and continue making 15 more crêpes in the same manner. Cover and refrigerate if not preparing the stuffed crêpes immediately.

3. Preheat the oven to 400 degrees. Bake the sweet potatoes on a baking sheet until they are tender, about 50 minutes. Leave the oven on.

4. Cut the sweet potatoes in half and scoop out the pulp. Mash with a hand masher with the butter, cream, spices, rum, and salt and pepper. Cool for 15 minutes.

5. Spoon about ½ cup of the sweet potato purée into the center of a crêpe. Fold the bottom up over the potatoes. Fold the sides in and roll up the crêpe into a fairly square package. Put the stuffed crêpe, seam side down, into a large greased roasting pan. Assemble the remaining 15 crêpes in the same manner.

6. Brush the tops of the crêpes with the melted butter and sprinkle lightly with sugar.

7. Bake the crêpes for 10 minutes; then pass quickly under the broiler until the tops are golden brown. Serve at once.

STEVEN GREGOR'S
ROQUEFORT POTATOES AU GRATIN

Here's another recipe from the talented chef, Steven Gregor.

SERVES 24

15 Idaho potatoes, peeled and very thinly sliced (with a mandoline, if possible)

¾ cup (1½ sticks) butter, or as needed

Salt and freshly ground black pepper to taste

3 cups heavy cream

4 ounces Roquefort cheese, crumbled

½ cup seasoned bread crumbs

1. Preheat the oven to 425 degrees.
2. Grease a large roasting pan, about 14 by 16 by 3 inches, with butter.
3. Arrange the potatoes in layered rows. Sprinkle with salt and pepper and dot randomly with butter.
4. Bring the cream to a boil in a large non-metallic saucepan. Stir in the cheese and cook over high heat, stirring, until the cheese melts. Season with salt and pepper.
5. Pour the mixture over the potatoes. Cover the potatoes tightly with aluminum foil and bake for about 1 hour and 30 minutes.
6. Uncover, sprinkle with the bread crumbs and dot with 3 tablespoons of butter, which has been cut into tiny pieces. Pass under the broiler until golden brown on top.
7. Let stand for 10 minutes before cutting into even-sized squares.

OPEN-FACED POTATOES WITH PARMESAN CHEESE AND BREAD CRUMBS

SERVES 24

24 small Idaho potatoes, washed and dried
1 cup (2 sticks) butter

¾ cup freshly grated Parmesan cheese
¾ cup plain dry bread crumbs

1. Preheat the oven to 400 degrees.
2. Prick each potato once with the tip of a small sharp pointed knife. Bake in the oven on the two lower shelves for 20 minutes. Rotate the potatoes and bake for about 20 minutes, or until done.
3. Remove the potatoes and cut them in half lengthwise. Arrange side by side on two large baking sheets with at least ½ inch sides.
4. Brush the potatoes liberally with the butter and sprinkle lightly with the combined cheese and bread crumbs.
5. Cook 5 to 6 inches from the heat in a hot broiler, one pan at a time, until golden brown. This will only take a few minutes. Serve immediately.

NEW POTATO SALAD DIJONNAISE

SERVES 36

1 cup Dijon mustard
1 cup sour cream
3 cups mayonnaise
½ cup chopped fresh parsley
  leaves
  Peanut oil for deep-frying
8 small yellow onions, thinly
  sliced and separated into
  rings

8 pounds hot new potatoes,
  boiled and cut into ¼-inch-
  thick slices
  Salt and freshly ground black
  pepper to taste

1. Combine the mustard, sour cream, mayonnaise, and parsley.

2. Heat 2 inches of the oil in a fryer or large deep pan and fry the onion rings until golden brown, stirring often. Drain on paper towels and cool.

3. Put the *hot* potatoes into a large bowl with the onions and pour the dressing over the mixture. Toss gently and season with salt and pepper. Serve warm or cold.

BAKED POTATO SHELLS STUFFED WITH GERMAN POTATO SALAD

SERVES 50

50 large Idaho potatoes, washed
  and dried
2 cups finely chopped red
  onion
2 cups finely chopped yellow
  onion
4 large garlic cloves, minced
½ cup Dijon mustard

¾ cup chopped fresh parsley
  leaves
  Salt and freshly ground black
  pepper
2½ cups olive oil
2½ cups vegetable oil
2 cups white wine vinegar
2 pounds bacon, cooked crisp,
  and coarsely chopped

1. Preheat the oven to 400 degrees.

2. Pierce each potato once with the tip of a small sharp knife.

3. Cook 25 potatoes in the oven for about 45 minutes, or until they are tender. Remove and cook the remaining potatoes for 45 minutes.

4. Meanwhile, prepare the dressing. Put the onions, garlic, mustard, and parsley in a large bowl. Season well with salt and pepper.

5. Heat the olive and vegetable oils and vinegar. Just before the mixture boils, remove and carefully pour over the onion mixture. Add the bacon and stir. Set aside to marinate.

6. Cut off about one third of the top of each potato lengthwise. Scoop out the potato pulp in spoonfuls from the top, and put it in a large bowl. Discard the tops. Scoop out the pulp from the potato shells, leaving the shells intact. When the next batch of potatoes is cooked, cool slightly and repeat this procedure.

7. Pour the dressing over the potatoes in the bowl and combine gently. The potatoes should remain lumpy. Season with salt and pepper to taste.

8. Spoon the mixture into the potato shells. Serve immediately or chill before serving.

RICE DISHES

Rice is extremely easy to cook for crowds, and the introduction of vegetables, fruit, nuts, meat, seafood, or herbs and spices can change rice from a side dish accompanying the main course to an entrée itself.

Paella or a rice salad are excellent examples of recipes in which rice becomes a special main dish by the addition of other easily prepared ingredients.

The three rules to remember when cooking rice are: Except when using Italian Arborio or Basmati rice (the Indian long-grained rice), never wash or soak rice; never stir it during cooking; and never overcook it. The following instructions and time chart are for rice dishes serving from eight to fifty.

Instructions for Cooking Rice in Large Quantities

Serves	Size of Pot	Rice	Water or Broth	Butter	Salt
8	2½ quart	2 cups	3½ cups	1 tbl.	1 tsp.
12	4 quart	3 cups	5 cups	2 tbls.	1½ tsps.
16	6 quart	4 cups	6 cups	4 tbls.	2 tsps.
24	8 quart	6 cups	8 cups	6 tbls.	1 tbl.
36	10 to 12 quart	8 cups	11 cups	8 tbls.	2 tbls.
50	12 to 14 quart	10 cups	14½ cups	10 tbls.	3 tbls.

Do not add salt if cooking with chicken or beef broth; there is plenty of salt in the broth.

1. In the proper-sized pot, bring the water or broth to a boil. Stir in the rice, salt, and butter. Bring back to a boil, immediately cover tightly, and cook for 20 minutes.

2. Remove the pot from the heat and let stand, covered, for 10 minutes. If the rice is still a little moist, cover and cook over very low heat for 1 or 2 minutes so that the moisture will evaporate. Fluff the rice with a metal fork. Cooked rice will keep in the refrigerator for up to 5 days. It can be tightly wrapped and frozen for several months. Thaw the rice in the package in the refrigerator before reheating it.

CONFETTI BROWN RICE TIMBALES

◊══════════════════════════════════════◊

SERVES 8

4 cups (1 quart) canned beef
  broth
2 cups long-grain brown rice
1 tablespoon butter, plus extra
  for greasing the timbales
1/4 cup minced scallions

1 10-ounce package frozen
  green peas, cooked and
  drained
1 large sweet red pepper,
  seeded and diced
3 tablespoons chopped fresh
  parsley leaves

1. Bring the broth to a boil in a 2-quart saucepan. Stir in the rice and butter and bring back to a boil. Cover tightly and simmer for about 50 minutes, or until the rice is tender and has absorbed all of the broth.

2. Remove the pan from the heat. Preheat the oven to 350 degrees.

3. Add the scallions, green peas, red pepper, and parsley to the rice and combine well.

4. Grease eight 1/2-cup timbale molds or the same-sized dessert ramekins or custard cups. Pack the rice mixture into the timbales in equal amounts and put them in a baking dish with about 1/2 inch of boiling water. Bake for 5 minutes.

5. Using a hot pad, invert each rice timbale onto a dinner plate and shake once to release. After putting the rice onto each dinner plate, add the portions of the other dishes in the menu and serve at once.

More Servings
Double the recipe to serve 16 and cook the rice in a 5-quart pot.

CREAMED WILD RICE

◊══════════════════════════════════════◊

SERVES 8

2 cups wild rice
1/4 cup finely chopped shallots
6 cups (1 1/2 quarts) canned
  chicken broth

1 cup sour cream at room
  temperature
Freshly ground black pepper
  to taste

1. Combine the rice, shallots, and chicken broth in a large heavy saucepan. Bring to a boil, cover, and simmer for about 45 minutes, or until the rice is tender.

2. Drain the rice and return it to the same pan. Stir in the sour cream and season with pepper. Serve immediately.

More Servings
Double the recipe to serve 16 and cook in a 5-quart heavy pot.

ITALIAN FRIED RICE

SERVES 12

- ²/₃ cup peanut oil
- 7 cups cold boiled long-grain white rice
- ½ cup chopped fresh parsley leaves
- ½ cup thinly sliced scallions
- 2 10-ounce packages frozen green peas, cooked and drained

- 1 cup diced Genoa salami
- ½ teaspoon dried basil
- ½ teaspoon dried oregano
- 4 large eggs, lightly beaten
- 2 tablespoons soy sauce
  Salt and freshly ground black pepper to taste

1. Heat the oil in a large wide curved-sided frying pan, wok, or paella pan (the latter is perfect for cooking this dish).

2. Add the rice and stir with a wooden spoon, separating any lumps of rice. Add the scallions, green peas, salami, basil, and oregano. Continue to stir-fry until the mixture is heated through.

4. Drizzle the eggs over the rice and immediately stir the eggs into the rice until they are solid. This will only take a minute or two.

5. Sprinkle the rice with soy sauce, stir, and season with salt and pepper. Serve immediately.

RISOTTO MILANESE

This magnificent classic dish served as a first course or side dish with roast meat, chicken, or seafood is savored by all. In northern Italy, risotto is often a meal in itself; this recipe will serve 6 as a main course.

SERVES 12

8 tablespoons butter
⅓ cup finely chopped shallots
1 cup dry white wine
3½ cups Arborio rice
7 cups (1¾ quarts) boiling homemade chicken stock or canned broth

¼ teaspoon powdered saffron
1 cup freshly grated Parmesan cheese
Freshly ground black pepper

1. Heat 6 tablespoons of the butter in a large heavy saucepan and cook the shallots over medium-low heat for 5 minutes, stirring often.
2. Stir in the wine and rice and cook, stirring constantly, until the wine is nearly absorbed.
3. Add 1 cup of the stock and cook, always stirring, until the stock has been absorbed. Continue adding the stock, a cup at a time, and cooking until all the stock has been used.
4. Stir in the saffron, remaining 2 tablespoons of butter, and the cheese. Remove from the heat and let stand, covered, for 5 minutes. Serve immediately and pass the peppermill at the table.

More Servings
Double the recipe to serve 24 and cook in two batches.

Variations
One and a half cups of chopped raw shrimp can be added to the risotto when adding the saffron, or add 2 cups of fresh asparagus cut into 1-inch lengths.

RICE WITH
BLACK BEANS AND VEGETABLES

SERVES 16

6 cups (1½ quarts) canned
 chicken broth
4 tablespoons butter
4 cups long-grain white rice
¾ cup minced onion
1½ cups scraped and diced
 carrots

1½ cups fresh string beans, cut
 into ½-inch lengths
2 16-ounce cans black beans,
 drained

1. In a 6-quart pot bring the broth to a boil. Add the butter, rice, and onion. Stir, cover, and bring back to a boil. Simmer for 20 minutes.

2. Meanwhile, cook the carrots and string beans together in 1½ quarts of boiling water in a saucepan for exactly 5 minutes. Drain well and set aside.

3. Heat the beans and their liquid in a saucepan and drain well.

4. When the rice is done, add the carrots, string beans, and black beans. Toss gently off the heat. Cover and let stand for 10 minutes.

More Servings

To serve 36, follow the instructions for cooking large quantities of rice on page 259 for amounts of broth, rice, and butter and the size of the pot. Double all the other ingredients and cook following the directions given in the recipe.

CURRIED RICE WITH RAISINS AND TOASTED ALMONDS

◇══════════════════════════════════◇

SERVES 16

6 cups (1½ quarts) canned
  chicken broth
4 tablespoons butter
4 cups long-grain white rice
½ cup thinly sliced scallions

2 tablespoons curry powder
1½ cups dark raisins
¼ cup peanut or vegetable oil
1 cup blanched sliced almonds

1. Bring the chicken broth to a boil in a 6-quart pot. Add the butter, rice, scallions, curry powder, and raisins. Stir and bring back to a boil. Cover and simmer for 20 minutes.

2. Meanwhile, heat the oil in a large frying pan and cook the almonds, stirring often, until they are golden brown. Drain.

3. When the rice is done, add the almonds and toss gently with a metal fork.

More Servings
To serve 36, follow the instructions for cooking rice in large quantities on page 259 for size of pot and amounts of broth, rice, and butter. Double all the other ingredients in the recipe.

PAELLA RICE

◇══════════════════◇

SERVES 24

8 cups (2 quarts) canned
  chicken broth
6 tablespoons butter
1 cup minced onion
1 teaspoon minced garlic
6 cups long-grain white rice
½ teaspoon powdered saffron
½ teaspoon ground turmeric

2 10-ounce packages frozen
  green peas, cooked and
  drained
1 cup finely chopped jarred
  roasted red peppers, well
  drained
½ cup chopped fresh parsley
  leaves

1. Bring the chicken broth to a boil in an 8-quart pot. Add the butter, onion, garlic, rice, saffron, and turmeric. Stir and bring back to a boil. Cover and simmer for 20 minutes.

2. Add the green peas, red peppers, and parsley and toss gently. Cover and let stand for 10 minutes.

More Servings
To serve 50, follow the instructions for cooking large quantities of rice on page 259 for the size of the pot and the amounts of broth, rice, and butter. Double all the other ingredients and cook following the directions in the recipe.

MOROCCAN RICE

SERVES 24

8 cups (2 quarts) water
6 tablespoons butter
1 tablespoon salt
6 cups long-grain white rice

½ cup chopped fresh mint leaves
½ cup chopped fresh parsley leaves

1. Bring the water to a boil in an 8-quart pot. Add the butter, salt, and rice. Stir and bring back to a boil. Cover and simmer for 20 minutes.

2. Add the mint and parsley, toss, and cover. Let stand for 10 minutes.

More Servings
To double the recipe, follow the instructions for cooking rice for 50 on page 259, using 1 cup of each chopped fresh mint and parsley.

PILAF PRIMAVERA

SERVES 36

11 cups (2¾ quarts) canned
   chicken broth
8 cups long-grain white rice
1 cup minced onion
½ cup (1 stick) butter
1 pound carrots, scraped and
   cut into fine julienne strips
2 10-ounce packages frozen
   Italian green beans, cooked
   and well drained

1 10-ounce package frozen
   chopped broccoli, cooked
   and well drained
¾ cup diced pimientos, well
   drained
1 tablespoon dried basil
1 teaspoon dried thyme
½ cup chopped fresh parsley
   leaves

1. Bring the chicken broth to a boil in a 10- to 12-quart pot. Stir in the rice, onion, and butter and bring back to a boil. Cover tightly and simmer for 20 minutes.

2. Meanwhile, cook the carrots in 1 quart of boiling water for exactly 4 minutes. Drain immediately.

3. As soon as the rice has cooked for 20 minutes, add the carrots, green beans, broccoli, pimientos, and herbs. Toss with a large slotted spoon. Cover and let stand 10 minutes.

More Servings
To serve 72, cook two batches of the rice.

MINCEMEAT RICE

SERVES 36

11 cups (2¾ quarts) water
8 cups long-grain white rice
½ cup (1 stick) butter

2 tablespoons salt
4 cups (1 quart) mincemeat at
   room temperature

1. Bring the water to a boil in a 10- to 12-quart pot. Stir in the rice, butter, and salt and bring back to a boil. Cover tightly and simmer for 20 minutes.

2. Remove the pot from the heat and add the mincemeat. Using a metal fork, gently fold it into the fluffed rice, cover, and let stand for 10 minutes.

More Servings
To serve 72, cook two batches of the rice.

Herbed Pilaf

◊ ══════════════ ◊

SERVES 50

14½ cups canned chicken broth
10 cups long-grain white rice
10 tablespoons butter
½ cup chopped fresh dill
1 tablespoon dried tarragon

1½ teaspoons dried thyme
1 cup chopped fresh parsley leaves
Freshly ground black pepper to taste

1. Bring the broth to a boil in a 12- to 14-quart pot. Stir in the rice, butter, dill, tarragon, and thyme and bring back to a boil. Cover tightly and simmer for 20 minutes.

2. Remove from the heat. Add the parsley and pepper, fluff with a metal fork, and let stand, covered, for 10 minutes.

More Servings
To serve 100, cook two batches of the rice.

Sandwiches

◊ ≡≡≡≡≡≡≡≡≡≡≡≡≡≡≡≡≡≡≡≡≡≡≡≡≡≡ ◊

Sandwiches are easy and quick solutions to cooking casual meals for crowds. But to be special, they should be composed of interesting and delicious fillings, breads, and spreads.

There are infinite combinations for sandwiches ranging from dainty cooling cucumber and dill on thinly sliced firm white bread, to hearty over-stuffed Dagwoods, standard favorites, such as fried clam or oyster Po' Boys, and Italian meatball or sausage and tomato sauce heros, to more contemporary combinations of arugula, goat cheese, and sun-dried tomatoes on whole wheat pita bread, to broiled mozzarella and Black Forest ham on fried croutons, or thinly-sliced rare roast beef with red onion and basil butter on poppy seed bagels.

The most unusual sandwich I have heard of recently has been popular in the north Midlands of England for many years. It is called a Chip Butty. Made with two thick slices of white bread, or a soft roll, and spread with butter, the sandwich is filled with hot "chips" (French fried potatoes), seasoned with salt and pepper, and sometimes a splash of vinegar—an acquired taste and definitely not for dieters.

Fillings and bread should complement each other in flavor and texture. Breads can be selected from the many excellent varieties available in bakeries or made right at home: all types of French or Italian breads and rolls, Portuguese sweet bread, challah, Indian fried breads, whole wheat, rye, pumpernickel, or black bread, bagels, toasted English muffins, biscuits, Kaiser rolls, pita bread, and so on.

Spreads add flavor, but also keep sandwiches moist, and can prevent bread from becoming soggy. Butter, mayonnaise, mustard, or cream cheese can be used plain or enriched with herbs, spices, ground nuts, or condiments, such as chutney, cranberry sauce, or relish. Tartar sauce, Russian dressing, and blue cheese dressings should also be considered.

Garnishes and side dishes must enhance the sandwich and balance out the menu. Crudités, Greek or Niçoise olives, cornichons, sour, dill, or sweet pickles, mixed green or tossed salads, raw or cooked vegetable salads, fruit salads, or pasta salads, and potato chips can make up a very satisfying menu.

Here are some favorite crowd-pleasing sandwiches, both hot and cold, to spark the imagination for your own creations.

FRIED SOFT-SHELL CRAB SANDWICHES

When soft-shell crabs are in season they make first-rate sandwiches for company. Beer goes nicely with these sandwiches.

SERVES 8

16 medium-sized soft-shell crabs, cleaned
Salt and freshly ground black pepper
All-purpose flour
4 large eggs, lightly beaten
3 tablespoons water
Plain dry bread crumbs

Peanut oil for deep-frying
8 6-inch long pieces French bread (2 or 3 loaves)
1 cup tartar sauce
1 medium-sized red onion, very thinly sliced and separated into rings
2 cups shredded iceberg lettuce

1. Season the crabs with salt and pepper.

2. Dust each crab with flour, dip in the combined eggs and water, and coat with bread crumbs.

3. Heat 2 inches of oil in a large heavy pot or fryer and cook the breaded crabs, a few at a time, until they are crisp and golden brown on each side. Drain well.

4. Cut each piece of the bread open and spread with the tartar sauce. Place two crabs on the bottom half of each piece of bread and top with

a few onion rings and the lettuce, equally divided among the sandwiches. Cover with the bread tops and serve immediately.

More Servings
Double the recipe to make 16 sandwiches.

HAM AND BRIE BAGUETTE SANDWICHES

SERVES 8

3 French baguettes, cut into 8- to 9-inch lengths

³/₄ cup (1¹/₂ sticks) sweet butter, softened

2 pounds Brie with rind removed at room temperature

2 pounds Black Forest ham, very thinly sliced

16 watercress sprigs

24 cornichons

1. Cut each piece of bread in half lengthwise. Spread one half of each half of bread with butter and the other half with Brie in equal amounts.
2. Top the bottom halves of the bread with equal amounts of the ham and watercress sprigs. Place the top on the sandwiches and cut each in half. Serve with the cornichons.

More Servings
Double the recipe to make 16 sandwiches.

SHREDDED
BARBECUED PORK SANDWICHES

◊ ═══════════════════════════════ ◊

MAKES 12 SANDWICHES

1 5½- to 6-pound fresh pork
   shoulder
½ teaspoon dried thyme
½ teaspoon dried oregano
1 tablespoon Dijon mustard

2 large garlic cloves, crushed
   Freshly ground black pepper
   to taste
12 hamburger buns

BARBECUE SAUCE
½ cup (1 stick) butter
1 large onion, finely chopped
1 large garlic clove, minced
½ cup packed dark brown sugar
½ cup red wine vinegar
¼ cup fresh lemon juice
1 tablespoon chili powder

1 16-ounce can imported
   Italian tomato purée
1 cup homemade beef stock or
   canned broth
   Salt and freshly ground black
   pepper to taste

1. Preheat the oven to 325 degrees.

2. Cut away the rind from the top of the roast. Leave the fat on top of the roast and score it.

3. Combine the herbs, mustard, garlic, and pepper and rub the paste into the surface of the roast. Put the roast in a roasting pan.

3. Roast for 3 hours and 30 minutes, or until the juices run clear. (The internal temperature on a meat thermometer should register 185 degrees.)

4. To cook the sauce, melt the butter in a large heavy pot. Stir in the onion and garlic and cook for 5 minutes. Add the remaining ingredients, combine well, and simmer for 30 minutes, stirring often. Cover and set aside.

5. Let the roast rest on a cutting board for 45 minutes. Cut the roast into thick slices and shred with a fork.

6. Add the pork to the sauce and simmer for 45 minutes, stirring frequently.

7. Toast the hamburger buns and fill each with the barbecued pork. The mixture can be cooled, covered, and refrigerated for up to 1 day; it can also be frozen.

More Servings
To serve 24, cook two pork shoulders, double the number of hamburger buns, and double the sauce recipe.

LOBSTER AND FENNEL SALAD ROLLS

A lunch or dinner of Lobster and Fennel Rolls, a mixed green salad, and dry white wine on a hot summer's day satisfies and rekindles the senses. For dessert: sorbet and fresh berries. My own favorite is lemon sorbet with blueberries. It should probably be a special occasion since lobster is so expensive.

SERVES 12

3½ pounds fresh cooked lobster meat, cooled and chopped
¾ cup diced fresh fennel stalks
1½ cups mayonnaise, or as needed
3 tablespoons fresh lemon juice
2 teaspoons Dijon mustard
½ cup diced red onion

3 tablespoons chopped fresh parsley leaves
Salt and freshly ground black pepper to taste
Softened butter
8 8-inch lengths of French baguettes

1. Put the lobster meat and fennel into a large bowl.
2. In a small bowl, combine the mayonnaise, lemon juice, mustard, onion, and parsley. Season the mixture with salt and pepper. Add the mayonnaise mixture to the lobster meat and combine it well.
3. Cut each piece of bread in half lengthwise, but don't cut through the opposite side; leave the sides attached. Open the bread and spread each lightly with butter.
4. Lightly toast the bread under the broiler on a baking sheet in two batches.
5. Divide the salad evenly between the 12 sandwiches. Serve at once.

More Servings
Double the recipe to serve 16.

BELLINI PANINI

SERVES 16　·　MAKES 32 SANDWICHES

32 small Italian rolls
 1 cup (2 sticks) sweet butter,
　 softened
2½ pounds prosciutto, very
　 thinly sliced
2½ pounds mozzarella, thinly
　 sliced

32 large fresh basil leaves (do
　 not substitute dried basil)
 6 firm ripe medium-sized
　 tomatoes, thinly sliced
 2 medium-sized red onions,
　 very thinly sliced and
　 separated into rings

1. Cut open the rolls. Lightly spread butter on each inside piece of bread.

2. On the bottom halves of the rolls, arrange equal-sized portions of the prosciutto, cheese, basil leaves, tomatoes, and onion rings.

3. Cover with the top pieces of the rolls. Serve at once, or cover with plastic wrap and refrigerate for no more than 3 hours.

More Servings
Double the recipe to make 64 panini or to serve 32.

ROAST BEEF AND GUACAMOLE BOCADILLOS

SERVES 16

16 Italian rolls
¾ cup (1½ sticks) butter
 4 pounds rare roast beef, thinly
　 sliced (Roast pork can also be
　 used.)

 4 cups Light Guacamole Dip
　 (see recipe page 69)
16 thin slices Monterey Jack
　 cheese
 6 large ripe tomatoes, thinly
　 sliced

1. Cut the rolls open, but not all the way through. Pull out any excess bread from the center of the rolls and save for making bread crumbs.

2. Spread the inside of the rolls lightly with the butter.

3. On the bottom half of each roll, put about 4 ounces of the roast beef and spread it with ¼ cup of the Guacamole. Top each with a slice of the cheese and equal amounts of the tomato slices. (Onion rings can be added, if desired.) Place the tops on the sandwiches, cut in half, and serve on individual plates or a large platter.

More Servings
Double the recipe to serve 32.

SHRIMP AND CRAB SALAD SANDWICHES

MAKES 24 SANDWICHES

3½ pounds medium-sized shrimp, cooked and coarsely chopped

3 pounds crab meat, cooked and coarsely chopped

3 cups mayonnaise, or as needed

¼ cup fresh lemon juice

½ cup thinly sliced scallions

¾ cup minced sweet green pepper

½ cup minced water chestnuts

⅓ cup chopped fresh parsley leaves

Salt and freshly ground black pepper to taste

24 Kaiser rolls

1. Put the shrimp and crab meat in a large bowl.

2. Combine the remaining ingredients, except the rolls. Add to the shellfish and combine.

3. Cut the rolls open and fill with equal amounts of the salad. Serve at once.

More Servings
Double the recipe to serve 48, adjusting the amount of mayonnaise to make the salad moist.

Lemon Chicken
Pita Bread Sandwiches

SERVES 36

12 large poached, skinned and boned chicken breasts (see recipe page 129)
1 cup finely chopped red onion
1 cup thinly sliced celery
3½ cups mayonnaise, or as needed
4 tablespoons fresh lemon juice
2 tablespoons grated lemon rind

3 ounces drained capers (about ½ cup)
1 teaspoon dried oregano
½ cup chopped fresh parsley leaves
Salt and freshly ground black pepper to taste
36 medium-sized pita breads
72 Greek olives

1. Cut the chicken into bite-sized pieces and put it into a large bowl with the onion and celery. Toss.

2. Combine the mayonnaise, lemon juice, lemon rind, capers, oregano, and parsley. Pour the mixture over the chicken and combine. Season with salt and pepper.

3. Cut about 1½ inches off of one edge of each pita bread and stuff each with equal amounts of the chicken. Serve with the Greek olives.

Tuna Caesar Salad Sandwiches

SERVES 50

50 8-inch lengths of French baguettes, halved lengthwise, but not all the way through one side
50 romaine lettuce leaves
9 12½-ounce cans solid white meat tuna, drained and flaked

2 2-ounce cans anchovy fillets
2 teaspoons chopped garlic
2 cups olive oil
½ cup fresh lemon juice
2 cups mayonnaise, or as needed

Freshly ground black pepper to taste

5 medium-sized red onions, very thinly sliced

2½ cups freshly grated Parmesan cheese

1. Put 1 lettuce leaf on the bottom half of each piece of bread.
2. Put the tuna in a large bowl.
3. Combine the anchovies, garlic, olive oil, and lemon juice in a food processor or blender. Add to the tuna, along with the mayonnaise and combine well. Season with pepper.
4. Spoon equal amounts over the lettuce leaves on each sandwich. Top with the onion rings and sprinkle lightly with cheese. Close the sandwiches and serve immediately.

Instant Hot Breads
and Other Specialties

◇ ━━━━━━━━━━━━━━━━━━━━━━━━━━━━━━ ◇

There is rarely time for preparing and baking fresh bread or rolls for a large gathering. Fresh bread can be baked and frozen in advance, of course. But buying excellent fresh bread or rolls from a favorite bakery on the day of the event is usually more practical.

There are a few exceptions in my household, which are quick and easy and very special. They are Great Big Buttermilk Biscuits, Corn Sticks, Blueberry Muffins, Foccaccia, Fried Flour Tortilla Crackers, Herb-Toasted Pita Bread, Fried Wonton Crackers, and French Walnut Bread. The French Walnut Bread, Foccaccia, Corn Sticks, and Blueberry Muffins can each be made weeks ahead and frozen.

When any of these breads fit into your menu, make an extra effort to serve them.

FRIED FLOUR TORTILLA CRACKERS
◇ ━━━━━━━━━━━━━━━━━━━━━━━━━━━━━━ ◇

SERVES 8 · MAKES 32 CRACKERS

1 10-ounce package flour   Peanut oil
   tortillas (about 6 inches wide)

1. Cut each tortilla in half twice, making four wedges.
2. Heat ½ inch of oil in a large frying pan and cook the tortilla pieces,

279

7 or 8 at a time until they are golden brown on each side. This will only take a few seconds. Drain on paper towels and serve immediately.

More Servings
Multiply this recipe by the number of guests.

HERB-TOASTED PITA BREAD

SERVES 8 · MAKES 32 PITA TOASTS

8 plain or whole wheat pita breads (about 5 inches wide)
¾ cup (1½ sticks) butter

2 tablespoons finely chopped fresh parsley leaves
1 tablespoon finely chopped fresh dill

1. Preheat the oven to 350 degrees.
2. Separate each pita bread in half by cutting into the edge. Cut each single side in half.
3. Melt the butter and stir in the herbs. Brush the pita bread on the inside with the butter.
4. Put the bread on one or two large baking sheets and bake until golden brown, about 15 minutes. The bread will curl slightly.

More Servings
Double the recipe to serve 16 or to make 64 pita toasts. Cook the toasts in several batches.

FRIED WONTON CRACKERS

Wonton wrappers are extremely versatile. Not long ago it was revealed that one of Paris' three-star Michelin chefs used the thinnest variety to make him famous lobster and foie gras-filled ravioli. These, of course, were stuffed, sealed, and poached in a broth and blanketed with an aromatic sauce.

The wonton wrapper or skin, is often fried. Working on a recipe for stuffed fried wontons, I found myself left with several of the wrappers. I cut them into circles and dropped them into hot oil. In seconds they turned into bubbly crisp golden brown crackers. These crackers remained crisp for several hours or for many days stored in a tightly closed tin box.

Any cheese, spread, or dip is good served on the delicate, crunchy crackers. Sprinkled lightly with a combination of sugar and cinnamon, they make instant cookies to serve with ice cream or sherbet.

MAKES ABOUT 100 CRACKERS

2 pounds wonton wrappers   Peanut oil for deep-frying

1. Cut the wonton wrappers, in stacks of 4 or 5, into circles using a 2-inch scalloped pastry cutter. Separate the wontons.

2. Heat 1 inch of the oil in a large frying pan to 360 degrees and fry the wontons, as many as will fit comfortably into the pan at a time. Drain on paper towels and cook the remaining wontons in the same manner.

More Servings
Multiply the wrappers according to the quantity needed, and keep the oil at the 1-inch level, reheating it as more oil is added.

GREAT BIG BUTTERMILK BISCUITS

At my grandparents' farm in north Texas, hot steaming biscuits were our daily bread. For breakfast, we slathered them with freshly churned butter and homemade preserves, usually peach. Sometimes we filled the biscuits with fried sausage patties or thick slices of grilled ham—and butter, always butter. The biscuits accompanied whatever appeared on the luncheon table. For dinner they were often as not split open and blanketed with hot chicken milk gravy. They remain one of my fondest memories of childhood.

MAKES 16 BISCUITS

3½ cups sifted all-purpose flour
2 tablespoons baking powder
1 teaspoon baking soda
2 tablespoons sugar
1 teaspoon salt
¾ cup (1½ sticks) butter
1¼ cups buttermilk

1. Preheat the oven to 425 degrees.

2. Combine the flour, baking powder, baking soda, sugar, and salt in a large bowl. Add the butter and, working with a pastry cutter, in a forward rolling motion, combine the mixture until it has the texture of coarse crumbs. Add the buttermilk and combine.

3. On a lightly floured work area, fold over the dough several times to form a ball. Flatten the dough with the palms of your hands and roll out into a circle about 1 inch thick. Using a 2½-inch round biscuit cutter, cut the dough into as many biscuits as possible. Place the biscuits on an ungreased baking sheet about 1 inch apart.

4. Reshape the dough into a ball and roll it out again and cut out into biscuits until all the dough is used.

5. Bake the biscuits on the middle oven shelf (or the one that is one up from the bottom shelf) for about 20 minutes, or until the tops are golden brown. Do not let the bottoms brown too much. Serve immediately.

More Servings
Double the recipe to make 32 biscuits.

FOCCACCIA

◇ ════════════ ◇

SERVES 16

2 13¾-ounce packages hot roll mix
2 large eggs
Olive oil
4 medium-to-small yellow onions, very thinly sliced and separated into rings
Salt and freshly ground black pepper

1. Prepare both packages of the dough together in a large bowl following the instructions on the package (the 2 eggs are in the directions).

2. Divide the dough in half. Use oiled fingers to pat out each piece of dough over lightly greased baking sheets, about 12 by 16 inches. Cover the dough with dish towels and let rise for 15 minutes.

3. Preheat the oven to 400 degrees.

4. Brush the tops of the dough with olive oil and scatter the onion rings over the surface. Sprinkle lightly with salt and pepper.

5. Bake the foccaccia in the oven for about 25 to 30 minutes, or until they are golden brown. Cut the bread into squares and serve immediately.

Variations
If desired, dried rosemary, poppy seeds, or sesame seeds can be sprinkled lightly over the surface of the bread after the oil is brushed on.

CORN STICKS

Corn sticks are a welcome special touch to any meal, whether breakfast, lunch, or dinner. When I'm serving a plain but deliciously honest meal of roast meat, fresh steamed vegetable, and a salad, corn sticks are often on the menu.

Corn-stick or corn-cake pans, as they are sometimes called, are made of cast ironware. There are usually seven molds or corn-shaped hollows per pan, so at least two pans will be needed.

Follow the manufacturer's instructions for seasoning the pans and always preheat the empty pans for a minute or two before adding the batter.

SERVES 12 · MAKES 28 CORN STICKS

2 cups cornmeal
1 cup all-purpose flour
1 tablespoon baking powder
1 teaspoon salt
¼ cup sugar

2 large eggs, lightly beaten
2 cups buttermilk
½ cup (1 stick) butter, melted and cooled

1. Preheat the oven to 400 degrees.

2. Put all the ingredients into a large bowl and combine well.

3. Heat two well-greased corn-stick pans in the oven for 1 to 2 min-

utes. Remove and spoon the batter into the molds, to just under each rim. Bake until golden brown, about 12 minutes.

4. Remove the corn sticks from the pans immediately. Grease the pans and make the remaining corn sticks in the same manner. Keep the first batch warm covered by a napkin in a basket. As soon as the second batch is done serve immediately with plenty of sweet butter.

More Servings
Double the batter recipe to make 56 corn sticks or to serve 24. The cooked corn sticks can be reheated in the oven for 5 minutes.

FRENCH WALNUT BREAD

The French serve this delectable bread with the cheese board before dessert. It is cut into very thin slices and served by the waiter. The bread is never left on the table for diners to take as much as they like. I fear that that is because so much would be eaten that dessert would be forsaken. I have learned my lesson, and when the bread is presented I greedily ask for more than the two slices generally offered.

SERVES 8 · MAKES 1 LARGE LOAF

3½ cups sifted all-purpose flour
1 tablespoon sugar
1 teaspoon salt
1 package active dry yeast
½ cup warm water

½ cup walnut oil, plus extra for greasing the bowl
¾ cup chopped walnuts
4 tablespoons vegetable oil
1 large egg, lightly beaten

1. Combine the flour, sugar, and salt in a large bowl.
2. Dissolve the yeast in the warm water.
3. Pour the yeast mixture, walnut oil, and milk into a well in the center of the dry ingredients and combine thoroughly.
4. Knead the dough until it is smooth and firm.
5. Brush a bowl with walnut oil and let the dough rise, covered, in a warm place, away from drafts, for about 1 hour and 30 minutes, or until doubled in volume.
6. Meanwhile, heat the oil in a large frying pan and cook the walnuts until lightly browned. Drain on paper towels and cool.

7. Punch down the dough and add the walnuts. Knead until they are evenly distributed into the dough. Shape the dough into a 14- to 16-inch baguette shape and put in a French bread pan or on a baking sheet. Cover and let rise for about 45 minutes.

8. Preheat the oven to 400 degrees.

9. Brush the bread lightly with the egg and bake in the oven for about 40 minutes, or until tapping on the bottom of the loaf makes a hollow sound.

More Servings
Double the recipe to make two loaves or to serve 16.

BLUEBERRY MUFFINS

MAKES 36 MUFFINS

4½ cups sifted all-purpose flour
1¾ cups sugar
2 tablespoons baking powder
1 teaspoon salt
3 large eggs
1½ cups milk

1½ cups (3 sticks) butter, melted, plus extra for greasing the muffin tins
3 cups fresh blueberries, stemmed, washed, and dried

1. Preheat the oven to 400 degrees.

2. Grease 36 muffin cups (3 pans).

3. Combine the dry ingredients in a large bowl.

4. Beat the eggs, milk, and butter together lightly and pour the mixture into a well in the dry ingredients. Combine but don't overmix. The batter should be slightly lumpy. Fold in the blueberries.

5. Divide the mixture evenly among the 36 greased muffin cups. Bake for about 25 minutes, or just until the muffins are lightly golden brown on top.

More Servings
Double the recipe to make 72 muffins and bake in several batches.

Desserts

◇ ═══════════════════════════════════════ ◇

Desserts are seldom major problem dishes when cooking for crowds, as it is possible, and even advisable, to prepare several desserts, giving guests a delectable selection from which to choose. A choice of Cold Banana Mousse, Walnut Tart, Brioche Cake with Vanilla Custard, and a large bowl of fresh strawberries served with sweetened whipped cream will delight your crowd, while taking into account individual taste preferences and passions.

Many desserts are easily prepared well in advance—even weeks or days before—since a wide variety freeze beautifully, notably cakes and cookies.

At the end of this chapter is a selection of quick and easy dessert recipes to consider for any occasion when time and taste are of the essence.

Hot Puff Pastry with Cold Chocolate Mousse and Crème Anglaise

This recipe was inspired by Chef Raymond Etchenis of Restaurant Léonie in St. Jean-de-Luz, France.

SERVES 8

CHOCOLATE MOUSSE

6 ounces semisweet chocolate
2 ounces unsweetened chocolate
1/4 cup (1/2 stick) butter
4 large eggs, separated

1 cup sugar
2 tablespoons Cointreau
1 teaspoon pure vanilla extract
1 cup heavy cream, whipped and chilled

1 pound homemade puff pastry or packaged frozen puff pastry, thawed

CRÈME ANGLAISE

6 large egg yolks
1/2 cup sugar
1 teaspoon pure vanilla extract

2 tablespoons Grand Marnier
3/4 cup heavy cream

1. Make the Chocolate Mousse the day before or at least 5 hours before serving. Melt the chocolate with the butter in the top of a double boiler over simmering water. Remove from the heat.

2. Beat the egg yolks with the sugar with an electric mixer until light and fluffy. Beat in the Cointreau and vanilla and add the chocolate mixture.

3. Beat the egg whites until stiff but not dry, and fold them into the chocolate mixture. Fold the chilled whipped cream into the mousse and turn it into a large bowl. Cover and refrigerate for at least 5 hours.

4. Preheat the oven to 425 degrees.

5. Roll the pastry to a 1/8-inch thickness and cut it into eight 2 1/2- by 4-inch rectangles.

6. Put the pastry on a large ungreased baking sheet and bake for about 18 minutes, or until puffed and golden brown.

7. Meanwhile, prepare the Crème Anglaise. Beat the egg yolks and sugar together in the top of a double boiler until slightly thickened and pale yellow.

8. Stir in the vanilla and Cointreau and whisk over just simmering water until the sauce thickens. Whisk in the heavy cream, cover, and set aside.

9. Split each puff pastry rectangle in half and put on a dessert plate. Spoon 2 heaping tablespoons of the mousse onto the bottom half and replace the top. Spoon the Crème Anglaise around the pastry. Assemble the remaining dishes in the same manner and serve immediately.

FRESH APPLE TART WITH CARAMEL GLAZE

SERVES 8

PASTRY

1½ cups sifted all-purpose flour	½ cup (1 stick) very cold butter
½ teaspoon salt	1 large egg yolk
2 tablespoons sugar	3 or 4 tablespoons ice water

TART FILLING

2 teaspoons all-purpose flour	2 tablespoons butter
6 to 8 Red Delicious apples, cored, peeled, and very thinly sliced	Sugar

CARAMEL GLAZE

1 cup sugar

1. Prepare the pastry: Combine the flour, salt, sugar, and butter with a pastry blender or in a food processor until it is the texture of coarse crumbs. Add the egg yolk and water and combine. Shape into a ball, cover with plastic wrap, and refrigerate for 30 minutes.

2. Preheat the oven to 425 degrees.

3. Roll out the pastry on a lightly floured surface until you have a

circle ⅛ inch thick to fit into a 10-inch tart pan. Fit the pastry into the pan and trim off the extra pastry by running a rolling pin over the top of the pan.

4. Brush the flour over the bottom of the pastry.

5. Beginning at the rim of the pan, overlap a circle of the apple slices. Make another circle of the apples and fill the center with a circle of the apple slices. Each apple slice should overlap the next by about half the width of the slice because the apples will shrink during cooking. Dot with the butter and sprinkle the apples with the sugar.

6. Bake on a baking sheet for about 40 minutes, or until the apples are golden brown.

7. Remove the cooked tart and cool it on a wire rack.

8. Meanwhile, melt the sugar in a heavy saucepan, stirring to dissolve any lumps of sugar, until smooth and a light caramel color.

9. Immediately pour the caramel over the top of the tart in a slow steady drizzle, in circles, It will sizzle! Cool and refrigerate until serving time.

More Servings
Bake two tarts to serve 16.

COLD BANANA MOUSSE

◇ ══════════════════════════ ◇

SERVES 8

1 envelope unflavored gelatin	1 cup sugar
½ cup cold water	¼ teaspoon salt
1 cup heavy cream	4 medium-sized bananas,
2 tablespoons fresh lemon juice	peeled and cut into chunks
5 large eggs, separated	

1. Put the gelatin in the cold water to soften it and set aside.

2. Whip the cream in a bowl and put it into the refrigerator.

3. In the top of a double boiler, put 1 tablespoon of the lemon juice, the egg yolks, ½ cup of the sugar, and the salt. Cook over simmering water, whisking constantly, until the mixture thickens enough to coat the back of a spoon. This will take about 10 minutes.

4. Pour the thickened egg mixture into a large bowl and stir in the softened gelatin.

5. Purée the bananas in a food processor with the remaining tablespoon of lemon juice. Add the banana purée to the egg mixture and blend thoroughly.

6. Beat the egg whites until they begin to hold their shape. Then gradually add the remaining ½ cup of sugar. Beat until the egg whites are stiff but not dry. Fold them into the banana mixture.

7. Fold the heavy cream thoroughly into the mousse.

8. Pour the mousse into a 2-quart soufflé dish or attractive bowl. Cover and refrigerate for several hours until set or overnight. (If desired, the mousse can also be divided equally among eight individual bowls.). Serve with cookies, if desired.

More Servings
Double the recipe to serve 16. When the mousse is mixed, either pour the finished mousse into two 2-quart soufflé dishes or one large bowl and refrigerate as directed.

CHOCOLATE-DIPPED STRAWBERRIES WITH ICE CREAM

SERVES 8

16 large fresh strawberries with stems left intact, washed and dried
6 ounces semisweet chocolate
3 tablespoons butter, plus butter for greasing the pan
½ cup chopped pecans or walnuts
1½ quarts ice cream (your choice)

1. Melt the chocolate and butter in a small heavy saucepan over low heat, stirring often.

2. Holding the stems of the strawberries, dip them, one by one, into the chocolate sauce about three quarters of the way up the strawberry. Place the dipped strawberries on a buttered baking sheet.

3. Sprinkle each with a few nuts and keep cool until served. Do not

refrigerate. For each serving, serve two strawberries with a scoop of the ice cream.

More Servings
Double the recipe to serve 16.

JULIE MCCLENNAN'S ORANGE SPONGE CAKE

SERVES 12

4 large eggs
1 cup sugar
¼ cup orange juice

1 cup sifted all-purpose flour
1 teaspoon baking powder

1. Preheat the oven to 350 degrees.
2. Separate the eggs and beat the yolks until they are light and fluffy. Add the sugar and beat with an electric mixer for at least 5 minutes.
3. Add the orange juice and beat for 2 minutes.
4. Add the flour and baking powder and beat for 2 minutes. The mixture should be very pale yellow and have a thick creamy consistency.
5. Beat the egg whites until stiff but not dry. Fold the egg whites into the batter and immediately turn the batter into an ungreased 10-inch tube pan. Bake for about 35 minutes. Cool before slicing. Serve with fresh fruit or Joelle's Fresh Peaches with Yogurt Sauce (page 310).

WALNUT TART

SERVES 12

4 large eggs
1 cup sugar
¼ cup (½ stick) butter, melted
1½ cups light corn syrup
2 teaspoons pure vanilla extract

½ teaspoon salt
1 cup finely chopped walnuts
1 recipe for pâte sucré for a
   10-inch tart (see recipe page 305)
12 unbroken walnut halves

1. Preheat the oven to 375 degrees.

2. Beat the eggs and sugar together for 5 minutes with a wire whisk in a large bowl. Add the butter, corn syrup, vanilla, salt, and chopped walnuts. Mix well.

3. Pour the mixture into the prepared pastry shell. Put the walnut halves around the edge of the top of the filling, spaced equal distances apart. Put the tart on a baking sheet and bake for 45 minutes. Serve warm or cold with vanilla ice cream, if desired.

MIXED BERRY
CRÊPES WITH CASSIS SAUCE

SERVES 12

3 16-ounce cans sour cherries, drained and pitted (reserve liquid in cans)
1 pint fresh blueberries, picked over, stemmed, washed, and dried
1 pint fresh raspberries or small strawberries

1 cup sugar
1 tablespoon fresh lemon juice
⅓ cup Crème de Cassis liqueur
2 tablespoons cornstarch
12 large crêpes (see recipe page 254, and add 3 tablespoons of sugar to the batter)

1. Put the cherries, blueberries, and raspberries in a large bowl and combine gently.

2. Combine the juice from the canned cherries, sugar, lemon juice, and cassis in a heavy saucepan and bring to a boil. Stir until the sugar dissolves. Meanwhile, dissolve the cornstarch in a little cold water and stir into the boiling liquid. Stir and cook for 1 minute, or until the sauce thickens.

3. Pour the liquid over the fruit, toss, and let stand for 10 minutes.

4. Spoon half of the fruit and sauce into the center of the crêpes in equal amounts on dessert plates. Roll up each. Spoon the remaining half over the crêpes in equal amounts. If desired, sprinkle with confectioner's sugar.

ZABAGLIONE CHEESECAKE

SERVES 12

1 tablespoon butter	1¼ cups sugar
⅓ cup graham cracker crumbs	5 large eggs
4 8-ounce packages (2 pounds)	¼ cup Marsala wine
cream cheese, softened	1 teaspoon pure vanilla extract
½ cup heavy cream	

1. Preheat the oven to 325 degrees.
2. Spread the butter over the sides and bottom of a 9-inch spring-form pan. Sprinkle the graham cracker crumbs over the bottom and sides of the pan. Shake the pan to evenly distribute the loose crumbs over the bottom of the pan.
3. Put the remaining ingredients into a large bowl and beat with an electric mixer on low speed for 1 minute. Increase the speed and beat until the mixture is smooth.
4. Turn the mixture into the prepared pan and bake on the center shelf of the oven for 1 hour. Turn off the oven and let the cake rest in the oven for 1 hour without opening the door.
5. Cool the cake on a wire rack, cover, and refrigerate. For easy cutting use a knife dipped into hot water and wiped dry.

More Servings
Make two cakes in two batches to serve 24.

FRESH POACHED WHOLE PEACHES WITH STRAWBERRY SAUCE AND PISTACHIO NUTS

I was first served this refreshingly simple, but elegant dessert in Cannes. It was June, and the fresh ripe peaches has been picked only hours before they were cooked. Friends I was dining with had brought them from Italy that morning. They were those gorgeous northern Italian peaches that fill the mouth with flavor with each bite.

SERVES 16

12 cups (3 quarts) water
3½ cups sugar
½ cup Cointreau
2 vanilla beans

16 large firm ripe peaches
¾ cup chopped skinned
   pistachio nuts

STRAWBERRY SAUCE

3 pints fresh ripe strawberries,
   washed, hulled, and halved

¾ cup sugar
3 tablespoons Cointreau

1. Bring the water, sugar, Cointreau, and vanilla beans to a boil in a 8-quart pot. Stir until the sugar dissolves.

2. Add the peaches and simmer for about 12 minutes.

3. Remove each peach carefully with a slotted spoon and drain on paper towels.

4. While they are still very warm, peel the peaches using a small sharp knife. Be careful not to pierce the flesh of the peaches.

4. Put the peaches in a large glass baking dish and spoon a little of the cooking liquid over each peach. Cover and chill for at least 3 hours.

6. Meanwhile, prepare the Strawberry Sauce. Purée the strawberries in a food processor with the sugar and Cointreau, half of the amounts at a time. Put into a bowl, cover, and refrigerate until served.

7. Serve the peaches topped with equal amounts of the Strawberry Sauce and the nuts.

FRESH LEMON TART

SERVES 16

1½ recipes for pâte sucré (see
    page 305)

1½ tablespoons all-purpose flour

FILLING

3 cups sugar
1 cup fresh lemon juice
8 large eggs

8 large egg yolks
1½ cups (3 sticks) butter

1. Prepare the pâte sucré recipe, first making a whole recipe and then half of a recipe. Combine the dough, tightly wrap in plastic, and chill for 30 minutes.

2. Preheat the oven to 400 degrees.

3. Roll out the dough to fit a 10- by 15-inch jelly roll pan. Trim off the edges and dust with the flour on the bottom. Put into the freezer.

4. Whisk the sugar, lemon juice, eggs, and egg yolks together in the top of a large double boiler over simmering water, until the mixture thickens. Whisk in the butter, a tablespoon at a time.

5. Pour the filling into the tart shell and bake for 25 to 30 minutes, or until the crust is golden brown.

6. Cool the tart and cut into 16 squares, or refrigerate and serve cold. If desired, garnish each serving with two mint leaves and two fresh raspberries or strawberries.

Brioche Cake with Vanilla Custard

SERVES 12

BRIOCHE DOUGH
- 2 envelopes active dry yeast
- 1/3 cup granulated sugar
- 3/4 cup warm milk
- 5 cups all-purpose flour
- 1 teaspoon salt
- 6 large eggs
- 1/2 cup (1 stick) sweet butter, softened, plus extra butter for greasing the pan
- 2 tablespoons heavy cream
- 2 tablespoons blanched sliced almonds
  Confectioner's sugar

CUSTARD
- 5 large egg yolks
- 3/4 cup granulated sugar
- 1/2 cup all-purpose flour
- 2 cups milk
- 1/4 cup (1/2 stick) butter
- 1 teaspoon pure vanilla extract

1. Proof the yeast with the sugar and milk in the bowl of an electric mixer for 10 minutes.

2. Combine the mixture with the flour, salt, 5 eggs, and butter until smooth. Add a few tablespoons of flour, 1 at a time, if necessary.

3. Transfer the dough to a clean bowl, cover, and let it double in bulk, about 2 hours.

4. Punch down the dough and shape it into a large round ball.

5. Put the dough in the center of a well-greased 13-inch deep-dish pizza or paella pan. Let the dough rise until it doubles in bulk.

6. Preheat the oven to 375 degrees.

7. Beat the remaining egg with the heavy cream and brush over the top of the dough. Scatter the almonds on top.

8. Bake for about 35 minutes, or until browned. Remove from the oven and cool.

9. Meanwhile, make the custard: Combine the egg yolks, sugar, and flour in a large heavy saucepan using a wire whisk. Over medium-low heat, gradually whisk in the milk until the sauce thickens. Turn the heat to very low and beat in the butter and vanilla. Cover and set aside.

10. When the cake has cooled, cut ½ inch off the top of the cake. Spread the custard over the inside and replace the top. Cut into 12 wedges.

More Servings
Prepare two cakes to serve 24.

AUNT IMA'S SOUR CREAM COFFEE CAKE WITH RASPBERRIES

SERVES 16

1 cup granulated sugar
½ cup (1 stick) butter, softened, plus extra butter for greasing the pan
2 large eggs
2 cups sifted all-purpose flour
1 teaspoon baking powder

1 teaspoon baking soda
½ teaspoon salt
1 cup sour cream
1 teaspoon pure vanilla extract
1 10-ounce package frozen raspberries, thawed and drained

TOPPING
¼ cup packed dark brown sugar
¼ cup granulated sugar

1 tablespoon ground cinnamon
1 cup chopped walnuts

1. Preheat the oven to 350 degrees.

2. To make the cake, beat the sugar and butter together in a large bowl with the eggs.

3. Combine the flour, baking powder, baking soda, and salt. Stir into the egg mixture. Add the sour cream and vanilla and mix well.

4. Lightly butter a 10-inch tube pan.

5. Combine the topping ingredients.

6. Spread half of the cake batter evenly in the pan. Spoon the raspberries in a circle over the center of the batter in the pan and sprinkle half of the topping mixture over the berries. Spoon the remaining batter carefully over all and sprinkle with the remaining topping mixture.

7. Bake for 1 hour, or until a cake tester inserted near the center of the cake comes out clean.

More Servings
Make two cakes in two batches to serve 32.

Variations
A 10-ounce package of frozen strawberries or blueberries can be substituted for the raspberries in the recipe. Completely thaw the fruit and drain it well.

BANANA-NUT BREAD

Everyone loves Banana Bread. It makes a fine dessert for lunches, picnics, and tailgate or outdoor parties. I frequently serve Banana Bread for breakfast with fruit salad and yogurt.

MAKES 2 LOAVES

1½ cups sugar
1 cup (2 sticks) butter, plus extra butter for greasing the pans
4 large eggs, lightly beaten
4 cups sifted all-purpose flour
2 teaspoons baking soda
2 teaspoons baking powder

2 teaspoons ground allspice
1 teaspoon salt
8 medium-sized ripe bananas, puréed in the food processor or mashed with a hand masher
2 cups chopped walnuts or pecans

1. Preheat the oven to 350 degrees.

2. Beat together the sugar and butter in a large bowl. Add the eggs and mix well.

3. Combine the flour, baking soda, baking powder, allspice, and salt in a separate bowl. Add the dry ingredients to the egg mixture and combine well. Add the bananas and nuts and mix thoroughly.

4. Lightly grease two 9- by 5- by 4-inch loaf pans and turn half of the mixture into each pan. Bake for 1 hour, or until a cake tester inserted into the center of the loaves comes out clean. Serve with ice cream, if desired.

Freezing Instructions
Cool the loaves completely and wrap each in plastic wrap or aluminum foil and freeze. To thaw the bread, leave it at room temperature in the wrapping for about 2 hours.

BAKED APPLES WITH MINCEMEAT AND WALNUT STUFFING

SERVES 24

24 Rome or McIntosh apples
 4 cups (1 quart) mincemeat
 2 cups chopped walnuts

½ cup (1 stick) butter
Sugar

1. Preheat the oven to 350 degrees.

2. Core each apple at the stem end about 1½ inches wide, but do not core all the way through the apple.

3. Combine the mincemeat and walnuts well. Spoon equal amounts into each apple. Dot with butter and sprinkle lightly with sugar.

4. Put the apples into two large roasting pans and bake for about 35 minutes. If desired, serve with sweetened whipped cream. The apples can be served hot or cold.

More Servings
Double the recipe to serve 48 and cook in two batches.

Judy Witty's
Twin Chocoholic Cakes

◇━━━━━━━━━━━━━━━━━━━━━━━◇

Judy Witty, the former actress and dancer, owns the Little Vienna restaurant in St. Thomas. She prepares most of the desserts herself. Here is Judy's quick chocolate cake recipe.

SERVES 24

1 cup (2 sticks) butter, softened
2 cups sugar
8 large eggs
2 cups self-rising flour

32 ounces Hershey's chocolate syrup
2 teaspoons pure vanilla extract

1. Preheat the oven to 350 degrees.
2. Cream the butter and sugar together in a large bowl. Beat in the eggs, one at a time. Add the flour, chocolate syrup, and vanilla and combine well.
3. Pour the batter, in equal amounts, into two ungreased 10-inch springform pans and bake for 1 hour. Cool the cakes before releasing them from the pans. Serve with chocolate frosting, sweetened whipped cream, or ice cream.

Double Chocolate Brownies

◇━━━━━━━━━━━━━━━━━━━━━━━◇

Four 9-inch-square cake pans are required for this recipe, or cut the recipe in half and bake in two batches.

MAKES 36 BROWNIES

2 cups (4 sticks) butter, plus extra butter for greasing the pans
24 ounces unsweetened chocolate

16 large eggs
8 cups sugar
1 tablespoon pure vanilla extract
5 cups sifted all-purpose flour

5 teaspoons baking powder
2 teaspoons salt

4 cups chopped walnuts

1. Grease four 9-inch-square cake pans.
2. Melt the chocolate and butter in a large heavy saucepan over low heat, stirring often. Cool this mixture for 5 minutes.
3. Preheat the oven to 350 degrees.
4. In a large bowl, combine the chocolate and butter with the eggs, sugar, and vanilla. Add the flour, baking powder, and salt and mix well. Stir in the walnuts.
5. Pour the batter into the prepared pans in equal amounts and bake for exactly 25 minutes. Do not overcook.
6. Cool completely and cut each pan into 9 brownies each. Cover and refrigerate until served. The brownies can be wrapped individually and frozen. Thaw the brownies in the wrapping at room temperature.

CRULLERS

*Inspired by Crutchley's famous Cruller bake shop
in Southampton, Long Island, now closed*

MAKES ABOUT 10 DOZEN
(PREPARATION BEGINS THE DAY BEFORE)

1 cup sugar
2 large eggs
1 large egg yolk
¼ cup vegetable oil
1 cup milk
1 tablespoon pure vanilla
   extract

4 cups sifted all-purpose flour
1½ tablespoons baking powder
1 teaspoon salt
1 teaspoon freshly grated
   nutmeg
Peanut or vegetable oil for
   deep-frying

1. Combine the sugar, eggs, and egg yolk with an electric mixer in a large bowl. Add the oil, milk, and vanilla and blend well.
2. Combine the flour, baking powder, salt, and nutmeg and gradually add to the batter, mixing well.
3. Cover and chill, overnight, in the refrigerator.

4. Knead the dough for 3 or 4 minutes and roll it out to a ½-inch thickness on a lightly floured surface. Cut into cruller shapes or dough-nut centers with a 1-inch-thick round cutter. Reshape the dough and cut into cruller shapes until all the dough is used.

5. Heat 3 inches of the oil in a deep wide heavy pan or fryer to about 375 degrees. Fry the crullers in batches until golden brown. Drain and cool. Dust with confectioner's sugar or a combination of granulated sugar and cinnamon, if desired.

LEMON-POPPY SEED CAKE

Make one cake at a time, or, for 36, triple the ingredients and bake in three 10-inch tube pans, dividing the batter among in the pans in equal amounts.

12 SERVINGS PER CAKE

1¼ cups (2½ sticks) butter, softened, plus extra butter for greasing the pan	½ cup poppy seeds
	2½ cups sifted all-purpose flour
	1½ teaspoons baking powder
2 cups sugar	1½ teaspoons baking soda
6 large eggs, separated	½ teaspoon salt
½ cup fresh lemon juice	Confectioner's sugar
1 teaspoon pure vanilla extract	

1. Preheat the oven to 350 degrees. Lightly grease three 10-inch tube pans.

2. Cream the butter and sugar together in a large bowl with an elec-tric mixer. Add the egg yolks, one at a time, combining after each addi-tion. Stir in the lemon juice, vanilla, and poppy seeds.

3. Combine the flour, baking powder, baking soda, and salt and mix into the batter.

4. Beat the egg whites until stiff but not dry, and fold into the batter.

5. Turn the mixture into the greased pan. Bake for 1 hour, or until a cake tester inserted into the center of the cake comes out clean.

6. Cool the cake for 15 minutes. Remove from the pan and sprinkle lightly with confectioner's sugar. The cake freezes beautifully.

KENTUCKY FRUITCAKES

MAKES 6 CAKES

1 pound chopped candied citron

½ pound chopped candied lemon peel

½ pound chopped candied orange peel

1½ pounds chopped candied pineapple

2 pounds halved candied cherries

2 pounds pitted dates, chopped

2 pounds dark raisins

1 pound pecan halves

1 pound walnut halves

10 cups sifted all-purpose flour

4 cups (8 sticks) butter, softened, plus extra butter for greasing the pans

4 cups sugar

18 large eggs, lightly beaten

1 teaspoon ground cinnamon

1 teaspoon freshly grated nutmeg

1 teaspoon ground allspice

2 teaspoons salt

2 cups bourbon, plus extra for marinating and soaking the cheesecloths

1. In a very large bowl, combine the candied fruit, raisins, dates, and nuts with 4 cups of the flour.

2. Cream the butter and sugar together using an electric mixer. Beat in the eggs. Add the spices, salt, and bourbon and combine well. Beat in the remaining 6 cups of flour.

3. Pour the fruit and nut mixture and thoroughly mix with your hands.

4. Preheat the oven to 300 degrees.

5. Grease six 9- by 5- by 4-inch loaf pans and line them with wax paper. Pack the mixture, in equal amounts, into the pans. Bake the cakes in two large roasting pans with water coming up the sides of the pans about 1 inch for 2 hours.

6. While still warm, sprinkle the tops of the cakes in the pans with about 3 tablespoons of bourbon each. Cool completely.

7. Remove the cakes from the pans and peel off the paper. Wrap each cake in bourbon-soaked cheesecloth and either store in a tightly covered tin box or wrap tightly in aluminum foil. Store in a cool place (not the refrigerator) for 2 to 3 weeks before serving. The cakes will keep for several months. If desired, moisten the cheesecloth with bourbon after 1 month.

"3" FRESH ZUCCHINI CAKES WITH BUTTER-CREAM CHEESE FROSTING

SERVES 50

2¾ cups vegetable oil
1½ cups (3 sticks) butter, melted, plus extra butter for greasing the pans
12 large eggs, lightly beaten
4¾ cups granulated sugar
6 cups shredded zucchini
6 cups sifted all-purpose flour
3 tablespoons baking powder

3 tablespoons baking soda
1 tablespoon salt
1½ teaspoons ground cinnamon
Freshly grated nutmeg to taste
1 tablespoon pure vanilla extract
3 cups chopped walnuts

BUTTER-CREAM CHEESE FROSTING

3 8-ounce packages, cream cheese, softened
1½ cups (3 sticks) butter, softened

1½ pounds confectioner's sugar
1 tablespoon pure vanilla extract

1. Preheat the oven to 350 degrees.

2. In a very large bowl, combine the vegetable oil, butter, eggs, and sugar well. Add the remaining ingredients, except the walnuts, and mix thoroughly. Stir in the walnuts. Turn the mixture into three greased 10-inch tube pans in equal portions. Bake for about 1 hour, or until done. Cool the cakes.

3. Meanwhile, prepare the frosting: In a large bowl, beat the cream cheese with the butter until smooth with an electric mixer at medium speed. Add the confectioner's sugar, a little at a time. Stir in the vanilla.

4. Remove the cakes from the pans and spread the frosting evenly over each. If desired, decorate the tops of the cakes with walnut halves. The unfrosted cakes can be wrapped tightly and frozen for several weeks.

PASTRY FOR 10-INCH TART (PÂTE SUCRÉ)

1½ cups all-purpose flour
2 tablespoons sugar
½ teaspoon salt
9 tablespoons very cold butter,
cut into tablespoon-sized
pieces

1 large egg yolk
2 to 3 tablespoons ice-cold
water

1. Combine the flour, sugar, salt, and butter in a food processor. Through the feed tube, add the egg yolk and and the ice-cold water and run the machine until the dough forms a ball and rolls around the blade.

2. Remove the pastry and shape it into a ball. Tightly cover the pastry with plastic wrap and refrigerate for 30 minutes. The dough can also be frozen.

3. On a lightly floured surface, roll the pasty out into a ⅛-inch-thick circle slightly larger than the tart pan. Roll the pastry around a rolling pin and fit it into the tart pan. Fit the pastry into the corners of the pan with the top draping slightly over the rim. Roll the pin across the edge of the pan to cut off the excess pastry. Before filling the tart shell, brush 1 tablespoon of flour over the bottom of the pastry. This will absorb liquid and help prevent the tart from becoming soggy on the bottom.

4. If not using a food processor, combine the flour, sugar, salt, and butter in a bowl with a pastry blender or two forks until the texture of coarse crumbs. Add the egg yolk and water and combine thoroughly. Follow the rest of the instructions given above.

Variation
To make Pâte Brisée, or unsweetened pastry, eliminate 1½ tablespoons of the sugar and prepare in the same manner.

The recipe can also be made without an egg yolk. Increase the ice-cold water to 3 or 4 tablespoons.

CHOCOLATE CHIP, WALNUT, AND RAISIN COOKIES

◊ ══════════════════════════════════ ◊

MAKES ABOUT 100 COOKIES

2 cups (4 sticks) butter, softened, plus extra butter for greasing the baking sheets
1½ cups dark brown sugar
½ cup granulated sugar
2 large eggs
1 teaspoon pure vanilla extract

4 cups sifted all-purpose flour
1 tablespoon baking soda
1 teaspoon salt
1 cup chopped walnuts
1 cup dark raisins
12 ounces semisweet chocolate chips

1. Preheat the oven to 375 degrees.

2. Beat together the butter, sugars, eggs, and vanilla in a large bowl with an electric mixer for 3 minutes, or vigorously by hand for 5 minutes.

3. Combine the flour, baking soda, and salt in another bowl and add it to the butter mixture. Mix thoroughly by hand. Stir in the nuts, raisins, and chocolate chips.

4. Lightly grease two 18¼-inch baking sheets. Drop heaping teaspoons of the dough onto the baking sheet about 1½ inches apart. Bake for about 10 minutes, or until the cookies are golden. Take care not to let the bottom of the cookies burn. Cool the cookies for 1 minute before removing them with a spatula to a wire rack. Continue baking the cookies in batches in the same manner until all of the dough is used.

More Servings
Double the recipe for 200 cookies.

CRESCENT COOKIES

MAKES ABOUT 50 COOKIES

1 cup (2 sticks) butter, softened
¾ cup sifted confectioner's
    sugar
2 cups sifted all-purpose flour
2 tablespoons cold milk

2 cups finely chopped pecans
All-purpose flour
Confectioner's sugar for
    coating the cookies

1. Preheat the oven to 275 degrees.

2. Cream together the butter and the ¾ cup confectioner's sugar. Add the flour and milk and mix well. Stir in the pecans. The mixture will be quite stiff.

3. Shape one rounded tablespoon of the mixture into a crescent shape with lightly floured fingers. Shape the remaining dough in the same manner.

4. Bake the cookies on greased baking sheets for 1 hour.

5. While the cookies are still warm, roll them carefully in confectioner's sugar. Store in an aluminum foil-lined box at room temperature.

More Servings
To make 100 cookies, double the recipe and bake in batches.

COCONUT-OATMEAL COOKIES

MAKES ABOUT 100 COOKIES

1 cup granulated sugar
1 cup packed light brown sugar
1 cup (2 sticks) butter,
    softened, plus extra butter for
    greasing the baking sheets
2 large eggs

2 cups all-purpose flour
1 cup shredded coconut
1 teaspoon baking powder
1 teaspoon baking soda
1 teaspoon pure vanilla extract
½ teaspoon salt

1. Preheat the oven to 350 degrees.

2. Cream the sugars and butter together. Beat in the eggs and then the remaining ingredients. The dough will be on the dry side.

3. Lightly grease a baking sheet. Roll one rounded teaspoon of the dough into a ball. Put it on the baking sheet and flatten it slightly. Continue shaping the cookies and putting them on the baking sheet, about 1½ inches apart, until you've filled the sheet. Bake for 10 to 12 minutes, or until the bottoms of the cookies are light golden brown. It will be necessary to bake the cookies in several batches.

4. Cool the cookies on racks. Wrap tightly and store at room temperature.

QUICK AND
EASY DESSERTS

The best finale to an elaborate meal for crowds is a simple dessert. Twelve recipes follow for delicious quick and easy desserts that will satisfy the sweet teeth of guests, and bring the meal to a delightful conclusion.

While these dishes are not strictly summer recipes, they are especially welcome in warm weather months, because they require little or no time over a hot stove.

Select seasonal fruit when the flavor and price is right, combining sherbets and ice cream with fresh berries or slices of ripe fruit, such as nectarines, plums, and peaches. Create dazzling parfaits with layers of ice cream, mangoes, or cherries; each topped with a splash of Cointreau or Frangelico, and crushed caramelized sugar.

Freeze layers of softened ice creams in springform pans, sprinkling ground or chopped roasted walnuts or almonds and toasted coconut over the frozen top.

I hope that these suggestions and recipes will ignite your own creative instincts into improvising your own quick and easy masterpieces.

LEMON SHERBET
WITH FRESH BLUEBERRIES

One pint of lemon sherbet, 1 pint of small stemmed, washed, and dried blueberries will serve 4. Multiply the ingredients according to the number of guests.

For each serving spoon ½ cup of the sherbet into a dessert bowl and top with ½ cup of the blueberries.

JOELLE'S FRESH PEACHES WITH YOGURT SAUCE

Four medium-large peeled ripe peaches and 1 cup of plain yogurt, plus ⅓ cup of sugar and 1 teaspoon of pure vanilla extract will serve 4. Multiply the ingredients according to the number of guests.

Cut each of the 4 peaches into 8 slices each and put into a large bowl. Combine the yogurt, sugar, and vanilla in another bowl and pour over the peaches. Combine well and chill until serving time.

LICHEE NUT, STRAWBERRY, AND BLUEBERRY PARFAITS

One 11-ounce can of lichee nuts, 1 pint hulled and sliced small strawberries, 1 pint stemmed, washed, and dried blueberries, 1 cup of heavy cream, whipped with ½ cup of sugar, and ¼ cup of brown sugar will serve 4. Multiply the ingredients according to the number of guests

In four parfait or balloon wineglasses put equal amounts of the combined lichee nuts and strawberries. Spoon half of the sweetened whipped cream over the top in equal amounts. Spoon the blueberries over the cream and then top with equal amounts of the remaining cream. Sprinkle each with 1 tablespoon of brown sugar. Serve at once or refrigerate until dessert time.

MIXED BERRIES WITH VANILLA WHIPPED CREAM

Two pints of raspberries, 2 pints of small strawberries, and 2 cups of blueberries, plus 2 cups of heavy cream, ¾ cup sugar, and 1½ tablespoons of pure vanilla extract will serve 8. Multiply the ingredients according to the number of guests.

Put the berries in a large bowl, combine gently, and chill. Whip the cream until soft peaks form; add the sugar and vanilla and beat until light and fluffy. Cover and chill. Serve the berries in balloon wineglasses or dessert bowls in equal amounts topped with the cream.

COFFEE ICE CREAM CRÊPE SUNDAES

One and a half quarts coffee ice cream, 8 crêpes (see recipe page 254), 2 cups fudge sauce, and 1 cup chopped pecans or walnuts will serve 8. For more servings, multiply the ingredients times the number of guests for every 8.

For each sundae put 1 large scoop of the ice cream in the center of a crêpe and fold the edges underneath. Spoon ¼ cup of heated thick fudge sauce over the crêpe and sprinkle with 2 tablespoons of pecans. Serve at once.

BUÑUELOS

As easy and unpretentious as Buñuelos are, they are a consistent hit with guests. I will also admit that when alone, I'll quickly make one for myself.

Peanut oil for frying, eight 8-inch flour tortillas, ¾ cup of sugar, 2 teaspoons of ground cinnamon, 1½ quarts of chocolate ice cream, and 1 cup of toasted almond slices will serve 8. For more servings multiply the ingredients times the number of guests.

In a medium-sized frying pan, heat ½ inch of oil. Cook one flour tortilla a few seconds on each side until it is golden brown and crisp. Drain and immediately sprinkle with the combined sugar and cinnamon. Top with a scoop of the chocolate ice cream and sprinkle with about two rounded tablespoons of the almond slices. Serve immediately and continue cooking and assembling the other buñuelos. It's a great help to have someone in the kitchen to help you put the cinnamon sugar, ice cream, and nuts on the fried tortillas while you continue cooking them.

AMBROSIA COMPOTE

Four navel oranges, 1 large fresh pineapple, peeled, cored, and cut into bite-sized pieces, 3 cups seedless green grapes, 1 cup shredded coconut, ½ cup freshly squeezed orange juice, and ⅓ cup Grand Marnier will serve 8. For more servings, multiply the ingredients times the number of guests.

Peel the oranges, including the pith, and cut them into ¼-inch-thick slices. Discard any seeds. Put into a large bowl with the remaining fruit and combined orange juice and Grand Marnier. Combine gently. Cover and chill. Serve with macaroons, if desired.

CINNAMON ICE CREAM WITH TOASTED ALMONDS

One and a half quarts of vanilla ice cream, 3 tablespoons ground cinnamon, and 1½ cups of toasted sliced almonds will serve 8. Multiply the ingredients according to the number of guests.

Soften the ice cream in a large bowl. Stir in the cinnamon and combine thoroughly. Refreeze. Serve equal-sized scoops in eight dessert bowls and top with equal amounts of the toasted almonds. Serve with cookies, if desired.

ORANGE SLICES WITH PURÉED STRAWBERRIES

Eight navel oranges, two 10-ounce packages of frozen strawberries, and 3 tablespoons of Cointreau will serve 8. Multiply the ingredients according to the number of guests.

Peel the oranges, including the white pith, and cut them into ¼-inch-thick slices. Discard the seeds. Arrange each sliced orange across eight dessert dishes. Purée the thawed strawberries with the Cointreau in a blender or food processor. Spoon the mixture, in equal amounts, over the center of the rows of orange slices. Serve at once or chill. If desired, garnish each dish with a sprig of mint or chopped pistachio nuts.

COMPOSED FRUIT SALAD WITH RASPBERRY SAUCE

Two large cantaloupes, 5 kiwi fruit, 6 ripe plums, 1 large pineapple, 5 medium-sized ripe bananas, and 2 pounds of seedless green grapes, plus three 10-ounce packages frozen raspberries, and 3 tablespoons of freshly squeezed lemon juice will serve 12. Multiply the ingredients according to the number of guests.

Cut the cantaloupes in half and remove the seeds. Cut the flesh into thin slices and remove the rind. Peel and cut the kiwis into thin slices. Pit the plums and cut them into wedges. Peel and core the pineapple and cut it into wedges. Peel the bananas and cut them into 1/4-inch-thick slices. Arrange the fruit on a very large platter or in shallow bowl with the bunch of grapes in the center. Purée the thawed raspberries in the blender, 1 1/2 packages at a time and add the lemon juice. Serve in a well-chilled bowl with the fruit. Serve immediately.

ALL-CHOCOLATE BROWNIE SUNDAES

On eight dessert plates, top each of 8 brownies (see recipe page 300) with a large scoop of chocolate ice cream (you will need about 2 pints). Spoon a few tablespoons of hot fudge sauce over the ice cream and serve immediately. Multiply the ingredients according to the number of guests.

EMILY McCORMACK'S "IN A PINCH" CHOCOLATE CHOCOLATE CAKE

◇ ═══ ◇

This cake freezes beautifully.

SERVES 16 TO 20

Preheat the oven to 350 degrees and lightly grease a 10-inch tube pan.

Combine an 18¾-ounce package of devil's food cake mix, one 3½-ounce package instant chocolate pudding mix, 1 cup sour cream, 4 large eggs, ½ cup vegetable oil, ½ cup rum or water, 1 cup chopped walnuts, 5 ounces chocolate chips, and 1 teaspoon pure vanilla extract in a large bowl. Mix well.

Turn the mixture into the prepared pan and bake for 55 to 60 minutes, or until a cake tester comes out clean. Cool on a wire rack. Dust the cake with confectioner's sugar before serving, if desired.

Menu Suggestions

◇ ≡≡≡≡≡≡≡≡≡≡≡≡≡≡≡≡≡≡≡≡≡≡≡ ◇

DINNER FOR EIGHT

Crab Meat Rumaki Squares
Tagliatelle with Radicchio and Prosciutto in Basil-Cream Sauce
Sole Carolina
Hot Cooked Asparagus
Endive and Diced Radish Salad with Cream Vinaigrette Dressing
Hot Puff Pastry with Cold Chocolate Mousse and Crème Anglaise

DINNER FOR TWELVE

Mallorcan Marinated Mussels on the Half Shell
Cornish Game Hens Amandine
Hot Cooked Baby Carrots
Cherry Tomato Salad with Herb Vinaigrette and Scallion Dressing
Fresh Berries with Crème Fraîche

DINNER FOR SIXTEEN

Sautéed Cashew Nuts with Curry
Frances Bangel's "Faux Crab Meat" Artichoke Bake
West Indian Meat Pates
Chicken Cutlets Pojarsky with Mushroom-Dill Sauce
Zucchini, Tomato, Yellow Squash, and Onion Tian
Tossed Green Salad
Walnut Tart

DINNER FOR TWENTY-FOUR

Fruited Shrimp Wrapped in Prosciutto
Robbie Robinson's Fresh Hot Sausage Balls
Martha Rose Shulman's Black Bean Chalupas
Chicken and New Potato Salad with Celery Leaves and Parsley and
    Mustard Sauce
Buñuelos

DINNER FOR THIRTY-SIX

Country Pâté Loaf
Brie with Granny Smith Apple Slices and Walnuts
Open-faced Reuben Canapés
Baked Garlic Chicken Legs
Fusilli with Green Primavera Vegetables and Italian Parsley Sauce
Sliced Beefsteak Tomatoes with Herb Vinaigrette
All-Chocolate Brownie Sundaes

DINNER FOR FIFTY

Roast Beef Turbans with Creamy Roquefort Sauce
Dried Fruit with Toasted Coconut and Nuts
Shrimp Toast
Sylvia Putziger's Peanut Butter and Bacon Hors d'Oeuvre Rolls
Polynesian Chicken Curry with Condiments
Herbed Pilaf
Cucumber and Yogurt Salad with Fresh Herbs
"3" Zucchini Cakes with Butter-Cream Cheese Frosting

Index